THIS CAN'T BE HAPPENING!

RESISTING THE DISINTEGRATION OF AMERICAN DEMOCRACY

Dave Lindorff

Common Courage Press   Monroe, Maine

Library of Congress Cataloging-in-Publication Data is available
from the publisher on request.

ISBN 1-56751-298-4 paper
ISBN 1-56751-299-2 cloth

Common Courage Press
Box 702
Monroe, ME 04951

(207) 525-0900; fax: (207) 525-3068
orders-info@commoncouragepress.com

See our website for e-versions of this book.
www.commoncouragepress.com

First Printing

Printed in Canada

Acknowledgments

There are many people who helped me with this book—some who don't even know they played a role. There's no way I can thank them all, but I'll try to mention as many as I can.

First and foremost, I want to thank my editors, Alex Cockburn, Jeffrey St. Clair at *CounterPunch* and David Talbot, Joan Walsh and Ed Lempinen at *Salon.com*, for giving me the space and band-width in their magazines to publish my exposés and opinion columns, and for their work in helping me to achieve what focus and clarity these articles can claim (and in *Salon's* case, where I'd sold the rights, for graciously returning those rights to allow publication in this volume).

I also want to thank my editor and publisher at Common Courage Press, Greg Bates (who edited and published my prior book *Killing Time*), both for his confidence and enthusiasm in offering me the opportunity to publish this volume, and for his always on-target editing.

Many journalistic comrades, among them Chuck Young, Rip Rense, Allen Baker, Bernie Beck, Lisa Bergson, Bert Schultz, Linn Washington and Matt Miller, and others too numerous to mention, have offered encouragement and needed criticism along the way. And then there is John Hess, who has long inspired me not just with his own pithy and biting essays, but by showing that it's possible as a journalist, despite all odds, to hang on to that sense of outrage without which we'd all just sink into a pointless cynicism—and that one can maintain a sense of humor at the same time.

Thanks to my daughter Ariel, already at 20 the most exacting and talented of editors, for her help with both some of the wording of the text, and with the title. Thanks to my 11-year-old son Jed for his welcome distractions. And thanks especially to my wife Joyce for putting up with me on yet another book project—no small task—and for being my most enthusiastic reader and most demanding critic.

Thanks to the U.S. Fulbright Foundation, to the Taiwan Foundation for Scholarly Exchange, and to National Sun Yat Sen University and the NSYSU America Center in Kaohsiung for providing me with the stipend and residency that gave me time to complete this book.

Finally thanks to George Dubya Bush and his team of crazed zealots, for providing so much unbelievable material about which to write.

Much effort has gone into vetting this book for errors, both of fact and of style. I thank all those who have helped to make it better, but assume all responsibility for those errors, problems and shortcomings that may remain.

Contents

Foreword: Lighting Bonfires
by Alexander Cockburn   xi

Introduction
Shock and Awe at the Breakfast Table   1

Chapter 1
Mission Accomplished

Liberating Iraqis...*From* Their Homes: IOUs for Looting   14

And a Big Hand for...The Coalition of the Willing   16

War and Peace in New York: Against the War at Ground Zero   18

Bombing Saddam into Glory: A Hero Made in Washington   21

America's Dirty Bombs:
These WMDs are Right in Front of Their Noses   23

Secret Bechtel Documents Reveal: Yes, It *Is* About Oil   29

The Iraq Moneypot   36

Consider the Parallels with Vietnam:
An Iraq War and Occupation Glossary   39

Legitimizing Terrorism?
Making America Safer...for Iraqi Fighters   43

Rumsfeld v. Belgium: "Leave Us Alone or We'll Move NATO   45

Takoma Goes AWOL: The Dolphin Who Refused to Fight   47

Paying For War: $2150 Per Family and Counting   48

Chapter 2
Occupation: Lost in the Bush

Calling All Occupiers: Talking Turkey About Iraq   51

Shooting Ali in the Back:
Why the Pacification is Doomed   53

From Occupation to Guerrilla War:
A New Kind of Dancing in Iraq   55

The Longer it Goes On, the Worse It Gets:
Friendly Fire Will Doom the Occupation   58

Hiding the Dead Babies: Infanticide as Liberation   60

A Marine in Transit: "Spray and Pray" in Iraq   62

Dumb and Dumber in Iraq:
Human Trophies on the White House Wall   64

Now What? The Saddam Dilemma   65

Recalling LBJ in Vietnam: Bush's Baghdad Pit Stop   67

Good Morning Vietnam! A Strategic Rhetorical Retreat   70

The Bush Speech: Spinning a Fiasco   73

A Draft in the Forecast?
The Pentagon Puts Out the Help Wanted Sign   75

Bush's War on Veterans:
The White House Attack on the Troops   78

Misers of War: Troop Strength and Chintzy Bonuses   80

Weapons in Search of a Name:
Let's Reserve WMD for the Really Big Ones. You Know,
Those Made-in-America Bombs   82

Coronado in Iraq: Laughter in the Dark   86

Will He Replace Ari?
The Catch and Release of "Comical Ali"   88

The New Bush Slogan: "Case Closed. Just Move On"   89

The Poll of the Shirt: Bush Isn't Wearing Well   91

Bush's Torturous Logic: Shocked, Shocked, Shocked   94

My Grandfather's Medal: A Final Memorial Day Thought   96

Chapter 3
Bush and Hitler: Gleich oder Änlich?

Bush and Hitler: The Strategy of Fear   103

Bush and Hitler…Compare and Contrast:
A Response to the WSJ's James Taranto   107

The Bush Election Strategy: The Politics of Fear and Blood   110

RNC Plays the Hitler Card:
MoveOn Shouldn't Apologize for Those Ads   113

Scare Tactics and Elections: A Spanish Parallel   115

Chapter 4
<u>The Assault on Civil Liberties</u>

When Neighbors Attack   121

Grounded   126

Snoops' Night Out: FEMA's Paranoid Communities   132

Keeping Dissent Invisible:
How the Secret Service and the White House Keep
Protesters Safely Out of Bush's Sight—and off TV   135

Reaping What Has Been Sown:
Prisoners, Torture and Hypocrisy   142

About Those Kids in Camp X-Ray:
Day Care in the Name of National Security   145

What's Next: You Call This Security?   146

Expanding Power, Gutting Liberty:
The Meaning of September 11   149

Ashcroft Rebuked: Lynn Stewart's Big Win   152

Fighting the Patriot Act: Alaska Turns a Cold Shoulder   154

John Walker Lindh, Revisited:
A First Glimpse at Bush's Torture Show   157

That Terrorism Report:
The Warning the State Department
Sent Its Own People, But Not You   160

Chapter 5
<u>The Inbedded Media</u>

The Failure of American Journalism:
War, Protest and the Press   165

Killing the Messengers:
Deliberate or Accident, It Doesn't Really Matter 169

Ari "the Fabulist" Fleischer Quits the Scene:
The Liar's Gone, the Enablers Remain 171

WMD Damage Control at The New York Times:
Many Presidents Have Lied,
But This Time the Press Went Along for the Ride 174

The Importance of Tipping:
Is the Media Finally Turning on Bush? 177

War Dispatch from the NYT: God's On Our Side 180

The Spinelessness of U.S. Journalism:
No Solidarity Among the Scribes 182

The Press and Fallujah: Barbaric Relativism 184

Imagination Deficit Disorder:
Finally, Bush Unites...the Resistance 187

Chalabi as Prosecutor:
An Appointment to Shock and Awe 190

This Couldn't Have Been Happening! (But It Was):
The Times' Okrent on the Credulous Judy Miller 193

Chapter 6
The So-Called Opposition

Clinton, Bush and Impeachment: It was the Lying, Right? 197

The Democrats in 2004:
Perfect Storm or Same Old Doldrums? 200

Facing the Music: Courage and the Democrats 202

General Hysteria: The Clark Bandwagon 206

A Black Day for Democracy:
Schwarzenegger and the Failure of the Dems 208

Take a Ride in God's Humvee:
A General Theory of Theology 211

Big Lies and Little Lies:
The Meaning of "Mission Accomplished" 213

Bush's Brand of Leadership: Putting Himself First 215

Al Gore's Judas Kiss: Dean Joins the Party 218

Histrionics about Howard:
Dean and His Democratic Detractors 220

Selling Out Democracy: Kerry's China Connection 224

Dude! Where's Your Politics?
Michael Moore Smears Kucinich 227

Beware the Iraq Election Blowback:
Rigged Votes and Puppet Governments 229

Presidential Occupations:
Bush and Kerry Share a Problem 232

Where is John Kerry?
A Campaign Coasting Toward Disaster 235

Chapter 7
Other Indignities, Assaults and Affronts

Will Rendell Act?
Race and the Death Penalty in Pennsylvania 237

There He Goes Again!
Michael Moore Proclaims Mumia Guilty 240

Not My Day in Court: How the System Rigs the Jury Pool 243

Bush's Scare Tactics May Backfire:
The Coming Senior Revolution 245

Social Insecurity: Fear Mongering for Privatization 250

Hypocrisy at the Fed: Greenspan's Pension 253

Marketplace Medicine: America's Healthcare Scandal 255

Lights Out Baby: Where's Arnold when We Need Him? 258

The Great Oil Gouge: Burning Up That Tax Rebate 260

Beef, the Meat of Republicans:
Deregulating Themselves to Extinction? 263

Memorializing a President Who Could Really Lie: 266
Put Reagan on the $3 Bill

Saigon Revisited:
Bush's Evacuation Moment?   268

Epilogue

Making Breakfast Safe Again   271

Appendix

Great Websites for Alternative News and Information   272

Notes   273

About the Author   274

Foreword

Lighting Bonfires

It was Dave Lindorff, in February of 2004, who launched the vogue for Hitler/Bush comparisons with an article on the *CounterPunch* website (www.counterpunch.org), edited by Jeffrey St Clair and myself. In an onslaught on Bush-as-warmonger, Lindorff swept into an impassioned finale, declaring that "we must begin exposing George W. Bush and his War Party for what they are: craven usurpers aiming at nothing less than the undermining of all those things that most of us hold dear."

Then Dave, ever the gent, raised a cautionary finger to his readers. "It's going a bit far to compare the Bush of 2003 to the Hitler of 1933. Bush simply is not the orator that Hitler was. But comparisons of the Bush Administration's fear-mongering tactics to those practiced so successfully and with such terrible results by Hitler and Goebbels on the German people and their Weimar Republic are not at all out of line."

I thought Lindorff's measured assessment of the two leaders' rhetorical talents indicated appropriate objectivity, but our *CounterPunch* inbox was soon crammed with furious denunciations of Lindorff from Bush supporters. Then in July, 2003, one of *the Wall Street Journal's* mad-dogs-in-residence, James Taranto, did us a favor by taking a passing jab at *CounterPunch* as "an outfit whose staple is stuff comparing Bush to Hitler". There were other useful attacks in the *National Review* and *Washington Times*.

Of course this allowed Lindorff to return to the scene of the crime, with further measured comparisons between the Bush administration and the Third Reich, such as shared propensities to warmongering, melding of corporate and political elites, recourse to the Big Lie, contempt for civil liberties and due process. Such kinship notwithstanding, and in that spirit of fair play for which *CounterPunch* is justly renowned, Lindorff reminded our readers that "we may not yet have a dictatorship" and that

> while he has rounded up some Arab and Muslim men purely because of their ethnicity or religion, Bush has not started gassing them—at least not yet.

I don't think you'd get that sort of gentlemanly sense of fair play and politeness from the likes of Taranto or Limbaugh.

This same Lindorff indirectly caused Katrina vanden Heuvel, editor of

The Nation to snort in disgust and make a rare phone call to Petrolia, California, home of the present writer. After the uproar about Lindorff's Hitler analogy, I decided to give the issue an airing in my column in *The Nation*. I came up with what I considered to be a frisky lead and soon had a thousand vigorous words winging their way to *The Nation*, beginning thus:

> Beyond the shared enthusiasm of the Fuehrer and all US presidents for mass murder as an appropriate expression of national policy, I've never seen any particularly close affinity between Adolf Hitler and the current White House incumbent but the Republican National Committee seems peculiarly sensitive on the matter.

My phone rang and it was vanden Heuvel, expressing outrage at my opening sentence. I said I couldn't see anything there to take exception to. It turned out she didn't care for the comparison of any U.S. president to A.H. She suggested I reconsider. I did, and inserted the words "with the possible exception of Warren Harding", on the grounds that Harding was too busy stealing, there weren't too many Native Americans left to wipe out and anyway, in the 1920s war wasn't popular.

Harding aside, I stood by what I wrote, including my reservations about Bush/Hitler comparisons. It's like comparing Pee Wee Herman to the Marquis de Sade. Vanden Heuvel said she'd enter a statement of editorial dissent in the same issue as my column, which she duly did. A bunch of letters came in, running (so the letters editor told me), 90 per cent in my favor.

So you see the kind of rows Dave sparks with his splendid chronicles of the passing show.

He lit the same sort of bonfire under the national snitch program know as TIPS, sprung from Ashroft's head. Lindorff called the Justice Department offering his services as a citizen-snoop and asked whither he should forward the fruits of his labors. They gave him an 800 number and it turned out to be the hot line for Fox's "America's Most Wanted". His story got picked up by the networks and soon the bold denizens of Congress scented TIPS was a turkey and denied it funding.

Lindorff wrote a fine, fair book on the Mumia case, and he brings the same qualities of independence, hard work and a radical-populist perspective to this great journal of the Bush years. It's Lindorff and writers like him—and we are proud to publish them in *CounterPunch*—who have saved the honor of American journalism when the mainstream pundits had their heads buried deep in the sand.

—Alexander Cockburn
Petrolia, July, 2004

Introduction

Shock and Awe at the Breakfast Table

The bad news just keeps popping up each morning:

"Supreme Court Rules Bush Wins Presidency"

"John Ashcroft Named Attorney General,"

"Gale Norton Named Secretary of the Interior"

"World Trade Center Towers Collapse"

"Iraq Invasion Begins"

"Katherine Harris Elected to Congress"

"Bush Nominated for Nobel Peace Prize"

This can't be happening!" How many times have we all involuntarily blurted out this phrase over the morning coffee these past few years!

I remember the first time I had that awful thought—a mixture of shock and dismay. It was back in November 1980, as the returns poured in showing that Ronald Reagan, second-rate actor, shill for Westinghouse, and conservative political icon, had decisively defeated the hapless incumbent Jimmy Carter and won the presidency, and that Republicans had also captured the Senate. The next morning, in what could have been a scene from "Night of the Living Dead, " dazed people were wandering around my Upper West Side neighborhood in New York City, zombielike, all muttering the same thing: "This can't be happening!" And indeed how could it have happened? After all, revolution was on the march in Central America, the CIA and FBI had been leashed and muzzled by post-Watergate reforms, and the global environment was finally getting some attention. Heck, only a few years earlier, we lefties had helped defeat the American war machine in Indochina, And now this! Yet the shock and chagrin ended quickly. In short order, liberal and progressive forces steeled the resolve of Democrats in the House and President Reagan found himself blocked from pursuing much of his troglodyte agenda. His effort to undo Social Security foundered almost immediately, and over the eight years of his presidency, the American left, faced with a clear enemy, actually thrived.

Election 2000 and the Bush Presidency that followed, has been alto-

gether different, though. In part, this can be attributed to those eight dispiriting years of the Clinton presidency; years which did incalculable damage to
progressive politics in America by co-opting the language of liberalism and
progressivism, while promoting policies that belonged in a Republican platform. With Clinton in the White House cutting deals with Republicans, the
American left was confused, splintered and demoralized. The Clinton administration over two four-year terms slashed welfare supports, casting the poor
onto the streets, it weakened environmental protections, subverted the Bill of
Rights with passage of the so-called Anti-Terrorism and Effective Death
Penalty Act, it undermined American workers with the passage of the North
America Free Trade Act, it sabotaged Social Security, promoting the idea of
opening up the fund to private investment and letting inflation eat into the
benefit amount, it intentionally threw away a chance to pass some kind of
national healthcare by handing the whole process over to the insurance
industry, and even undermined the Bill of Rights, endorsing a weakening of
habeas corpus, a right to a fair trial that dates back to ancient British
Common Law.

Then, to top it all off, Al Gore's whole presidential campaign was one of
corporate co-option, political cowardice and missed opportunities. Even with
this background, however, the actual election debacle was beyond belief. The
Florida presidential balloting was a clear case of conspiracy, intimidation,
fraud, theft and denial of the constitutional right to vote by the Republican
Party, and of stupidity and cowardice on the part of Democrats, including
Gore himself, who refused to demand from the outset, as was his right, a full
recount of the state's votes. Forget butterfly ballots and hanging chads; it was
clear from the start that African-American voters by the tens of thousands
were being denied the right to cast votes by Florida's corrupt county voter registrars and Secretary of State, that voting machines were systematically rejecting Democratic votes, and that clearly marked ballots were being misclassified
as void—all in numbers that dwarfed candidate George W. Bush's at best
miniscule lead in what was ultimately declared to be the official count.*

As the charade of a battle worked its way through the courts to an inexorable Bush win in the Republican-dominated U.S. Supreme Court, I found
myself once again, along with countless other Americans, sitting at the breakfast table each morning, looking at my local paper's front page, and exclaiming involuntarily: "This can't be happening!"

But this time, the feeling of shock and disbelief hasn't abated. With the

---

* Anyone interested in knowing all the details of this electoral coup should read Greg Palast's book,
  The Best Democracy Money Can Buy (Plume Books, 2004).

anointing of President Bush by the Supreme Court, there was no subsequent rallying of the Democratic opposition, as there had been in the days following Reagan's win in 1980. Instead, despite the fact that this was a president who had been the choice of a minority of the electorate, cowed Democrats in Washington began to seek "common ground," to accommodate themselves to the new Washington power structure. They behaved, in short, as if Bush had won a mandate, not stolen an election.

The result: more shock and awe at the breakfast table.

Look at the record:

- Democrats in Congress acquiesced in the passage of $1.3 trillion in tax cuts, massively skewed to favor the very rich—and this was in 2001, coming right out of the starting gate for the administration.
- Democrats did nothing to block horrific appointments to the cabinet—most infamously the naming of a bible-thumping, Confederacy-praising racist and proto-fascist, John Ashcroft, to the post of Attorney General—a man so demonstrably unpopular that voters in his home state of Missouri had only recently spurned him in favor of a dead Democrat (and here I'm talking about an actually dead guy, Democrat Mel Carnahan, who died in a plane crash during the campaign, not Gore or someone like him who only appeared or acted dead). More recently, even Ashcroft's own pancreas tried to dump him.
- Democrats caved in and passed a Bush education bill that placed huge burdens on local schools while providing them with no new funds, and that implicitly blamed teachers for educational failures that in large part are really the result of defunding of schools in poorer districts.
- On the environment, Democrats largely failed to block Bush rollbacks in air and water quality regulation. Ditto for the area of women's rights, which have seen a series of successful attacks, particularly undermining the right to a safe, legal abortion.
- Meanwhile, on the international stage, Democrats stood by silently while Bush withdrew U.S. support for such international treaties and institutions as the World Court, the Kyoto Protocol on global warming, the ABM treaty with Russia, etc.

And remember, all this was happening *before* the 9-11 attack on the World Trade Center and the Pentagon. That truly unbelievable day then provided the Bush Administration, much as the Reichstag Fire did for Hitler's National Socialists in Weimar Germany, with an opportunity to push its long-planned right-wing agenda of constitutional demolition harder and faster. Hyping the threat of terrorists and deliberately frightening the public by claiming (on the basis of no real evidence) that there were horrible weapons of mass destruction—nuclear, biological and chemical—poised and ready to be used, the Bush Administration introduced, in the coming days and months, the cynically named USA PATRIOT Act and the even more cynical War on Terror, and finally, the unprovoked "pre-emptive" War on Iraq. In all these cases, the Democrats in Congress rolled over and voted massively in support of these profoundly anti-democratic measures and actions.

It has been a dizzying parade of right-wing power grabs since 9/11, made the more remarkable by the Republicans' razor-thin majorities in the two houses of Congress.

This can't be happening!

But it is.

Back in the early 1970s, as the dark saga of Nixon's Watergate crimes unfolded, most mainstream pundits scoffed at the notion that the scandal-plagued president and his circle of advisors and co-conspirators had actually been engaged in not just one petty burglary and cover-up, but a massive project designed to use all the powers of government to undermine democracy and in effect establish a one-party state. There were martial law war games, there were huge data banks created, with over 10,000 files on known or perceived critics of the government, plans for a round-up and incarceration of thousands of political activists, and untold numbers of dirty tricks and black-bag jobs—even murders—all designed to undermine and weaken the Democratic and progressive opposition. Some of this stuff was uncovered in the course of the Watergate and Cointelpro investigations, but Congress and the Justice Department were unwilling to investigate seriously, and the mainstream press never followed up on obvious leads—for example the evidence of plans, collectively code-named Operation Garden Plot, to establish martial law.

Today, the same thing is happening, though much more openly. Far from simply ignoring anti-democratic developments, however, the Democrats have this time helped them along. The media have, in large part, ignored them entirely or, particularly in the case of the Fox network, and to a lesser extent the other major networks—CBS, ABC, NBC and CNN—have actively championed them.

Let's step back for a minute and look at this situation for what it is (something that is easier for me to do as I write these words from a mountainside office seven thousand miles from the U.S. in profoundly and rambunctiously democratic Taiwan):

The U.S. is currently being led by a blueblood Connecticut Yankee who, after barely graduating from a prestigious private New England prep school where he made a name for himself as a male cheerleader, barely graduated from Yale University, where he had been admitted thanks to his familial connections (his grandfather had been a U.S. Senator from Connecticut), and where he spent his time drinking and, allegedly, snorting.

But wait. I'm not done. It gets worse.

This is also a man who escaped the Vietnam War by joining the Texas Air National Guard (again thanks to political pull—his daddy was a congressman at the time), from which service he proceeded to go AWOL for a year without punishment. This ne'er-do-well East Coast scion, who shamelessly poses as a Texan, barely reads, indeed can barely talk intelligibly without cue cards or a teleprompter, and who claims that he not only speaks with God *but that God speaks back to him*, has—without having been supported by a majority of the electorate, which voted for his opponent—become president of the most powerful nation in the world. Worse yet, as president, he has started not just one but two full-scale, bloody wars, neither of which is likely to end for years, and at least one of which will require upwards of 135,000 American occupation forces to remain in hostile territory indefinitely. He has declared a third war—the so-called War on Terror—which, while not a real war, or really even anything approximating a war, is being used to justify an indefinite suspension of American democratic principles and laws such as habeas corpus (the common law right to bring any case before a federal judge) and the right to a fair trial, a lawyer, and to be charged and to face one's accuser. (Already, we've seen one disastrous result of this abrogation of basic rules of civilized behavior—the horrible abuse and torture of Iraqis, Afghanis and other alleged enemies of America, which finally came to light in May 2004.)

Incredibly, this gilded goof-off—surely one of if not the worst and most willfully ignorant of presidents the republic has ever had to endure—was nonetheless in 2004 being considered a strong contender for a second term as president of the United States.

This is all quite shocking. Sometimes it's enough to make the coffee blow out your nose, as when Bush, in the middle of a bloody war in Iraq, pulled his aircraft carrier stunt announcing "Mission Accomplished," or when he offered up, apparently to demonstrate "vision," a harebrained scheme to build a moon base as a future launching site for a manned mission to Mars. In the first case, the Iraqi resistance quickly forced an initially complicit media to start challenging Bush's premature victory claim, but that same media treated, and continues to treat Bush's space fantasy respectfully, as if it were for real—I guess because it came with good graphics, courtesy of the NASA art department.

This can't be happening!

But it is.

So what is to be done?

The first thing, it seems to me, is to restore a sense of reality in the American body politic (no small challenge, given that we're talking about a public that still widely believes that Saddam Hussein masterminded the World Trade Center bombings, that the Creation myth is actual history, and that Wonder Bread builds strong bodies 12 different ways).

We—both ordinary citizens and journalists—need to learn to start saying "That's ridiculous!" when something like a moon base, or a budget with a built-in $540-billion deficit, or some plan for a new war is announced. Americans have to begin applying at least the same level of skepticism to political promises and policies that we apply to a come-on for aluminum siding or the purchase of a used car. If it looks like a Nigerian email fund solicitation, don't vote for it. We need to learn to laugh when the president says America is in a life-and-death war of survival against the agents of terror. Heck, does anyone really believe that the U.S. or our vaunted Way of Life is seriously threatened by a bunch of high school dropouts and religious school grads from Saudi Arabia and Egypt? We need to learn to be stunned and outraged when the Attorney General says it's okay to strip an American of his citizenship rights and to imprison him indefinitely. We need to be dumbfounded when that same Attorney General proposes establishing a network of millions of citizen spies to snoop on their neighbors. I mean, is that how anybody wants to live, really?

Let's all get a grip.

We need to hold on to that feeling that "This can't be happening!"

And we need to start insisting that it *won't* happen.

In fact, things aren't all bad. *New York Times* "reporter" Judith Miller may still believe, or pretend to believe, that there are piles of nukes stacked up in some basement in Baghdad, and Dan Rather may think catching Saddam Hussein is a Big Story, but the good news is that millions of Americans no longer buy it. They have simply stopped watching the news on TV and aren't reading the mainstream daily papers (which have lost 11 percent of their readers over the past ten years), because they don't believe them. Indeed, if we can believe the numbers, millions are instead reading publications like *CounterPunch* magazine (www.CounterPunch.org), Salon (www.Salon.com), (both of which, in the interest of disclosure, I write for), and other alternative media. And the anger that propelled the Democratic primaries in early 2004, and that made it so embarrassingly difficult for the plodding and over-cautious Kerry to make a really strong showing anywhere until he was the last man standing, is rooted in a massive rejection by a significant amount of the electorate of everything that is happening in Washington.

The New York Times itself belatedly acknowledged this situation when it published a 1100-word mea culpa on May 26, 2004. In this article, the editors confessed to having allowed slanted pro-war propaganda to run as news stories, to have been slip-shod about the usual insistence on verification of sources and balance, and to having failed to correct those pro-war stories when they were shown to be false or overblown. While the Times was less than forthright about the extent of its dissembling and propagandistic coverage of the Iraq invasion and the run-up to the war, and declined to name the guilty reporters and editors who perpetrated the scam on readers, it was still a remarkable admission, given the unique role the Times plays in setting the national journalistic agenda. As my friend and colleague John Hess, a former Times reporter and author of a wonderful and revealing recent book on the paper of record (My Life and Times: A Memoir of Dissent), put it in Counterpunch, "Halleluya! On this 26th day of May, 2004. The New York Times confessed to having helped promote the lies that got us into war with Iraq."[1] Even more remarkable than the editors' confession was a scathing indictment of the Times' war coverage published four days later by the paper's ombudsman, Daniel Okrent. Okrent publicly accused Miller and another of the paper's reporters of writing pro-administration stories that failed to meet basic journalistic standards, and said the paper's editors had virtually enlisted in the war effort.

My goal, writing in these unbelievable times, has been to help nurture that crucial sense of shock, awe and anger—to show just how off-the-wall and frightening the Bush administration is, and yet how ludicrous, too. But not just the Bush Administration, for there are unbelievable things happening all over. The conduct of the Iraq War itself, sometimes in violation of law and decency, sometimes just stupid, the treacherous behavior of Democrats and even of some on the left, like Michael Moore, with his weird endorsement of the unblinking Gen. Wesley Clark, the nation's continuing obsession with the death penalty, all cry out for attention.

Sometimes it hasn't been hard at all to point out the madness and craven behavior. Back in 2002, I decided to investigate Ashcroft's TIPS scheme by volunteering to be a citizen spy, and called the Justice Department asking where I should call with the tips I claimed to have gathered about my suspicious neighbors. I was given an 800 number that turned out to be the hotline for Fox TV's "America's Most Wanted" crime-stopper show. That bizarre discovery—I thought it was the last word in privatization until dis-abused of that notion by the Bush administration's even more incredible pri-vatization of the army and of military prison torture operations in Iraq—caused such an outcry that my *Salon* story was picked up by CBS's "Evening News" program and by some other mainstream news organizations, after which Congress effectively killed the program, denying it any funding.

Other times, it's been more of a challenge.

Take the attack on Social Security for instance. The Bush administra-tion is filled with people whose goal is to undermine and destroy this most enduring and popular legacy of the New Deal, and has gone so far as to have the supposedly non-partisan Social Security Administration include a dire warning printed in the annual notice of benefits it sends to all taxpayers say-ing: "Without changes, by 2042, the Social Security Trust fund will be exhausted. By then, the number of Americans 65 or older is expected to have doubled. There won't be enough younger people to pay all the benefits owed to those who are retiring. We will need to resolve these issues soon to make sure Social Security continues to provide a foundation of protection for future generations as it has done in the past."

This is pretty discouraging and depressing news if you, like most average Americans, were counting on Social Security to help you get through your declining years. The thing is, though, it's utter bull. First of all, the govern-ment's dire predictions are based upon notoriously unreliable projections about future economic performance. Furthermore, as the Social Security Administration's own actuarial experts are happy to tell any reporter who will just bother to call them,* it would take only minor tinkering with the system to ensure its ability to pay current benefit levels on out for the next 75 years, well past the time that the last baby boomer would have already checked out. There is no need to undermine the system by converting some of the Social Security fund into voluntary private pension accounts—the favored Republican "reform" scheme, and one which would actually help sink the sys-tem by pulling current workers' contributions *out* of the fund right when they're needed most to pay benefits to a wave of current retirees. The real question that should be asked is this: What other problem, or potential prob-

---

* The problem here is that reporters in today's pared-back, entertainment-oriented media, don't do that kind of reporting. They only get soundbites from political figures or use the handouts those politicians give them. My guess is that most reporters who write about Social Security don't even have the phone number for the SSA's actuarial office in their rolodexes, or even know the right area code to call for information. (The media office number is 410-965-8904.)

lem, facing this country that is that far off in the future (or even a fraction as far off) gets *any attention at all* from Republicans (and conservative Democrats)? Certainly not global warming, which clearly threatens to make the alleged threat of a Social Security fund crisis in 2079 shrink to insignificance, if not moot it altogether. Certainly not the federal budget deficit, which threatens to turn the U.S. into a third world nation in as little as 10 years if it keeps rising at the current rate thanks to Bush's tax cuts for the rich. Certainly not the AIDS crisis, which is starting to rival the Black Plague of Middle Ages fame and which threatens to become a destroyer of nations. So why this obsession with Social Security's survival, especially on the part of a group that doesn't like the program in the first place, and that nowhere else shows the slightest concern about the welfare of the poorest among us? Could it be that it's all a charade, and that what they and their corporate backers are really doing is trying to destroy the system before all those politically savvy baby boomers realize they have a stake in making sure Social Security provides people with a genuine retirement program—and the political clout to do it?

This is a hard sell, and yet it's so obvious that the attack on Social Security really is nothing more than a con game when you just look at the numbers, and when you consider how absurd it is to imagine that Republicans and the Bush Administration (or their allies among the more conservative "New Democrats") really give a rat's ass about the welfare of the working poor in their declining years.

Okay, I have to admit: the nearly four-year run of the Bush pResidency has been a grand time to be a journalist. The abuses of power, the high crimes and misdemeanors, the war on Iraq, the fake "war on terrorism." the assault on the Bill of Rights, the religious posing and pandering, as well as the bold efforts of progressives to resist, provide an endless source of material. But as much fun and excitement as this provides to those in my line of work, I'm reminded of that stellar journalist I.F. Stone, who recalled once how as a young cub reporter at a small New Jersey daily, he had found himself covering a tenement fire, in which several families were trapped and dying. Turning to another reporter, he said, "What a great story!" Only then did he realize that his "great story" was actually a horrible tragedy in the making. And so it is too with these years of the Bush Administration outrages, only on a much grander scale. Yet strangely, the corporate media have been silent, or at best timorous, in reporting on most of these stories. It's almost as if the crazier things have gotten, the more blatant the power grabbing and hustling of the political establishment and its corporate paymasters, the less the media has had to say about it. Mainstream journalism has increasingly become an unwitting, or sometimes (certainly in the case of Fox News or the *New York Times*) even a willing accomplice or publicist for the state. In part this is a matter of professional cowardice, but there is another reason for the problem too. As they have become increasingly concentrated in the hands of a few powerful corporate conglomerates, the media have turned the long-held American press tradition of "objectivity" into a kind of straitjacket that prevents journalists from pursuing truth even when they might want to. Forced to "give both sides of the story," and thus to treat official liars with the same or even, because of their high positions, undeserved and greater respect than their critics, the media have forsaken their role as a Fourth Estate. Power is no longer suspect. It is revered.

It is my hope that these commentaries and investigative reports, all of them done during the Bush II era, most of them during the run-up to the Iraq war and on up through the occupation and the presidential election campaign, will give readers a sense of the madness, the nuttiness, and the venality and greed that has gripped this nation since the Florida coup of 2000.

The first group of columns deals with Bush's war, clearly both the biggest of this administration's crimes, and also the foundation for its broader agenda of undermining American democracy and enriching its corporate sponsors and friends. These articles and columns expose some of the hypocrisy of some of the administration's claims—that it is bringing democracy to the Middle East, that it is making the U.S. safer, that it adequately planned for the war and occupation. Other articles make it clear that a very real motive for the war was an imperial scheme to control Iraqi oil, and that the unanticipated resistance to occupation makes a return to the draft increasingly likely.

This is followed by a series of columns concerning the so-called "occupation"—actually a continuation of the war, but now against an increasingly popular insurrection, instead of against the regime of Saddam Hussein.

The third group of articles, particularly dear to my heart, examines the stunning parallels between Bush's shameless use of the 9/11 tragedy and the early Nazi Party's use of the torching of the Reichstag (the German parliament building). It is my view that Bush and his handlers, particularly Karl Rove, deliberately stoked the fears of the American public in the wake of that shocking incident, in order to gain public approval for their assault on American democracy. In that regard, the war on Iraq—a country that never remotely threatened the U.S.—was much like Germany's attack on Poland. Both were exercises in imperial expansion and ploys to put the public on a war footing, in which appeals to blind patriotism could be used to blunt criticism of otherwise politically impossible domestic policies.

Drawing parallels between Bush and Hitler apparently really struck a nerve, leading to my being attacked in everything from the *National Review* to the *Wall Street Journal* and on Fox TV—a good indication that I was on to something. In fact, while even *Nation* editor Katrina Vanden Heuvel apparently finds it distasteful to link Bush with Hitler, to the point that she actually felt the need to publicly dissociate herself and the *Nation* from a column on the subject by my colleague and editor Alex Cockburn, there are undeniable and highly disturbing similarities to the way the two parties, the National Socialists and the Republicans, have used jingoism and public fears, and of course the Big Lie, to aggrandize power and crush any opposition.

The fourth group of columns looks at the domestic war on civil liberties and democracy. This war, it is clear, is closely linked to the war in Iraq and the "war" on terror, which, together with the 9/11 attack, are being used as a justification, or excuse, for all manner of assaults on American freedoms.

Fifth, there is a section on the media, which has clearly abrogated its assigned role as a Fourth Estate with the task of exposing and serving as a brake on the activities of the other three branches of government. One of the benefits of living and working in Asia as I have—in China, Hong Kong and Taiwan—is that one gets to see how media in other nations work. For me, it was an eye-opener to find when it comes to news reports on government-related affairs, whether it be war, space programs or tax policy, it's sometimes hard to see much difference in the way stories are handled by CNN's Wolf Blitzer or NBC's Tom Brokaw on the one hand, and by the guys on Central China TV on the other. Similarly, the overt bias of the mostly party-aligned newspapers in Taiwan don't seem that outlandish or strange anymore, with papers like the *N.Y. Times* and the *Washington Post* so uncritically reporting on administration activities or statements.

A sixth chapter looks at the opposition to the Bush administration and its international and domestic actions, for while Bush and the Republican Congress have largely gotten away with murder in their efforts to drag the country back into the 19th Century, there has been resistance, particularly from outside the traditional Democratic Party. Massive popular resistance in the form of unprecedented global demonstrations, the overturning of a U.S. client regime in Spain, and a Democratic primary campaign that put opposition to the war front and center among key issues, have acted as a brake on Bush's schemes, for example forcing the U.S. to cut back on troop strength in Iraq even as the resistance grows, and to back off, at least temporarily, on some of the most egregious attacks on civil liberties—for example the TIPS domestic spying plan or the passage of a PATRIOT II Act.

Finally comes a group of columns on a range of other issues, from Social Security attacks to international relations, the death penalty and attacks on

Chapter 1

Mission Accomplished

Much fun has been made of the Bush photo-op aircraft carrier landing and his speech to a bunch of sailors proclaiming the "end of major combat" in Iraq while standing under a banner reading "Mission Accomplished." On its face the stunt was ridiculous. People were still dying every day in Iraq, the U.S. had 135,000 troops in the country with no idea when they'd be coming home, and here was the commander-in-chief, all dolled up in flight gear, declaring that it was all over.

What most Americans missed, though, was that in fact, the sign was absolutely correct. We were all simply confused because we didn't realize what the mission was. It was not the much-touted "liberation" of Iraq or, god knows, the elimination of those mythic Weapons of Mass Destruction. Hell no. The mission was the war itself! And so the banner on the carrier Lincoln was accurate. The Bush administration wanted a war, and by god, it had gone out and made itself a dandy one.

Today, it is clear that the fanatics and zanies in the White House and the Pentagon got a lot more than they had bet on. Wars can have a funny way of doing that, as Lyndon Johnson and Richard Nixon both discovered (and as Napoleon and Hitler discovered too, in their day). But the fact remains that this was a war that was long in the planning, and that was going to happen because the Bush White House had decided it needed a serious national crisis—and only a war would do— to achieve its goal of Republican hegemony in Washington.

It is with this context in mind that the following columns, all written between Feb. 1, 2003 and the summer of 2004, should be read.

There is much that is grotesquely wrong with the way Bush and his people have conducted the war in Iraq. There has been enough pigheadedness, ignorance, stupidity, duplicity, corruption and criminality in the course of the build-up to and the fighting of this latest American war to rival anything that happened during all the decades of the Indochina conflict. But we need to be clear about a fundamental difference. In Vietnam, several successive presidential administrations were sucked deeper and deeper into a quagmire. Each president in his turn was guilty in his own way of making it worse, but the Vietnam War was never entirely a disaster of one president's or one administration's own making. In the case of the current war, it is safe to say that everything we see happening is the result of deliberate actions of the Bush administration, which wanted this war so badly it hurt.

By Spring 2004, with events spiraling rapidly out of his control, George W. Bush no doubt had begun to wish he never started the thing, but there's no question that when he stood on the flight deck of the Abraham Lincoln back on May 1, 2003, he really did feel like his mission had been accomplished. He had his war!

This first set of columns addresses some of the roots of the war, how it was begun, how it was fought, and what some of the consequences have been and are likely to be.

Liberating Iraqis...From Their Homes: IOUs for Looting

As the U.S. Army's Seventh Combat Support Group, a unit of the Third Infantry Division, moved northward in the Arabian desert west of the Euphrates River towards the town of Najaf on March 26, 2003 the commander, realizing his exhausted men faced shortages of food and water, was looking for a place of refuge. He found it in the form of two Bedouin families.

Drew Brown, reporter from Knight Ridder News Service who was embedded with the unit, reported that Col. John P. Gardner ordered the two families to leave their land and turn it over to his men. He reportedly gave them "receipts" for the tents, dogs, chickens, bowls, pots and other possessions they left behind—receipts that neither he nor anyone else could tell them how they could redeem—and sent them off "befuddled"[2] into the desert.

If any incident illustrates the true nature of the Anglo-U.S. invasion of Iraq, this one is it. A modern army unit, bristling with the latest in high-tech, high-powered weaponry, purportedly in the country to "liberate" the natives from the tyrant who "enslaves" them, summarily casts two defenseless groups of men, women and children out of their homes into the barren desert, handing them worthless IOUs for their trouble.

Obviously Col. Gardner the Liberator didn't do much studying of American history or he would have known that the Third Amendment of the U.S. Constitution, the one that bans the billeting of troops in private households, was a direct result of the British practice of taking over colonial farms and households at will for the quartering of Redcoat troops. It was this obscene imperial behavior, perhaps more than the issue of "taxation without representation", that really fed the fires of rebellion in the U.S. colonies. Brown doesn't tell us what the two "nomad" families felt or said as they were driven by Gardner and his men from their homes and lands, but it's a fair bet they weren't awash with feelings or gratitude at their liberation.

As this war continues to look more and more like a quagmire, this and other actions by the Bush/Blair army of liberation are likely to cause problems for the liberators.

Take the U.S. attacks on Iraqi television and on the telephone headquarters in Baghdad. Under the doctrine of reciprocity, a country that suffers any type of attack during a war is entitled to respond in kind, even if the initial attack was outside the bounds of normally acceptable rules of war. This means that should Iraq decide to respond by sending sappers (explosives experts) to the U.S to blow up the headquarters of CNN or Fox TV, for example, such attacks would not be acts of terrorism, but of war.

President Bush said he was invading Iraq to make America safe. In fact, by going to war in Iraq, he has, legally speaking, made the entire U.S. a potential battlefront in this war, inviting Iraq to send its agents into the country, or to get sleeper agents already here activated.

It's unlikely that Iraqi sappers would be billeting themselves in American households, but should they do so, in an effort to hide from Ashcroft's minions, or simply to seek temporary refuge, they could always cite the precedent of Col. Gardner, saying they were just behaving reciprocally.

Hopefully, if they force any American families out of their homes, those Iraqi agents will be as thoughtful about providing their unwilling hosts with receipts, as was the Seventh Combat Support Group.

— *CounterPunch.org, March 31, 2003*

Certainly a big part of the propaganda campaign beamed at Americans during the run-up to the invasion was aimed at creating the illusion that this was a global campaign against Iraq, not just an American imperial adventure. (No one abroad was likely to swallow such a con job, which required the participation of a jingoistic media.) Accordingly, after a lot of diplomatic arm-twisting, outright bribery and extortion, a list of "allies" was announced. As we've subsequently seen, aside from the British, no other countries actually did much fighting, though a few nations' troops did do a significant bit of dying.

And a Big Hand for...The Coalition of the Willing

Here they are, the Coalition of the Willing, courtesy of Colin Powell and your friends at the White House. This is the entire State Department list of the so-called "Coalition of the Willing," those countries that are allegedly backing our pre-emptive war on Iraq. Let's take a look at who's with us:

- Afghanistan—Well, they should be a big help. Aren't we still trying to help them create an army? And isn't that army likely to be pretty well tied up at home?
- Albania—Um, okay.
- Australia—Just promised to send over 2000 troops. Thanks, mates!
- Azerbaijan—Takes one dictatorship to know another.
- Bulgaria—Our ace in the hole on the Security Council, but they are so important to the campaign that our plucky commander-in-chief forgot to invite them to the Azores for his big Allied leadership confab.
- Colombia—Taking time out from the war on drugs to take out Saddam. Maybe they'll ship some of those defoliant-spraying helicopters we've provided them with over to the Gulf to help clear away all that messy swamp grass lying between the Tigris and the Euphrates.
- Czech Republic—Let's see Mr. Havel—Mister Peace and Human Rights—explain this one!
- Denmark—To be or not to be part of an independent Europe, that is the question.
- El Salvador—This act of solidarity must be in gratitude for America's staunch defense of democracy there over the years.
- Eritrea—I guess they're glad to see the weapons flying anywhere outside their own benighted land.
- Estonia—Russia's against the war, so they're for it.
- Ethiopia—Maybe the U.S. will reward them with some sacks of surplus grain.
- Georgia—Shevardnadze's bid for recognition as still being globally significant.
- Hungary—Count the troops being provided. One, do I hear one?
- Italy—Well, let's say Berlusconi. After deducting all the Italians who have demonstrated against this war, and remov-

ing the Vatican, he's about the only one left supporting Bush's war in the entire country.

- Japan—Anxious to move the focus of guns and bombs away from the Korean peninsula. While Japan is not providing any troops for battle, the State Department points out they are willing to help out with the post-war clean-up. After we bombed them at Hiroshima and Nagasaki, they're good at that kind of thing.
- South Korea—see Japan above. Also Eritrea.
- Latvia—see Estonia
- Lithuania—ditto
- Macedonia—This is a bit hard to fathom, but I'm sure they'll make an important contribution to the war effort.
- The Netherlands—seeking relevance before global warming renders the entire country irrelevant. Thanks to massive opposition at home, no Dutch combat troops are being offered. Sort of a Dutch Treat kind of ally.
- Nicaragua—see El Salvador
- The Philippines—Hoping to keep American troops busy, so they won't pile into Mindanao, ignoring Filipine government statements, and start mixing it up with Islamic rebels.
- Poland—Needs a diversion from economic disaster at home.
- Romania—see Poland, only more so. Don't expect to see a Romanian battalion marching towards Baghdad. The government's having trouble rustling up boots for them to wear.
- Slovakia—Hey, State Department dudes! Didn't this country change its name a while back, to Slovak Republic? Shouldn't we get our allies' names correct? Oh well, no matter. Whatever they're called, they're on board.
- Spain—See Italy. With only 14 percent popular support for the U.S. war, this is really just the governing elite. There's nobody willing to shoulder a gun and join the Brits and the Americans in battle. Spain, supposedly America's biggest backer, along with Britain, the country whose flag was flying alongside America's and Britain's as a backdrop at the Azores summit, is sending how many troops? Answer: zero.*
- Turkey—Excuse me? This is one of our partners in the

---

*Eventually, Spain did send about 1200 troops, and suffered some casualties. That was enough to sink conservative Prime Minister Anzar's re-election bid. In March 2004, he and his party were defeated by the Socialists, who promised to pull Spain's troops out of Iraq by June 30.

Coalition of the Willing? Didn't their parliament just stick it to us and say they weren't going to play? Okay they did finally say our planes could fly over their airspace enroute to Iraq, but added that they'd better not stop in Turkey along the way. Sort of makes you wonder about some of the others being listed as allies. With friends like these...

- United Kingdom—Okay, this one's for real at least. Though with 80 percent of the British public against war, Tony Blair may not be with us for long.
- Uzbekistan—And thank goodness for that!

—*CounterPunch.org, March 19, 2003*

Shortly after the Iraq War was launched, a massive demonstration was organized in New York City. At that march, several hundred thousand protesters peacefully demonstrated their opposition to the hostilities that had been begun by America. Despite provocations by some elements of the New York Police Department, and a few hostile spectators, the march was remarkably peaceful, if determined. I include the following report because it is so at odds with the mainstream media accounts, which focused on a few minor incidents that involved confrontations with police.

War and Peace in New York: Against the War at Ground Zero

New York City, March 22, 2003—The first thing I noticed as I walked up from the 38th Street ferry pier towards the Broadway march assembly point was row upon row of police buses—the paddy wagons used for mass arrests—lined up along 12th Avenue.

As I walked past the entrance to the Lincoln Tunnel, another jarring sight greeted my eyes: clusters of National Guard soldiers in camouflage uniforms, M-16 assault rifles at the ready.

The image was of a city in the grip of war.

...Until I reached Broadway. There, the mood was entirely different. Stretched from Times Square at 42nd Street, down to almost Herald Square at 34th Street, the entire Great White Way was jammed, elbow to elbow, with a still growing throng of anti-war demonstrators.

The day was sunny, the temperature was heading for the 60s, and the mood of the crowd was upbeat but determined.

It was an astonishing display. Even as the nation was engaged in a ferocious assault on the nation of Iraq, and as the first reports of American casualties in that war were coming in, what was shaping up as one of the largest peace demonstrations in the history of New York was getting set to march through the heart of the very city where this new round of global violence had started. New York, N.Y.

That the march was happening at all was a remarkable testament to the power of protest. A month earlier, the administration of Mayor Michael Bloomberg, reportedly under pressure from the Bush Administration and with the support of a compliant federal district court and appellate court, had denied a march permit to the coalition seeking to march past the United Nations to protest the looming war. That time demonstrators, who numbered between 100,000 and 400,000, had been penned in and in some cases brutalized by police on horseback. Several hundred had been arrested.

This time the city, which had suffered an enormous public relations black eye for its handling of legitimate protest on a day when much larger protests had gone off peacefully around the world, had agreed to grant a march permit, allowing demonstrators to walk from Times Square all the way down Broadway to Union Square at 14th Street, and then on down to Washington Square in Greenwich Village.

But nobody, either the police or the city or the march organizers, had anticipated how enormous this demonstration would prove to be. At 11 am, an hour before the lead marchers—a group of World Trade Center Survivors and families of Trade Center victims—were to step off, police, who had set up barricades limiting the march to only half of the width of the street, realized that this would not work. They pulled the barricades over to the sidewalks, surrendering all of Broadway to the mushrooming throng.

In the end, when the march finally got moving, the densely packed but orderly crowd reportedly stretched for 40 blocks—a distance of about three miles.

There were no speakers, either during the march or at its start or terminus. Demonstrators were left to convey their messages via signs, which were both focused and creative. "Bush, pull out like your daddy should have!" was popular. So was "Money for jobs, not for war."

Some people carried fake tombstones with the names of young Palestinians killed in the Intifada. Others wore berets and hoisted baguettes, in honor of the French, who had led the successful campaign to block U.S. efforts to gain Security Council approval for the war on Iraq. One man carried an elaborate 3-D mural of a red, white and blue elephant defecating missiles onto a map of Iraq.

The remarkable thing about this march, which one officer said police were estimating at 100-200,000, and which CNN put at 175,000, but which rally organizers estimated at over 400,000, was how little opposition it engendered. From my vantage point in the rough middle-point of this stream of humanity, during the entire course of the march I saw only three individuals along the sidelines holding signs in support of the war or heckling marchers.

Among marchers, the sentiment of supporting the troops was widespread. I saw no signs criticizing American soldiers, but many signs saying things along the lines of, "Support our troops. Bring them home."

As a veteran of the October 1967 mass march on the Pentagon (when I and hundreds of other peaceful protesters were arrested and carted off to the federal prison in Occoquan, VA, where we faced criminal trespass, resisting arrest and various other charges), I found both the sophistication of the marchers, and the non-antagonistic, even supportive response of bystanders, simply astounding, particularly in a city that had been the target of such a horrendous attack only a year and a half earlier—an attack which the U.S. government has been trying to link to America's current wartime foe, Iraq.

While marchers expressed support for U.S. soldiers, and appeared for the most part to get along with local police lining the route, there was considerable unconcealed anger at the mass media, however.

When an NBC camera crew set up a video camera atop a van at Herald Square, for example, demonstrators in the surrounding area pretty much deep-sixed any chance of favorable coverage by hoisting their middle fingers and chanting "NBC—National Bullshit Corporation!" A similar angry reception was given to a young woman and cameraman from WB's local Channel 1 News.

Fox TV—the network owned by the openly pro-war News Corp. of Rupert Murdoch—came in for special rebuke. A reporter attempting to interview one marcher had her microphone repeatedly brushed aside as she leadingly tried to ask him why he was demonstrating while American troops were overseas fighting.

For the most part, the 2000 police who lined the march route were relaxed and even, in many cases, friendly with marchers, though at certain points, particularly in the various open areas such as Herald and

Union Squares, there were numbers of officers dressed in riot gear as if prepared for the worst.

The only incidents came at the end of the march, when some demonstrators decided not to disperse as ordered by police, but to remain in and around the area of Washington Square.

At about 5 PM, an hour after the parade permit had expired, police attempted a pincer move to trap a group of over a thousand demonstrators on the block running along the north of the park. With police and police vans blocking a rear escape, a large contingent of police in riot gear began advancing on the group from the other end of the street. It started to look tense, and some mace was sprayed (both sides accused the other of spraying it). Then a 75-year-old woman stepped forward and confronted the advancing officers. "Why are you doing this?" she asked them. "We are being trapped here."

Confronted with a choice of moving forward and arresting the woman or backing off, the police relented, and allowed the protestors to move forward.

There were, however, several dozen arrests as the march was breaking up. As one young black woman was dragged off, handcuffed, by police, she shouted out several times, "I have the constitutional right peaceably to assemble."

In New York City on March 22, 2003, apparently, only until 4 PM. As another demonstrator nearby me who was watching the incident commented wryly, "She obviously hasn't heard about the changes Bush and Ashcroft have made in the Constitution."

—*CounterPunch.org, March 19, 2003*

Bombing Saddam into Glory:
A Hero Made in Washington

You've got to hand it to President and Commander-in-Chief George W. Bush. Only last month, virtually the entire world was in agreement that Saddam Hussein was one of the world's great villains. Not only was there near universal condemnation of his domestic tyranny, there were also rigorous sanctions being applied against his regime, and the U.N. was conducting an aggressive campaign of searching out and destroying his more dangerous weapons.

Now, in less than a week, our own benighted maximum leader has managed to do something that this grotesque megalomaniac had failed to accomplish for 30 years despite billions of oil dollars spent on arms and millions more spent on blanketing his country with statues and murals: He has made the Butcher of Baghdad into a hero of Third World resistance.

Incredibly, the U.S. military's massive, illegal invasion of Iraq has almost overnight galvanized at least some of the people of Iraq into death-defying guerrilla fighters willing to take on Apache helicopters and Abrams tanks of the most powerful military machine the world has ever known with hand-held weapons, and has reportedly even convinced exiled opponents of Hussein to sneak back into the country to help defend their country against the aggressors.

And it can only get worse.

Each Iraqi fighter (and each innocent civilian bystander) killed now leaves behind a grieving family that can be counted on to harbor a blood hatred for the countries that caused their loss. Ergo: more recruits for Osama Bin Laden's Al Qaeda and those "Al Qaeda-type" organizations which Bush keeps referring to.

Each nomad family driven from its home by American troops holds bitter thoughts of revenge.

Each family that watches its home demolished by American or British cannons will remember the loss. Each family that loses a child or a parent to American bombs will become a potential enemy.

None of this can be very comforting to think about for the American troops who will have to serve as occupiers over the coming months and years if things go well for America—or for their families back home.

Meanwhile, across the vast stretches of northern Africa, the Middle East and South Asia, and on out into the island nations of the Pacific, Islamic peoples watching on television the wholesale destruction of one of Islam's oldest regions, are cheering the astonishing and indeed inspiring resistance being displayed by the vastly outgunned Iraqis.

In a few short days of battle, the War on Iraq has become a no-win situation for the U.S.

If America wins at this point after an inevitably bloody battle for Baghdad, the resulting country will be ungovernable, except under the most brutal of martial law regimes—a quagmire-type situation that promises an endless string of American casualties and another grim monument to insanity on the increasingly crowded Washington Mall.

If America loses—something that is at least being contemplated by some military experts because of the inability of the military to secure the 350-mile supply line from the Persian Gulf to the Baghdad front line—it could undermine the carefully cultivated myth of U.S. invincibility, leading others to challenge U.S. hegemony.

If there is a stalemate, with the slaughter continuing on both sides and no likelihood of a resolution of the fight, the pressures from around the world, from Europe, the Middle East and elsewhere, for a cease-fire will become irresistible, even as the peace movement at home will mushroom. Bush bet mightily on this war to secure his position as a powerful leader, harkening to the ill-conceived advice of a group of narrow-minded ideologues with little knowledge of either military strategy or Middle East history.

Now he appears doomed to become another Lyndon Johnson, throwing more and more ordnance at and spilling more and more blood in a country far from home, while his political future drains away. In the wake of the 9-11 terror attacks on America, George Bush looked unstoppable for a second term as president.

No longer.

— CounterPunch.org, March 28, 2003

In the run-up to the invasion, and during the heavy fighting in March and April particularly, very little was said in the mainstream American media about the U.S. use of depleted uranium weaponry, though it has been condemned by the U.N., and has been a major concern among American GI's, who suspect that it may be the reason for the high numbers of veterans of the 1991 Gulf War suffering from mysterious ailments collectively referred to as Gulf War Syndrome. By May 2004, a year after the weapons had been used, the first reports of uranium poisoning of American veterans, and of Iraqi civilians—had started to come in. But we should have known this would happen. The Pentagon *did* know, but has been covering it up with the help of the embedded media.

America's Dirty Bombs:
These WMDs are Right in Front of Their Noses

The Pentagon has announced plans to send several thousand specialists into Iraq to join the search for Saddam Hussein's "weapons of mass destruction"—remember the ones that Iraq was supposedly brimming over with, and which were the stated reason for America's invasion? But while it is stepping up that effort, the Pentagon says it has no intention to do anything about the consequences of America's own "dirty bomb" campaign against Iraq. Although the U.S. and Britain reportedly dropped as much as 2000 tons of depleted uranium weapons on Iraq, including in the center of densely populated Baghdad, a Pentagon spokesman last month told the BBC that it has "no plans to do a DU clean-up in Iraq."

Nor is the U.S. allowing inspectors from the U.N. environmental Program into Iraq to look for signs of DU contamination. It seems that just as the U.S. government doesn't want U.N. weapons inspectors to come into Iraq where they might undermine any U.S. claims to have found evidence of Saddam's WMDs, they don't want any U.N. environmental inspectors to come in and find evidence of U.S. use of a weapon that the U.N. has condemned as a weapon of mass destruction.

If U.N. estimates of the quantity of depleted uranium ordnance used in the current war in Iraq are correct, it would mean six times as much of the super-toxic and carcinogenic substance was used this time as in 1991, and already there are disturbing reports of dramatically higher incidences of cancer and birth defects in Southern Iraq following the 1991 war. But at least in that war, virtually all the DU ammo was used against Iraqi armor out in the desert. This time, bunker-busting bombs and anti-tank weapons were used in Iraqi cities, including Baghdad, putting in jeopardy tens or hundreds of thousands of civilians who might come in contact with the radioactive dust from those explosions. Of course, U.S. troops, now playing the role of an occupying army in those bombed cities, are also at risk. Many veterans of the last Iraq war suspect that the notorious "Gulf War Syndrome" that many came home with was the result of their having breathed in or ingested uranium dust from the weapons used in that war.

The U.S. has been firing off "dirty bombs" in the form of depleted uranium (DU) weapons now since the 1991 Gulf War against Iraq. Depleted uranium, a radioactive metal that is part of the waste stream from nuclear weapons and power plants, turns out to be a highly effective armor-piercing material. 1.7 times as dense as lead, it also has the unusual property of self-sharpening: as a rod of the stuff slams into a sheet of steel or a wall of reinforced concrete, instead of mushrooming into a flat, broad projectile that then is slowed or stopped by the obstacle, uranium sheds its exterior layers and becomes sharper as it is propelled by momentum deeper and deeper into its target. Uranium is also highly flammable at the kinds of high temperature generated by a high-velocity collision, and so it incinerates itself and whatever target it hits.

In the 1991 Gulf War, depleted uranium was used extensively in two types of weapons—the 120 mm anti-tank shells fired by Abrams tanks and other anti-tank cannons, and the 30 mm anti-armor guns on the A-10 Warthog ground attack jets. An estimated 300 tons of the stuff was fired off in the Iraqi and Kuwaiti desert during that war. In Kosovo, the same weapons were used, this time reportedly a total of about 12 tons, mostly in the form of small 30-mm projectiles fired by aircraft.

In Afghanistan, in addition to those two kinds of shells, the Pentagon introduced a third category of uranium weapon—the so-called bunker-busting bomb—a depleted uranium "smart bomb" or missile that can burrow deep into the ground or through thick concrete walls to hit heavily shielded shelters or cave hideouts. The Pentagon has not released information about how much depleted uranium was used in weapons in Afghanistan, but estimates have ranged from several hundred tons to as much as 1000 tons—and this was in a conflict that was tiny compared to the likely war in Iraq. (The Center for Defense Information reports that the patents for America's bunker-busting bombs include both tungsten and uranium-clad versions, making it clear that these weapons exist in the U.S. military arsenal. Given the Pentagon's public stance that uranium weapons pose no appreciable health risk, it seems clear that these dangerous weapons of mass destruction are being used.)

Critics of depleted uranium weapons—and these run the gamut from the U.N. World Health Organization to Gulf War veterans groups—note that the new use of uranium bunker-buster bombs raises the danger of radioactive contamination dramatically, because of where such bombs get used.

For the most part, anti-tank weapons, at least to date, have been used where tanks are generally deployed, which is out in the open, where population density is low. When a depleted uranium round explodes, the uranium is incinerated, becoming a dangerous aerosol of minute inhaleable particles of uranium oxide, though out in the desert the risks are relatively low of many people becoming contaminated. Absent a wind, most of that radioactive residue settles within 50-100 yards of the target.

Even so, there are reports from both the Basra area of Southern

Iraq, where use of depleted uranium shells by British and U.S. forces in 1991 was heavy, and in Afghanistan, of higher than anticipated cancer rates and birth defects. There is also some suspicion that at least some of the cases of what has become known as Gulf War Syndrome among returned U.S. Gulf War veterans are the result of their having inhaled the residue of uranium weapons. Researchers from a British non-profit organization, the Uranium Medical Research Center, for example, claim that during an investigation of bombed areas in Kabul and especially Jalalabad, Afghanistan, they encountered widespread evidence of illnesses and birth defects, which they said, were consistent with uranium poisoning and radioactive contamination. They also reported finding elevated levels of uranium in the vicinity. They called their findings "shocking". Similar findings have been claimed in the area around southern Iraq where uranium anti-tank weapons were widely used.

But earlier reports of dirty bomb after-effects could be dwarfed once reports start coming in of the effects of DU contamination in urban areas of Iraq. For one thing, the amount of uranium vaporized in an explosion of one bunker-busting bomb would be vastly greater than any anti-tank shell. There are, for example, "only" about three kilograms of uranium in 120mm anti-tank round.

But the DU explosive charges in the guided bomb systems used in Afghanistan and now Iraq (for example Raytheon's Bunker Buster-GBU-28) reportedly can weigh as much as one and a half metric tons. Besides, U.S. troops, which had to fight their way into Baghdad and other heavily fortified Iraqi cities, made use of their uranium anti-tank weapons there too, not just out in the desert approaches to urban centers.

The notion of Baghdad, a city of five million, being dusted with uranium oxide, is grim, as it will likely produce widespread injuries and death, particularly among children, who are closer to the ground and who routinely play in the dirt.

No wonder the U.S. government is so anxious to keep U.N. environmental experts at bay. The risks of uranium weapons to soldiers and civilians is a topic of some controversy, even among critics, though no one except the Pentagon and NATO disputes that it is a health threat.

Indeed, the Royal Society, whose studies the Pentagon spokesman cited in saying that fears of DU health threats have been debunked since 1991, pointedly disagreed, saying that in the society's view, DU poses both short and long-term risks in Iraq.

A government study prepared for Congress in the mid 1990s

offered the following assessment of the dangers of the radioactive weapons: "As much as 70 percent of a DU penetrator can be aerosolized when it strikes a tank. Aerosols containing DU oxides may contaminate the area downwind. DU fragments may also contaminate the soil around the struck vehicle." It adds that there are many paths by which the resulting particles may enter the body—by inhalation, ingestion, or through open wounds. The report then states, "If DU enters the body, it has the potential to generate significant medical consequences. The risks associated with DU in the body are both chemical and radiological."

Once inside the lungs or kidneys, uranium particles tend to stay, causing illnesses such as lung cancer and kidney disease that may take decades to show up. According to Dr. J. W. Gofman, a leading expert and critic of low-level radiation risks, particles of uranium smaller than 5 micron in diameter can become permanently trapped in the lungs. By one estimate, a trapped, single uranium oxide particle of this size could expose the adjacent lung tissue to approximately 1,360 rem per year—about 8,000 times the annual radiation dosage considered safe by federal regulations for whole body exposure.

Uranium, which besides being carcinogenic is also highly toxic chemically (like lead or mercury), also concentrates in the kidneys and reproductive organs if ingested orally. Even Dan Fahey, of the Persian Gulf War Veterans Resource Center, a Navy veteran who has criticized as overblown some anti-war organizations' charges concerning the dangers of uranium weapons, says that they were "probably a contributor to Gulf War Syndrome" among returning U.S. Gulf War veterans. Although he debunks as "propaganda and science fiction," a report by the Uranium Medical Research Center, a U.K.-based organization which claims to have found uranium contamination and signs of radiation-sickness and radiation-induced birth defects in people who live around suspected uranium weapon targets in Kabul and Jalalabad, Afghanistan, Fahey himself is critical of the U.S. military's ever-expanding use of these weapons. In one article he wrote on the subject, he quotes a 1990 Pentagon memo on the health risks of exploded uranium ordnance which concludes that, in order to avoid criticism of the weapons' battlefield use, "we should keep this sensitive issue at mind when after action reports are written."

His conclusion: "The military's view is that unless you can prove something is dangerous, we'll keep using it. My view is that given the known health concerns about depleted uranium weapons, unless you can prove it's safe, don't use it."

There is no question about whether or not the US and British are using uranium weapons in the current war against Iraq. Robert Fisk quoted a U.S. general on the eve of battle as saying, "We have already begun to unwrap our depleted uranium anti-tank shells." (In the 1991 Gulf War, one in seven Iraqi tanks destroyed by the U.S. was hit by a uranium projectile. This time, the percentage of Iraq's 1800 tanks hit by uranium weapons was clearly far higher. As for the more serious use of uranium-tipped missiles and bombs in urban settings, the best evidence that they were used is that the Pentagon, absent rules that limit its behavior, uses whatever it has in its arsenal that the generals think works best—and clearly uranium-tipped weapons outperform any alternative in terms of their ability to penetrate armor and other heavy shielding. According to Pentagon studies, uranium projectiles are at least 10 percent more effective at penetrating shielded bunkers and armor than the next-best alternative—tungsten clad weapons. That alone was a powerful incentive to use them.

Given the Pentagon's public stance that uranium weapons pose no appreciable health risk, there is no reason to believe that these dangerous weapons of mass destruction were not used. Moreover, given the controversy surrounding DU, it seems likely that if the Pentagon had decided not to use DU weapons inside Iraqi cities, it would have trumpeted that fact. No such disavowal was made.

Civilians in the future "liberated" Iraq will likely be paying the price for years—maybe generations—to come. Meanwhile, after they're through watching their president play airman on an aircraft carrier, American veterans of the Iraq war might want to consider the fate of those soldiers whom the Pentagon sent to participate in early nuclear weapons tests. Fifty years later, after most of those soldier/guinea pigs have died, many of them from suspicious cancers, the government is finally admitting that they received far larger radiation doses than it ever was willing to acknowledge.

—CounterPunch.org, May 12, 2003

It is my firm belief that the Bush administration invaded Iraq primarily for political reasons: it wanted a war—neat, short and victorious—ahead of the 2004 election to ensure a Republican sweep of the White House and Congress. That said, there were other ancillary reasons invading Iraq looked like a great idea to oilman Bush and his oil-soaked cabinet and campaign contributors. This article, which ran initially in *CounterPunch's* print edition in April 2003, reported on a study that received little attention in the mainstream corporate media.

CounterPunch Special Report

Secret Bechtel Documents Reveal: Yes, It Is About Oil

Is the war against Iraq all about oil? Not to hear Defense Secretary Donald Rumsfeld tell it. Back on Nov. 15, he called the notion that oil was the real reason behind the Bush administration's drive against Saddam Hussein "nonsense," saying, "It has nothing to do with oil, literally nothing to do with oil."

But a new study released by the Institute for Policy Studies, based upon secret diplomatic cables just declassified by the National Archives, and internal communications of the Bechtel Corporation, suggests just the opposite: that oil is the underlying cause of this war.

The study, which discloses the intimate links between the Bechtel Corporation and Bechtel executives and U.S. policy towards Iraq, also shows that some key players in the push for America's war against Iraq, including Rumsfeld, Vice President Dick Cheney, and other former Reagan administration officials Roger Robinson, Judge William B. Clark and Robert McFarlane, have been intimately involved in issues relating to Iraqi oil as far back as the1980s.

Titled "Crude Vision: How Oil Interests Obscured US Government Focus on Chemical Weapons Use by Saddam Hussein," this report traces an intense effort by Reagan officials in the mid1980s to win Hussein's approval for a $2-billion oil pipeline to be built by Bechtel, running from the Euphrates oilfields in southern Iraq westward to Jordan and the Gulf of Aqaba.

A key player in that effort was Rumsfeld, then the CEO of Searle drugs, the giant pharmaceutical company (whose chairman is a leading right-wing backer of Bush and conservatives in congress).

One particularly revealing 1983 memo, declassified for the first time in February by the National Archives, concerns a trip by Rumsfeld to Iraq. Acting as a special White House "peace envoy" allegedly to discuss the bloody war between Iran and Iraq with Hussein and then foreign minister Tarik Aziz, Rumsfeld turns out according to this memo to have been talking not about that war, but about Bechtel's proposed Aqaba pipeline.

In his memo to Secretary of State George Schultz reporting on the meeting with Hussein, Rumsfeld talks at length about the pipeline discussion, but makes no mention of having discussed either the war or charges that Hussein's army was using chemical weapons against the Iranians.

The intense focus of Rumsfeld, Schultz (a former president of Bechtel), Cheney and other Reagan officials, in concert with Bechtel, on the pipeline, reads like an abbreviated, or mini "Pentagon Papers," laying the groundwork for a collapse in relations between the U.S. and Iraq, and eventually to war. The documents also cast Bechtel's current position as one of two top candidates for the lucrative contract to "rebuild Iraq" in a troubling light.

As American troops press into Baghdad, and Iraqi casualties run into the thousands, *CounterPunch* speaks with Jim Valette, director of research at the Sustainable Energy and Economy Network, and one of the three authors of "Crude Vision."

Q: What prompted this study?

A: We were examining the interconnections between private corporations and the U.S. government in the pursuit of oil worldwide since 1995—principally the U.S. financing —through the World Bank and US agencies like the Export-Import Bank and the Overseas Private Investment Corporation (OPIC), etc. of that pursuit. But what has clearly occurred in recent months has been an even more serious expression of this pursuit of fossil fuels for the benefit of Big Oil, which is an extension of this relation into the military role. And so we're looking at the deployment of troops and paramilitaries financed by the U.S. government worldwide, and of course the most serious conflict of interest is in Iraq. In the course of that research we saw the beginning and end of the story of American efforts to gain control of Iraq's oilfields, the beginning being Rumsfeld's meeting with Saddam Hussein in December 1983 to the end, which was the Independent Counsel's investigation of the Attorney General, at the time, Edwin Meese, and his relationship with one of the brokers of the pipeline, E. Robert Wallachs. Before this, nobody had connected the dots between Rumsfeld and the Meese investigation and nobody had examined exactly how dominant this pipeline project was in the diplomacy and the burgeoning relationship between the Reagan administration and Saddam Hussein. It was in that context that we came across corporate records and government memoranda related to the Aqaba pipeline project. It was a real eye-opener to us to see how interwoven Bechtel's interests were with the Reagan Administration.

Q. We're talking about stuff that happened almost 20 years ago. How is this relevant to what's happening in Iraq now?

A: This story, I think, is timely even though it's 20 years old because Bechtel is back now, as the likely winner of the contract to rebuild Iraq's infrastructure, and many of those Reagan administration officials are back, and they are poised to get their hands on Iraq's oil again.

Q: So what is new here?

A: The release in February by the National Archives of cables back and forth between Washington and U.S. diplomats in the Middle East around the time of 1983 and 1984 disclose for the first time what really transpired in Rumsfeld's meetings with Saddam and other Iraqi officials. What had previously been reported was that Rumsfeld had a cozy meeting with Saddam in Baghdad in December 1983. In the past, the focus was on whether or not he had raised the issue of Saddam's use of chemical arms against Iran. But what the actual memoranda show is that a big part of Rumsfeld's discussion with Saddam Hussein was this new proposal from Bechtel to build a pipeline form Iraq to Jordan. I mean Rumsfeld was executing the marching orders of George Schultz, who was the Secretary of State, but who came directly from the presidency of Bechtel to the Reagan administration. The documents released by the National Security Archive suggest that what was going on then had quite a bit to do with oil—certainly more than had been known before.

Q: Before the release of those documents we didn't know that Rumsfeld was talking about a pipeline?

A: Right. Right. I mean it was reported that when he was there he didn't raise an issue with Saddam about the use of chemical weapons, even though there were reports coming out of Iran that Saddam was dropping chemical bombs on Iranian troops.

Q: So we knew before what he didn't talk about, but not what he was talking about, and that was the pipeline?

A: Right, he was there sort of as a bagman for Bechtel. And then there were documents I found in the government's National Archives that showed the extensive involvement of Reagan officials and the very close relationship they had with Bechtel officials, in pursuing this pipeline over the next two years. We sort of connected the dots between what was in these National Security Archives and what was known in the general coverage over the last 15 years.

Q: How important was this pipeline in terms of U.S.-Iraqi relations?

A: It was the focus of U.S. relations with Iraq for several years, right through the period that Iraq was locked in a bitter war with Iran. In one 1984 internal company memo, Bechtel executive H. B. Scott exhorts his colleagues at Bechtel, after it appeared that all this diplomacy by Rumsfeld seemed to be paying off, "I cannot emphasize enough the need for maximum Bechtel management effort at all levels of the U.S. government and industry to support this project. It has significant political overtones. The time may be ripe for this project to move promptly with very significant rewards to Bechtel for having made it possible." And in these documents we see how tightly interwoven this management effort is with their former colleagues such as George Schultz in the State Department in implementing this initiative. It shows how corporations take advantage of U.S. geopolitics in the region and how they try to profit from those geopolitical developments. Another important memo was in July of 1985, after Bechtel had run into some difficulties in assuaging Saddam's fears about potential Israeli threats to the pipeline. Bechtel and the State Department were having trouble getting the right degree of assurance from the Israeli Labor Party [then the ruling party in Israel] that the pipeline would be off limits to attack. Bechtel and the Reagan administration officials were trying to get absolute assurance from the Labor Party that the pipeline would absolutely not be attacked. There were some frustrations to that approach in 1985, and so Bechtel hired a couple of very close friends of the Reagan administration to sort out the deal. In July of 1985, pipeline promoters hired Judge Jim Clark, who was considered Reagan's right hand man. He had just left government to go into private business. There's a memo from Judge Clark saying that he's "on board" and laying out the terms of his involvement, which were $500 an hour, and saying he'd be flying to Baghdad, not as a private consultant, but representing himself as a White House representative. That memorandum, which is available on our website (<www.gwu.edu/~nsarchiv /NSAEBB/NSAEBB82>), shows how blurry that revolving door had become. He's working for the government while he's simultaneously getting paid as an agent for Bechtel.

Q: Okay, so we have the evidence that there was this big concern about getting this big pipeline for Bechtel, and the interest in getting oil out without it having to go through the Persian Gulf. But wasn't that a legitimate national security concern for the U.S., given Iran's political situation and its hostility towards America?

A: Well, it has been long-standing US national security policy on paper that threats to the free flow of oil are threats to national security, and this is what we're getting at here. Is this pursuit of oil or the pursuit of empire? Some folks define what's going on in Iraq as U.S. pursuit of empire, but right now it's really two sides of the same coin. And this policy of pursuing oil and empire is coming up against all sorts of realities now that weren't well understood back in the 1980s. On the National security side, this pursuit of oil wealth at all costs has huge costs to democracy and human rights. It's creating a backlash in the Middle East and elsewhere that has had some horrible expressions recently.

Q: The pipeline never got built though. What happened?

A: In the end, Saddam decided that Bechtel was trying to charge too much for the project, and so he killed the project and instead went with a pipeline connecting into pipelines in Turkey and into Saudi Arabia, but avoiding the Straits of Hormuz.

Q: Do you expect to see the Aqaba pipeline revived?

A: Maybe, maybe not. I've seen reports now of Israel looking to build a pipeline from Iraq to the Golan Heights. It's not the same project as Bechtel's Aqaba pipeline idea. Bechtel asked the Commerce Department to keep the Aqaba pipeline registered as an active project for years, but it's probably less necessary now for the U.S. and Bechtel. The pipelines to Saudi Arabia and Turkey give an alternative route for oil to the Persian Gulf, and Bechtel gets into Iraq as a contractor to rebuild Iraq after the war. Right now, according to an article in the *Wall Street Journal*, Bechtel is one of the two finalists for the Iraq reconstruction job, along with Parson's group, which has Halliburton as a secondary contractor. Halliburton is Vice President Cheney's former company [Note: Cheney is still receiving payments from Halliburton]. That was reported in the *Wall Street Journal* today (April 2). They're both on the short list. Halliburton sort of stepped back for obvious reasons but they're still in there with Parsons.

Q: Aside from the unseemly picture of two well connected companies getting an inside track for all that post-war business in Iraq, why do you find the Bechtel involvement in this situation so troubling?

A: Schultz worked at Bechtel. So did (Reagan Defense Secretary) Caspar Weinberger. There were a lot of Bechtel people in the government in the '80s at the same time that the Iraqi's were gassing the

Iranians. The same people are now formulating the plans for a coming U.S. occupation of Iraq, and in turn, the same people will be given the spoils of war—whether it's Parsons and Halliburton or Bechtel. It's all kind of circular back to the 1980s, you know—completing unfinished business—getting American companies back in there after their being shut out since 1991 and the first Gulf War. Bechtel was also listed by Iraq in its report to the U.N. weapons inspectors as one of the companies that helped supply Saddam with equipment and knowledge for making chemical weapons. Bechtel in the 1980s was prime contractor on PC 1 and 2, two petrochemical plants constructed in Iraq which had dual-use capacity. So I guess the bottom line is that the Bush-Cheney-Rumsfeld squad is now holding Saddam Hussein accountable for chemical weapons of mass destruction—the same weapons which these same officials ignored in pursuit of the Aqaba pipeline project. And now we are going to reward the pipeline promoter with massive contracts for reconstruction resulting from this policy. There is just such hypocrisy in all this.

Q: This all seems like a kind of mini-Pentagon Papers, laying out the early roots of this war.

A: It's not as much of a blueprint as was the Pentagon Papers, but these memos and documents do show how business gets done in Washington, how it was conducted in the 1980s and how it's probably being conducted now behind closed doors under secret bidding processes. And it shows how the origins of American conflict with Iraq involve control of and access to oil.

Q: Can you see any signs that the current war is linked directly to oil? I mean the administration has given so many reasons for going to war I'm surprised they haven't gotten to oil. I remember in 1991, the first Bush said it was about jobs, which equates pretty quickly to oil. But they didn't say that this time around.

A: Yeah, they've redacted any reference to oil from their language. Maybe that's the best evidence that that's what it's really about, because it's logical. I mean Bush the first in his national security papers defined the free flow of oil as a national security priority, as did President Clinton in his final months in office. He released a national security paper that said that the free flow of oil is a national security priority that must be enforced with military might if necessary. The current Bush came out with the national security strategy that redacted this long-standing text dating back to the Carter administration, but at the same time you had this Cheney energy policy that continues this idea of the necessity of a "diverse and free supply of oil" without the military language. And actually you had Cheney kind of kick off the whole war fever last August in a speech to the Veterans of Foreign Wars. He cited the specter of Saddam Hussein with his weapons of mass destruction threatening the flow of oil from the region. Then immediately afterwards, any kind of reference like that vanished from the Bush administration's rhetoric, to the point that Secretary of Defense Rumsfeld called any kind of association of the current conflict with oil an "absurdity." So there is no document or strategy paper now that says, "We must invade Iraq because our US oil companies have been shut out of this second largest reservoir of oil for the last 20 years," but who knows what we'll find in the National Archives 20 years from now? It's a circumstantial case, but that's as good as we can do now. And logic certainly has its place as well. I mean, the question is why are the weapons of mass destruction today a cause for war when these very same weapons were ignored by the same officials 20 years ago when they were being used. What has changed is that other national oil companies—French, Russian and Chinese—have gotten into Iraq, while U.S. companies were being frozen out. I'm sure there are other factors. Certainly the Kuwait invasion didn't help U.S relations with Saddam, and since Kuwait, Saddam signed very lucrative oil contracts with the French, Russians, Chinese and others.

Q: You made the point in your paper that US relations started to tank with Iraq after the rejection of the oil pipeline.

A: That's true. There was a shift away from Iraq to Iran right at that time, but I should say that Reagan and Bush the First both played both sides of the fence for a while, even after the pipeline project collapsed. You had the Iran Contra deal, but at the same time the U.S. was providing Iraq with intelligence about Iranian troop movements. And the U.S. did extend commodity credits through the Agriculture Department that Saddam then parlayed into arms. And there were the chemical plants that Bechtel helped build. So it's been quirkier than that. But certainly the end of the pipeline destroyed oil relations.

Q: What do you think led to the current war. What's the oil link?

A: Look at what's in Iraq and what's undeveloped. Iraq represents a major insurance package against any kind of political overhaul in Saudi Arabia or problems elsewhere in the Middle East. Look at the policy that people like Rumsfeld and others were recommending in the 1990s leading up to this war and they certainly cited the threat of Saddam Hussein to regional oil supplies as a cause for war. Certainly if the Bechtel pipeline had been built, the course of Iraqi-U.S. relations would have been much different. The failure of that pipeline set into motion a much different course for those relations.

A: So having control of Iraqi oil is still a key issue?

Q: It's the sole reason why the Persian Gulf region and Iraq have been a United States national security concern for so long. It's not geography.

Q: So what would you say is the lesson of all this?

A: The lesson is that when it comes to oil, a dictator is friendly to the U.S. when he's willing to do business and he's a mortal enemy when he's not. That has been the driving force behind national security policy, especially since the fall of the Soviet Union. Oil and national security policy were all submerged in the context of the Cold War. But once that Cold War collapsed, now it's a no-holds-barred battle for oil globally, and the U.S. has seen itself cut out of the world's second largest reserve of oil—and oil that is very inexpensive to extract. So with the U.S. shut out of Iraq, certainly it makes the trigger fingers of U.S. policy-makers itchy. And whether it's a blood feud or a war for oil, it's just a tragedy that the people of Iraq and our own sons and daughters and brothers and sisters are paying the price.

—*CounterPunch* (print edition), *April 9, 2003*

Of course, whatever the motives for the war, it was only natural that once it got going, the Friends of Bush—a mercenary lot to be sure—would be there vulture-like to gobble up whatever they could of the reconstruction money that was sure to follow the wave of destruction, as this next column, one of the earlier reports on this unseemly war profiteering, explains.

The Iraq Moneypot

A little money goes a long way in the war-profiteering business
And war profiteering is the name of the game in post-war Iraq.

Long before the bombs started dropping in Baghdad, some well connected companies that wanted a piece of the reconstruction action were dropping bundles of cash on the Republican Party and on George W. Bush's campaign committee.

According to the Center for Responsive Politics, which tracks such things, five big winners in the rigged game of getting contracts in

Iraq, between 1999 and 2002, gave a total of $3.6 million in campaign donations. Two-thirds of that money went to Republicans, with the rest going to the right-wing Democratic Leadership Council crowd.

According to the center's website (www.capitaleye.org), the biggest donor among that group—and the biggest winner so far in the Iraq "reconstruction" contracts business—is the Bechtel Group, Inc. This San Francisco-based company, which has close ties to Secretary of Defense Donald Rumsfeld and the Bush family, as well as many other revolving-door connections to the White House and the Pentagon (US Agency for International Development Administrator Andrew Natsios, who oversees the awarding of post-war contracts, earlier oversaw the "Big Dig" tunnel project in Boston, for which Bechtel was the prime contractor), has already won an Iraq reconstruction contract worth up to $680 million. Even if Bechtel didn't win more of the estimated $20 billion per year in reconstruction contracts still to be awarded, $680 million in return for Bechtel's campaign contribution of $1.3 million (59 percent, or $770,000 of which, went to the Republican Party and G.W. Bush) represents a remarkable 52000% return on investment!

It's hard to know what the rate of return will be on Halliburton's contracts in Iraq. That's because the contract awarded to this uniquely well-connected Dallas-based oil-services and construction company to rebuild Iraq's war and sanctions-devastated oil industry is open-ended. Halliburton, besides donating $709,000, 95 percent of it to Republicans, between 1999 and 2002, was run by Vice President Dick Cheney until his election, and the secretive VP still collects some $1 million a year form the company while hiding out at his undisclosed locations (his not-so-blind trust still includes a big chunk of Halliburton stock, too). While Halliburton discretely removed itself from the bidding for Iraq reconstruction contracts because of the firm's prominent connection to the Bush Administration, the huge oil industry contract was awarded to a Halliburton subsidiary, Kellogg, Brown & Root.

Halliburton will be in Iraq in another hidden guise, too. That's because Halliburton will be a principal subcontractor of Parsons, another major contractor in the running for Iraq rebuilding contracts. Parsons gave $249,000 in campaign contributions over the pre-war period examined by the Center for Responsive Politics, 63 percent of it to Republicans.

Another big winner in the Iraq rebuilding sweepstakes is the Fluor

Corp., another California-based company which gave a whopping $483,000 in campaign contributions, 43 percent of that amount to Republicans.

The other big winner which was also a big contributor to the GOP and the Bush campaign was Stevedore Services of America, which won a $4.8 million initial contract to start rebuilding the Umm Qasr port facilities in Iraq, and which gave $28,000 in campaign contributions, 80 percent to Republicans.

The Bush Administration has conceded that the bidding for the first round of Iraq reconstruction contracts, worth a total of some $1 billion, was "restricted" to certain few firms (all foreign-owned companies were excluded, even including British firms), ostensibly for reasons of "national security." So far, despite protests from Britain and other countries, these restrictive bidding rules are expected to continue in place.

But particularly with the war largely over, the national security argument rings increasingly hollow. The close alignment between campaign contributions and contract awards offers a much more convincing explanation for the tightly controlled bidding process, however.

It also raises disturbing questions about the level of damage caused by American bombs. To what extent was damage to Iraqi infrastructure a payback for campaign contributions made by firms eager for the contracts to rebuild that same damage?

While a compliant and complicit Congress cannot be expected to delve into these kinds of issues, Bechtel, Halliburton, Fluor and others would do well to grab as much of the reconstruction funding as they can get up front. The way things are going in Iraq, with Shiite clergy moving into positions of political power, many of those contracts may quickly go the way of Enron's corruption-plagued Dabhol Power Plant in India, which was cancelled after a new party took power in Maharashtra state and Enron's links to the corrupt prior state government were exposed.

—*CounterPunch* (print edition), *April 23, 2003*

As the occupation has dragged on, and the killings and maimings in Iraq have mounted—over 11,000 Iraqi civilians and over 700 U.S. servicemen and servicewomen killed by the anniversary of the invasion, with no end in sight—there have been increasing references to Iraq as "another Vietnam." The truth is, the grim similarities between the two American invasions of these long-suffering Third World nations were apparent from the outset.

Consider the Parallels with Vietnam: An Iraq War & Occupation Glossary

As the war in Iraq grinds on and American casualties mount, the situation there is increasingly coming to resemble the one in Vietnam some 35-40 years ago. We even have a Defense Secretary who, like Robert McNamara before him, is an over-confident egotist devoid of self-doubt and incapable of tolerating criticism, and who thinks himself so brilliant that he can outsmart a popular insurgency and overpower it with fancy weaponry. What makes this historic parallel particularly haunting is the return of terminology, some of which hasn't been heard in years. To help readers understand likely future developments in Iraq, here is a glossary of some of those terms:

Guerrilla war—An unconventional conflict, in which the enemy can hide among the people, popping out to fire on U.S. soldiers and ducking back before he or she can be challenged or identified. Are we in a guerrilla war in Iraq? Ask Don Rumsfeld. His denials are starting to sound like his claims before the war about WMD's: empty.

Quagmire—A sticky situation in which the military cannot hope to win victory, but cannot retreat for fear of losing the entire war—and face. Is Iraq becoming a quagmire? The latest testimony by Rumsfeld and Gen. Tommy Franks (who has, it is worth noting, quit his post as head of the military in Iraq before things can get worse and damage his reputation), is that at least 150,000 troops will be needed in Iraq "indefinitely."

Body count—A tally of how many of our guys and their guys get killed each day. The U.S. body count has been averaging about one a day until recently, but now we're starting to see two people a day get hit, and larger-scale attacks are becoming more common. We haven't been getting the enemy body counts that used to be *de rigueur* (and massively inflated) at Pentagon press conferences during the Vietnam War, but as the U.S. body count mounts, the pressure will rise on the Pentagon to respond to public dismay by showing that the "score" of dead is always in our favor. (Obviously, the fact that 10 times as many Vietnamese troops were dying as Americans didn't affect the outcome of that conflict, any more than it is likely to affect the outcome of this one.)

Light at the end of the tunnel—This gloomy image was popular for years in the White House and Pentagon during the interminable Indochina conflict. We haven't heard it used yet with respect to Iraq, but if "quagmire" starts to be more in vogue, can this grizzled phrase be far behind?

Search and Destroy—This was a favorite tactic of U.S. forces in Vietnam. It had the effect of killing the occasional Vietcong or Vietcong sympathizer as well as many innocents. It also had the effect of driving entire rural populations into the arms of Vietnamese insurgents. Search and destroy efforts in Iraq are already having the same effect, as innocent bystanders get killed in droves each time the U.S. mounts a campaign. (Search and destroy is likely to be even more counterproductive as a strategy in Islamic Iraq than it was in Buddhist Southeast Asia, given the Arab culture's deep-rooted tradition of eye-for-eye vengeance.)

Allies—As in the Indochina War, the U.S. in Iraq is twisting arms to compel a few weak client states (in the Vietnam era it was Korea and Australia, now it's Poland, Bulgaria and maybe India, a particularly weird choice given that nation's fundamentalist Hindu government and its militant crackdown against Muslims), to send a token few troops to make the occupation and counterinsurgency look like an international effort. This is, in other words, not your grandfather's allies of World War II.

Letting Iraqi boys defend Iraq—Nixon's "secret plan" to end the Vietnam War was to "Vietnamize" it. The strategy proved a dismal failure, because he was trying to get a corrupt government to battle committed nationalists. Current plans to create a new Iraqi army of 40,000 to fight with U.S. troops against Iraqi resistance are unlikely to fare any better. (Sound familiar? For a preview of how well it works, check out the performance of the new American-made Afghan "army.")*

Winning hearts and minds—This was what U.S. military efforts in Vietnam were supposed to accomplish. The idea was that somehow by napalming villages, terrorizing populations with high-tech weapons, defoliating cropland and littering it with hair-trigger anti-personnel bomblets, and then after all that distributing some goodies—chocolate bars, medicine and food rations for example—the people's hearts and minds would won over to the U.S. effort. This of course never happened in Vietnam, Laos or Cambodia. Now we're attempting the same thing in Iraq, where similar actions can be expected to produce similar results.

---

* By the spring of 2004, we were reading reports of the new Iraqi police providing intelligence to insurgents, even aiding them in attacks, and with the April uprisings in Fallujah and the Shi'ite south, of the new Iraqi army refusing to fight its own people, or even of turning on the Americans.

Vietnam Syndrome—This term came into vogue among Republicans and neo-con Democrats directly after the U.S. defeat in Indochina. The idea was that the loss in Vietnam had soured American policy makers and the public on foreign military actions of any kind. The Bush administration's war-mongering in Afghanistan and Iraq was supposed to drive a stake through that syndrome, by offering an example of successful use of military force in promoting American foreign policy. With Afghanistan quickly returning to its pre-invasion condition of feuding warlords and anarchy (and continuing to prove a hospitable place for Al Qaeda-type terrorists), and with Iraq becoming a guerrilla war quagmire that the U.S. has little hope of actually "winning," it seems Bush, Rumsfeld and National Security Director Condoleeza Rice are well on their way to reviving the syndrome, though it will probably eventually get a name change, to Iraq Syndrome. Another variant of Vietnam Syndrome was The Lessons of Vietnam, a phrase more popular among liberals). The irony is that the "lesson" of Vietnam (which was supposedly taken to heart too by Secretary of State Colin Powell), was that the U.S. should not get involved in future wars unless the objective was clear and the public was solidly behind it. Yet here we have a war that, like Vietnam, was entered into based on a series of lies to the American public, and that, like Vietnam, has no clear objective. Eventually, thousands of Iraqi and American deaths hence, we will, sadly, no doubt also be hearing about the Lessons of Iraq.

Peace with honor—This was the semantic contortion that Richard Nixon attempted to use to disguise America's embarrassing defeat by the peasant army of Vietnam. Again, as the American public loses patience with the continued slaughter of American troops in Iraq, and the lack of progress there towards some resolution of the conflict, we can expect Bush and Rumsfeld to come up with some version of peace with honor to describe their eventual humbling retreat from Iraq.

Escalation—During the Vietnam War, escalation was the term used for upping the intensity of the fighting. Whenever the U.S. found itself starting to lose the war, presidents, from Kennedy to Nixon would "escalate" the U.S. effort, adding troops and expanding the field of battle, first to North Vietnam, then to Laos, and finally to Cambodia. The more they escalated, the worse they got trounced. We're already hearing the term escalation applied now to Iraq. So far, it's the Iraqi resistance that has been escalating the fighting since the collapse of the Saddam Hussein regime. Inevitably, though, unless the U.S. decides to declare peace with honor and quit Iraq, we can expect to see the U.S. begin escalating the counterinsurgency effort, with the addition of more troops and more aggressive search-and-destroy tactics.

The Draft—One big difference between the Vietnam War and the current war in Iraq is that during the decades of the Southeast Asian conflict, the U.S. had a draft, and consequently an almost unlimited supply of soldiers to throw into battle. The U.S. military now, which numbers about 1 million, is largely dependent for front-line combatants upon reservists and National Guardsmen. Already some one-third of U.S. forces are directly committed to the war effort in Iraq, counting the 150,000 actually stationed in Iraq, and the 200,000 who play supporting roles in Kuwait and other regional countries. Given the enormous back-office operation required by today's technologically complex, highly bureaucratic, and managerially top-heavy U.S. military, there is actually little in the way of more troops that could be assigned to this conflict should it escalate in intensity. Moreover, with morale crumbling among the reservists and guard troops in Iraq, most of whom are older than typical soldiers in a draft army, and who have left behind jobs and families, the U.S. is facing a serious manpower crisis, just in terms of replacing current troops in the field. If it doesn't turn to a draft, it will have a hard time recruiting more reservists and guard troops, since most people join those units to make a little extra money, not to actually have to go overseas and fight. If it does restart the draft, popular support for war, such as it is—in Iraq or anywhere in the world—will evaporate completely. (The mechanism for a draft—the Selective Service office and local draft boards, and a lottery machine to allocate priority numbers by birthdate—is already in place, and a national call-up could happen within 30 days of a Congressional vote authorizing a return to compulsory service.)

—*CounterPunch.org, July 11, 2003*

When it became clear that there were no weapons of mass destruction to be found, and that there were no links between Saddam Hussein and Al Qaeda, the Bush administration, casting desperately around for a justification for its invasion of Iraq, began promoting the idea that it was all part of the so-called War on Terror, and that somehow, by tying up all available U.S. military assets in Iraq, Americans would be safer. In this next piece, I pointed out that far from it, the war was making it legal for Iraqis to attack American targets.

Legitimizing Terrorism?
Making America Safer... for Iraq Fighters

When the U.S. invasion of Iraq began, the new Homeland Security Department immediately raised the terrorism alert level to Orange because of intelligence suggesting that Iraq could be preparing acts of terrorism in response to the attack.

In fact, under international law, if Iraq were to attack the U.S. with teams of sappers, blowing up bridges, tunnels, TV stations, power plants, factories or refineries (all legitimate wartime targets), if the attackers were to wear military uniforms identifying them as Iraqi soldiers, legal scholars say they would not be terrorists at all, but rather soldiers engaged in acts of war.

The penalty, should such attackers be later apprehended, would be a prisoner of war camp for the duration of the conflict, after which time they'd be repatriated.

"It's a disturbing thought," says George Fletcher, a professor of jurisprudence and a specialist in the law of war at Columbia University. "Iraq, under the rules of war, has a clear right of self-defense which would permit it to blow up things in the U.S.," he says.

Nor would Iraq have to declare war against the U.S. for its agents in the U.S. to acquire military standing, according to Fletcher, because Iraq was attacked first by the U.S. "I think under the circumstances, they could certainly claim the right of self-defense," he said.

According to Fletcher, the key to establishing whether an attack by Iraqi agents in the U.S. was an act of terror or an act of war would be whether those agents were identifiable as Iraqi military personnel or not. "If they were dressed as civilians, then they would be considered to be unlawful combatants," he says, "and they would not come under the terms of the Geneva Convention. But if they wore their uniforms and were captured, they'd have to be considered prisoners of war.

This raises serious questions about the Bush Administration's claim to Americans that it was going to war against Iraq to protect Americans from terrorism.

By attacking Iraq, Washington has not only given Iraq a motive to counterattack in the U.S., it has made it possible for those Iraqis who are willing to fight for their country here in America to do so with much less risk. Assuming they were to opt for something other than a suicide bombing, Iraqi agents could at least contemplate being free before long even if they were captured, since the rules of war require that POWs be treated humanely, and that they be released at the end of a war.

That's a lot better treatment than what is in store for captured terrorists, who would likely face the death penalty.

Iraq has already said that in retaliation for the U.S. invasion, it will strike back at America. The longer the war lasts without a clear and decisive resolution, the likelier it is that Baghdad will make good on that threat. If it does, the U.S. may have little alternative but to add the perpetrators of any attack, should they be captured, to its growing list of captured soldiers in Iraq.

Of course, the Bush administration hasn't shown much regard for international law, so it's possible they'd ignore the fact that Iraqi fighters in the U.S. fall under Geneva Convention rules. It might just treat them like Al Qaeda suspects. That course of action, however, would put all American POWs in Iraq and other future conflicts at grave risk.

Meanwhile, even if Iraq never succeeds in opening up a front in the domestic U.S., or against American government, military or business assets overseas, Americans should be prepared for some ugly scenes. Fletcher notes that those Americans who are fighting in Iraq as special forces or as CIA operatives—that is, if they are undercover and not in uniforms that clearly identify them as American soldiers—do not have the protection of the Geneva Convention themselves, and could be treated themselves as unlawful combatants—which could mean torture or execution.

Is everyone feeling safer now?

—CounterPunch.org, April 2, 2003

I know one group of people who are feeling anything but safe: our supreme leader and his coterie of advisers. Ever since Augusto Pinochet, the dictator for life of Chile who was arrested and nearly prosecuted in Europe for his horrific campaign of slaughter against the supporters of Chilean democracy, and the later incident where former US Secretary of State and arch war criminal Henry Kissinger had to scuttle out of France to avoid similar arrest, American leaders like Bush, Rumsfeld and Cheney have had to worry about their safety traveling outside the U.S. They're not worried about assassination attempts—they have an army of Secret Service people to protect them. What they fear is arrest for their war crimes. That explains why our Secretary of War, Donald Rumsfeld, resorted to threatening the mighty state of Belgium (a stolid ally since World War II) because of its law giving it authority to prosecute war crimes wherever they may have occurred.

Rumsfeld v. Belgium:
"Leave Us Alone or We'll Move NATO"

Is Defense Secretary Donald Rumsfeld an idiot or just an unbelievable boor? And do the *New York Times* and the Associated Press have historical memories that reach past the prior day's news?

What prompted these ruminations was a comment made by our pompous war secretary during his current European tour, as reported in the NYT. Miffed by a 1994 Belgian law that empowers prosecutors to go after any war criminal regardless of nationality, for crimes against humanity wherever they may have occurred, Rumsfeld, who along with the rest of the U.S. government has been opposing inclusion of the U.S. in the jurisdiction of the International Criminal Court, actually groused that Belgium "appears not to respect the sovereignty of other countries." He went on to threaten removal of NATO headquarters to another jurisdiction if Belgian law wasn't changed.

This assertion comes from a guy who just weeks ago ignored the will of the United Nations and invaded, conquered and now occupies a country, Iraq, which posed no threat to the U.S.! Talk about respecting sovereignty!

And remember, this was no one-time transgression. We're talking about the United States of America, a country that, along with the former Soviet Union, surely shares honors as the biggest violator of national sovereignty in modern history, and which since the end of the Cold War holds that title alone.

A country that is illegally holding prisoners from its war in Afghanistan (including children) even though that conflict is over, and which still refuses even to recognize them as prisoners of war.

A country that has repeatedly, in recent memory, invaded other nations that posed no threat—Grenada and Panama, —not to mention North Vietnam and Cambodia, where the casualties numbered in the millions—and which actually kidnapped the head of state of Panama, brought him to the U.S., and tried, convicted and jailed him for crimes allegedly committed in his own country.

A country that a few years back bombed two foreign nations—the Sudan and Afghanistan—with no warning, and which did the same more recently in Yemen.

A country that for decades has engaged in an illegal embargo—an act of war under international law— against Cuba, causing untold damage to that country's people and economy.

A country that has repeatedly violated the sovereignty of other lands by forcing them (on pain of devastating trade sanctions), to permit the advertising of cigarettes, despite efforts in those nations to reduce smoking by banning such advertising.

A country that today talks casually of invading Syria and/or North Korea, and which is openly discussing the adoption of a policy of undermining the government of a sovereign nation, Iran, and which for decades has just as casually overthrown governments it didn't like, including democratically elected ones in states like Iran, Guatemala and Chile.

The point should by now be clear: Rumsfeld, who has had a hand in a fair number of the above gross violations of national sovereignty (and in plenty more that haven't been listed here), may be legitimately worried that he and a host of American military leaders may find themselves being charged under Belgium's statute, but he clearly has no business complaining about any country's concept of what is fair game when it comes to respecting sovereignty.

But what about the *Times* and the AP? *Times* reporter Craig S. Smith focused on European diplomats' complaints about Rumsfeld's "tactlessness." He and his editors let Rumsfeld's comment slide past without a line of comment about America's own history of trampling on national sovereignty. Meanwhile, Pauline Jelinek, writing for the AP (as published in the *Philadelphia Inquirer*), didn't even mention any complaints about tactlessness. She seemed more concerned that Iraqi theater commander Gen. Tommy Franks, 1991 Gulf War commander Gen. Norman Schwarzkopf, Vice President Dick Cheney and Secretary of State Colin Powell have already been sued under the Belgian law (the Franks suit was subsequently tossed out by the court).

Is this because Smith, Jelinek and their bosses are ignorant?

Possibly.

More likely though, they just don't think that Belgium and the U.S. operate by the same set of rules.

Under this editorial theory, other nations of the world are bound by a stern set of behavior guidelines, enshrined in the U.N. Charter and other global treaties—and of course enforceable by us, the world's self-appointed global prosecutor and cop.

The U.S., however, doesn't operate under these same rules. When we invade another country, meddle in its political affairs, impede its health or environmental or labor reform efforts, or kidnap its leader, it is not a violation of sovereignty. It is our right.

We can't expect someone like the strutting Rumsfeld to change, but we can insist that the *Times* and AP do better than operate as the defense secretary's recording secretary and PR flak.

—*CounterPunch.org, June 14, 2003*

Soldiers in wartime face a lot of stress, which can lead to desertion. Some soldiers in every war also desert for reasons of principle. Of course, our commander-in-chief should be lenient with these people, given his own history of going AWOL for a year during the Indochina War. Here's the story of an AWOL from the Iraq War.

Takoma Goes AWOL:
The Dolphin Who Refused to Fight

News that Takoma, the Navy's mine-detecting dolphin, has gone AWOL while on duty in the Persian Gulf, sets off a host of thoughts. First of all, do we know that Takoma is really AWOL, or is this just another example of the Pentagon's trying to hide war casualties from the American public by classifying slain troops as missing or AWOL. It would not just be tragic if one of the U.S. military's sea mammal soldiers was killed in action; it would surely raise a storm of protest from a group far more powerful than the peace movement: the animal rights crowd. Both Americans and Brits have always been much more troubled by cruelty to animals than to humans, and it's a certainty that this is a group Allied Forces has no desire to arouse.

The peace movement can be safely ignored by Washington, at least for a time, but a fired-up animal rights movement could bring down the government in no time. While the Pentagon may well be fudging its human casualty figures, though, there is reason to suspect that Takoma is safe. Dolphins, after all, are known to have brains that are larger than we humans are possessed of. And while they are known to be capable of extreme brutality, even towards others of their own species, on an individual basis, there is no indication that dolphins engage in humanity's uniquely barbaric practice of war.

It's possible then, that once he or she realized that her efforts were not a game anymore but were part of a campaign designed to enable one group of humans to kill large numbers of other humans, Takoma decided to split the oil-befouled waters of the Persian Gulf for the more tranquil and dolphin-friendly Indian Ocean.

One imagines that the Pentagon is now contemplating having to train a group of dolphin MPs (or perhaps they're working on sharks for this job), to keep the remaining dolphin mine-sweeping squad in line. If the military turns to coercion though, it will inevitably produce a counter-reaction in the dolphin community: militant dolphin pacifism—a movement that could see peace-minded dolphins luring Pentagon-trained dolphins away from their assignments and back to the freedom of the open sea.

—*CounterPunch.org, April 3, 2003*

Now, as you might suspect, training these dolphins, not to mention the care and feeding (and of course arming to the teeth) of those 138,000 troops in Iraq, and the hundreds of thousands more who are needed to back them up, costs money. Big Money. So much it's hard to get your mind around it. It's one thing to talk about the big numbers like $87 billion or $200 billion, but most Americans, for whom math has never been a particular strong point, have trouble even getting their heads around the idea of $5 billion a month. I mean what's a billion dollars anyhow? You have to think of a stack of a 10,000 C-notes just to imagine $1 million, and I'm not sure I can picture that. But a billion dollars would be 1000 of those stacks. It's gotta be a big pile. It's a lot easier to figure this out on a per family basis.

Paying for War: $2,150 Per Family and Counting

Sitting here working on my taxes at the last minute, after having just watched President Bush's appalling performance at his only press conference of 2004, and having just read about the plans for an all-out Marine assault on Fallujah and Najaf if truce negotiations break down, I found myself wondering how much of my taxes were going to support the Iraq atrocity.

A call to Bob McIntyre of Citizens for Tax Justice gave me the answer. About 25 percent of my income tax payment. Of course, that's a rough estimate, based upon the prediction that this year's income tax will bring in $765 billion in revenues, and that the Iraq war is costing almost $200 billion for the year.

That's something to think about as you're mailing your envelope to the IRS tonight. For a typical family with a taxable income of $60,000, and a typical tax bill of $8626, that works out to an Iraq War tax bill of about $2150. For a family making $100,000 in taxable income, with a typical tax bill of $18,614, that is a war tax of about $4650. Even a student making a taxable income of say $7000, and paying a tax of around $700 to Uncle Sam is paying around $175 to support the killing in Iraq.*

Oh, but that's not all. If you're one of those who pays your taxes on line, you should also remember that the federal tax you pay on the phone line you use for your dial-up or DSL service is, and always has been a war tax, pure and simple. Lyndon Johnson, trying to come up with ways to pay for his own war, hit on the idea of the federal phone tax which, once instituted, has remained with us ever since, funding Pentagon extravagance and now, Bush's war.

If that information doesn't get your blood boiling, you should go check the Citizens for Tax Justice website (www.ctj.org) and check out how much you're actually saving from Bush's trillion-dollar tax cut plan for the rich.

According to CTJ, if you're in the group of taxpayers whose family income is in the range of about $36,000, you'll be saving about $827 this year. That may sound like a nice piece of change, but it pales to insignificance when compared to the family in the big McMansion down the road that has an income of $200,000 and that's seeing their tax bill drop by $6800 this year. Go figure. If it were even moderately fair, that tax break of $827 you're getting should be no more than six times as great for someone earning six times as much as you, or about $4900. And for the family earning $1 million, assuming they're really paying their taxes, their Bush savings is over $52,000. Over the full 10 years of these tax cuts, the picture gets even more outrageous. The folks earning that puny $36,000 in taxable income will save a total of $6500, while the $200,000 family will net almost $90,000 and the millionaires will save a whopping $665,000! It's really another way of pointing out who's really paying for this war, when you come right down to it. The wealthy don't only get to avoid the fighting and dying. They also get to avoid having to pay for it in Bush's America.

I'd go into this some more, but as it is, I'm probably going to be racing down to the Philadelphia main post office tonight to file my taxes before midnight.

—*CounterPunch.org, April 16, 2004*

---

*The cost per person is actually much higher still, since most of the war is being financed by government borrowing, so there will be years of interest to be paid on the debt.

Chapter 2

Occupation: Lost in the Bush

The arbitrary distinction which the Bush Administration has tried to make, between a war that supposedly ended on May 1, 2003, and an occupation that began on that date, is about as real as the fictional handover of "sovereignty" to a handpicked group of Iraqi collaborators which Bush's re-election strategists decided had better happen by June 30, 2004. Tell it to the families of the hundreds of American soldiers who died, or the thousands who came home grievously wounded after "the end of major combat operations" that they were not victims of a war. Tell it to the families of many thousands more Iraqis who died at the hands of American troops since that illusory transition.

Yet words have power, and the Bush administration has known this perhaps better than most of its predecessors. When things are going badly, "occupation" sounds a lot better than "war," especially with an election coming up, so despite all the fighting you might see on your TV screen, and the steady stream of flag-draped coffins being flown home from Iraq, know that it's an occupation that's going on over there, not a war.

The problem, of course, is that while the word "occupation" may sound better, or at least less scary, than the word "war" to American ears, it doesn't sound so good in the ears of Iraqis, whose history is replete with nasty occupations. And that's been the real problem, hasn't it? I mean, with this whole "Mission Accomplished" thing, the big question has always been: who was the message aimed at? Clearly it was the American voter. After all, if the mission, as now claimed, was to rid Iraq of totalitarian rule and to introduce Western democracy and freedom, what Iraqi would agree that the mission was "accomplished"? People are still arrested for saying the wrong thing, newspapers are arbitrarily shut down by the petulant American proconsul, L. Paul Bremer, if he gets upset at breakfast, there are military checkpoints everywhere and people get shot just for taking a walk at the wrong time. Some freedom and democracy.

In fact, I'd say if there was a single moment that demonstrated the complete ignorance, idiocy and self-delusion of the Bush braintrust, such as it is, and that showed that the Iraq adventure was doomed to failure, it was surely the attempt, early in the so-called "occupation," to bring in troops from neighboring Turkey—a country with a long history of conquest and abusive occupation of Iraq.

Calling All Occupiers: Talking Turkey About Iraq

Want to know how bad things are getting for the U.S. occupation in Iraq?

Let's talk Turkey, then.

Just for a moment, let's imagine a hypothetical situation. Say the U.S. was occupying Syria, and needed some help with the occupation—some troops who might help to put the occupied Syrians at ease. Would we invite in neighboring Israeli troops to help us? Unlikely you say? Or let's try Poland. Say we were occupying Poland and wanted some help there. Would we invite German troops in? No way.

Yet here we are in Iraq, losing a soldier a day, getting attacked somewhere between 50-100 times a day, resentment at the occupation growing, and domestic frustration and anger mounting at the cost of maintaining an army of 130,000 in the country. Where do we turn for help? Well, we tried the United Nations, but they quite understandably want nothing to do with the mess we've created. So we turn to Turkey.

Excuse me, but Turkey and its precursor state, the Ottoman Empire, was a brutal occupier of the land now known as Iraq for over four centuries. Its abuse of Arab peoples is the stuff of popular legend. On top of that, a third of the country is Kurdish, and there is a blood feud between Turks and Kurds that runs back farther even than that—one which includes a very current history of slaughter of Kurds by the Turkish military, both in Iraq and in Turkey itself where Kurds are a brutally oppressed minority. Add to this the fact that Turks are for the most part Sunni Muslims, while the majority of Iraq is Shiite. The Shias, long oppressed and subjugated by Iraq's Sunni minority, most recently at the hands of Saddam Hussein, are not going to be happy campers, watching a powerful Turkish Sunni army strutting around Baghdad.

If anyone needed a reminder of how unpopular the Turks are in Iraq, today's car bombing of the Turkish Embassy in Baghdad should do the trick. The suicide attack, which wounded two people, was greeted in the city with jubilation and dancing in the street.

The pressure being placed by the Bush Administration upon Turkey to send troops into Iraq to help the U.S. with the occupation of that country is also a threat to the government in Turkey, where the majority of the public wants nothing to do with this foreign adventure. Turks and their parliament last spring resoundingly defeated efforts to drag their nation into the war against Iraq, and in fact Turkey, a member of NATO, actually ended up denying the U.S. military the right to land its troops and equipment at Turkish ports, forcing the shocked and awed Pentagon at the last minute to drop plans for a full-scale northern front at the start of the war—an astonishing diplomatic affront by a supposed ally.

By pressuring Turkey to join in the occupation despite overwhelming public opposition, the U.S. could end up with a government in Turkey down the road that will be openly hostile to U.S. interests.

All this because the Bush Administration, in its unseemly and illegal rush to a unilateral invasion, so damaged American relations with its usual allies that it really has nowhere else to turn for help in Iraq.

I suppose one could argue that having Turkish troops in Iraq is better than having Indian Hindu soldiers there—another really dumb idea that almost happened until the Indian government thought better of it (and which could still come to pass).

While one is tempted to think that the planners in the Bush Administration—Pentagon, State and National Security Council alike—are ahistorical idiots and yahoos, coming up with bright ideas like this one, I suspect this is not the problem. Clearly there are some yahoos at work there, not least our Yahoo-in-Chief who still cannot pronounce nuclear or even eat a pretzel while watching the tube, but the decision to bring Turkish troops into Iraq is not an act of stupidity. Ill-conceived as it is, this is an act of desperation.

The sorry reality is that the U.S. has nowhere else to turn for help at this point.

The trouble is that once those Turkish troops move in, things are bound to get dramatically worse in a hurry. First of all, the Turks will quickly find themselves also under attack like the Americans, at which point they will begin to respond with the same kind of overkill that American soldiers have been using. And when Turks start killing Iraqis, all hell will break loose.

We might as well have turned to the Israeli Army for help.

Who knows, the way things are going, the Bush administration may end up trying that bright idea too.

—*CounterPunch.org, Oct. 13, 2003*

The idea of inviting Turkish troops to join the occupation party was truly an unbelievable moment in this mad Bush adventure, but there have been plenty of signs that this "occupation" would have little to do with what happened in Germany and Japan after World War II, much as the Bush team tried to conflate the two activities. Here follow some of the signs of looming disaster.

Shooting Ali in the Back:
Why the Pacification is Doomed

If you want to know why the U.S. campaign to pacify Iraq and make the country into a docile puppet state is doomed to failure, just look at what happened to 17-year-old Ali Muhsin.

Shot and killed by American soldiers on Tuesday, August 26, 2003, he died on his family's front stoop as neighbors gathered around, and frightened American soldiers pointed their guns at anyone who got too close.

According to Iraqis, including several who worked with the boy at a tire repair shop, Ali Muhsin was simply a kid in the wrong place at the wrong time, who, because of the color of the shirt he was wearing, was mistaken for someone who had just dropped two hand grenades onto a U.S. military patrol.

But even the account given in the New York Times on Aug. 27 by American troops involved in the incident raises serious questions about just what is going on in Iraq. According to those troops, a U.S. soldier, Sergeant Ray Vejar, saw something dropped from the street above as his Humvee approached a tunnel. Vejar didn't recognize the dropped object as a grenade until it exploded near him, but he did claim to have seen two men overhead on the street—one dressed in white and one in green, the latter of whom had "moved toward the railing."

Vejar says when his team raced up onto the street after exiting the tunnel, to pursue their attackers, they saw two figures in white and green start running. He says the man in green stopped and turned. "He looked right at me and I positively ID'd him as the guy who was at the railing," he says. Such a positive ID sounds dubious, considering that earlier, Vejar says he couldn't even tell what was being dropped, and surely was more focused on what was dropping, than on the face of whoever it was up on the street.

In any event, what happened next is particularly troubling.

Vejar says he and another soldier chased the fleeing man in green into an alley. But it was another group of soldiers in a Humvee who found Ali (who of course may or may not have been the same man Vejar was chasing).

When Ali tried to flee the Humvee, the soldier manning that vehicle's powerful mounted machine gun fired a warning shot, causing him to stop. As a soldier from the Humvee approached the boy, he tried to flee again. This time, the machine gunner shot him, hitting him several times.

Ali managed to stagger two blocks to his family's home before collapsing on the front stoop, where he died slowly.

It was at that point that Sgt. Vejar arrived, pushed his way through the gathering crowd (which included the boy's wailing mother), and identified him, saying, "I know he was at the railing."

Okay. If this account is correct (and the boy's neighbors say it is not—claiming that in fact he had been working at his job when the grenade was dropped, and had only gone out to see what the commotion was), we have to ask what kind of rules were being followed when the soldier in the Humvee decided to shoot a fleeing boy in the back that he knew was unarmed.

If this was rules of war, then perhaps it could be justified. Nasty perhaps, but a fleeing combatant can be shot in wartime. But is this a war or an occupation? In a war, the very outcome of the conflict is in question, making it perhaps necessary to shoot first and ask questions later. But at the point that, as our Commander-in-Chief claims, "major conflict is over," and the outcome of the battle has been determined, such Wild West behavior is no longer called for.

If what we have now in Iraq is an occupation, the occupier has to be a lot more restrained and careful about who gets terminated with extreme prejudice. An unarmed person fleeing a military patrol cannot automatically be presumed to be an enemy combatant. Fleeing a group of soldiers might be the logical and understandable—even if foolish— response of many innocent people. It is not a mistake for which anyone should be executed. And clearly the soldiers in the Humvee, including the one who fired the fatal shots that executed Ali, were not the ones who claimed to recognize him. They were purely guessing he was the one. It was only Sgt. Vehar, who was not on the scene at the time of the shooting, who claims he could identify the boy.

Bad enough that another young person, combatant or not, has died in this American war of aggression. Worse yet that it may have been an innocent lad who was shot and killed.

But even from the point of view of American policy makers-who clearly have little concern about the killing of civilians—this incident must be viewed as indicative of a disaster in the making.

Consider the situation in the U.S. We have a functioning Constitution, a set of laws and courts, and a whole bunch of legally constituted law enforcement agencies. Yet even with all the protections that are in place, our police all too often kill unarmed and innocent people in the heat of action. How much worse then in a country where there are no laws, are no courts to control the people doing the enforcing, and where those enforcers are not people who are trained in law enforcement, but rather are soldiers, trained in the art of killing.

Unless the Pentagon and Iraq viceroy L. Paul Bremer set a clear policy instructing occupying troops that they are not to shoot unarmed citizens—even those who are fleeing—the inevitable slaughter of innocents will produce a groundswell of hatred and blood vengeance within Iraq that will engulf occupying American soldiers, and eventually lead to the defeat of any efforts to create a new society and government in that benighted land.

—CounterPunch.org, Aug. 28, 2003

This next column talked about the foolishness of the election-driven plan to reduce U.S. troop levels in Iraq even as the guerrilla war was heating up, and of the ill-conceived plan to try and hastily create a new Iraqi army, which would supposedly be able to replace U.S. troops. As we saw in the spring of 2004, both those schemes blew up in the administration's face. The reduction in U.S. troops had to be called off, and more troops sent in because things have gotten worse, not better, with the passage of time. As for that new Iraqi army, it melted away at the first sign of a conflict during the April uprisings. So unreliable are its soldiers, we learned, that they were only being issued one clip of bullets each, in case they decided to switch sides (as some did during the April battles). As this column shows, even in early November 2003, five months before the pitched battles of April 1, it was clear that both policies were doomed to failure.

From Occupation to Guerrilla War: A New Kind of Dancing in Iraq

The Bush war plan has entered a new and much more dangerous phase.

Before, it was all about refocusing Americans on terrorism and patriotism, in hopes of getting our minds off the dismal state of the economy and the massive transfer of wealth to the rich that was and is still underway.

It was a bad bet, because the war, which was supposed to be short and sweet, with happy Iraqis dancing in the street, has turned into something else. (There has indeed been dancing in the streets, but only around the burning hulks of destroyed American military equipment and the charred bodies of dead GI's).

So now, with occupation turning into guerrilla war, the plan is to de-emphasize the ongoing war and try to refocus Americans on the domestic economy, which, while still in a mess, is at least less of a disaster at the moment than the Iraq war.

The new plan is to try and present the illusion of progress in Iraq, by at least temporarily "drawing down" the U.S. troop levels there, from the current 134,000 to "just" 100,000 by May 2004, when the presidential campaign will have begun in earnest.

It's a seemingly bizarre strategy, to be sure. How, one might ask, can the Pentagon be contemplating a reduction in the U.S. military presence in coming months even as the guerrilla resistance movement is growing in numbers, skill and daring?

Not long ago, of course, the publicly proclaimed strategy was to pull out American troops and replace them with foreign troops. Initial plans called for Pakistani or Indian soldiers, but those countries demurred. Then Turkish troops were proposed, but Turkey, faced with popular resistance and with fierce opposition to the idea within Iraq, also declined the invitation. European countries (with the exception of Poland, which may be reconsidering its decision after losing a major to a guerrilla attack, and after polls showing 57 percent oppose having troops in Iraq), were equally dismissive of the idea. So now, taking a page from President Nixon's book ("Vietnamization"), the Pentagon claims it will train 170,000 Iraqi soldiers to take over some of the job of pacification from the Americans.

This is quite a task, building from scratch in just half a year an army that, if successfully created, would stand right up there in the top ranks of the world's military forces, in terms of numbers. (Note that it takes that long just to get that many draftees out of civvies and suited up and trained in the U.S., a country over 10 times the size of Iraq, and with a 1.4 million-person military machine already in place to train and absorb the new recruits.)

The other surprising thing about this new Pentagon scheme is that no one—even the famously self-confident and vainglorious Defense Secretary Donald Rumsfeld—could reasonably predict how it would work. Would Iraq soldiers really aggressively go after, and kill fellow Iraqis, fighting loyally on the side of the American occupiers? Could they be entrusted with the heavy arms and air support that U.S. troops have, or would they be left to do the job with small arms? Would arming 170,000 Iraqis end up simply being a way of inadvertently training and arming a whole new cadre of anti-American guerrillas? Would the new Iraqi recruits resist the temptation to funnel arms—and information—to guerrillas?

It seems incredibly premature, with the establishment of this Iraqi army so speculative and untested, for the Pentagon to already be talking about and planning for significant U.S. troop reduction.*

But then, this appears not to be a generals' decision at all. Like the Vietnam War of yore, the military decisions in the Iraq war are clearly being made not by the brass, but by political operatives, headed by campaign "General" Karl Rove.

What this new plan means is that Rove and Bush's other political handlers are about to callously sacrifice both Iraqi civilians and American soldiers in the interest of winning re-election next November. It may be possible, that is, for the U.S. to draw down the number of soldiers in Iraq during the peak months of the presidential campaign, enabling Bush to claim, with the help of a demonstrably compliant and unquestioning media, that he is winning the war in Iraq, but this can only be done by a) exposing remaining troops to much greater risk of attack and b) having the remaining forces adopt even more deadly and indiscriminate tactics against guerrilla attacks—for

---

* As we found out some five months later, the idea of creating an Iraqi army to do America's imperial dirty work was another Bush-league fantasy. When the people of Fallujah decided they'd had enough of the U.S. military's abuse, and a group of Shi'ites headed by Sheik Muqtada al-Sadr decided it was time to throw the U.S. out, and began an insurrection in Baghdad itself and in some of the Shia towns to the south, the U.S. discovered that its new Iraqi police and troops didn't want to fight. In fact, according to the Pentagon's Central Command in Iraq, some 50 percent of the new Iraqi security forces either failed to appear for duty during the crisis, or went over to the insurgents. That's a pretty high desertion rate, and of course raises serious questions about the loyalty and reliability of the remaining half of those forces. The administration's response—to seek out higher officers of Saddam Hussein's old military—to take command of the new army, was one more unbelievable act in an unbelievable war. After all that blood and death, ostensibly spent to overthrow Baathist tyranny, the Bush administration is bringing back the Baathist military leaders to help it create the New Iraq!

example wider use of helicopter and fixed-wing gunships to spread death and destruction over wide areas whenever there is an attack, and a return to more aerial bombardment. Look, for example, for carpet-bombing of cities in the so-called Sunni Triangle, which will soon become Iraq's "Mekong Delta."

Longer term, of course, such a scorched-earth strategy will only lead to greater animosity towards the U.S. war and occupation, and to a more powerful guerrilla movement.

But that doesn't matter to Bush's political braintrust. Their goal now is clearly just to get past Election Day.

After that though, they, or Bush's Democratic successor, will have to confront the old Johnson/Nixon dilemma: keep sending in even more troops, or risk having the U.S. defeated and driven from the country in a humiliating defeat.

—*CounterPunch.org, Nov. 8, 2003*

The Longer It Goes On, The Worse It Gets: Friendly Fire Will Doom the Occupation

The crisis in Iraq has again jumped up and bitten the Bush war machine in the ass. In two separate incidents only a few hours and a few miles apart, there were clear signs that the American war against and occupation of Iraq is going badly.

In the first, a major firefight—actually it would be more appropriate to say battle this time—Iraqi guerrillas attacked a U.S. Army convoy, destroying several trucks, killing two GIs and wounding seven more. This was reportedly one of the biggest shootouts in recent weeks, and it suggests that the guerrillas are becoming bolder and more confident, ready to stay and fight it out with beleaguered U.S. troops instead of just laying mines or tossing the random grenade. This latest deadly shootout is liable to make the American occupiers even more jumpy and alienated from the people we are supposedly "liberating."

Worse yet was the killing—slaughter really—of eight Iraqi policemen and the wounding of another seven in what is being called a "friendly fire" incident.

"Friendly fire"—a wonderfully ironic bit of jargon coined by the Pentagon in the darker days of the Vietnam conflict as a way of trying to minimize casualty figures by separating out those U.S. deaths caused by our own guys—is hard enough to take when a soldier is shot by his own comrades, but it's not likely to go down well at all among Iraqis, for whom any allegiance to U.S. occupying forces is tenuous at best.

The Iraqi police force, still a work-in-progress of the American occupying authority, is in a precarious spot. Many of its members, especially at the officer level, are former police from the Saddam Hussein era whose loyalty to the occupation is purely practical. If they think that American soldiers are going to be mowing them down, that loyalty will quickly dissipate. Others, particularly at the street level, are men who, desperate for some income, have agreed to sign up for police duty. Again, whatever their attitude towards Iraq's former regime, their loyalty to the occupier is purely economic.

U.S. soldiers will have to be a lot less quick on the trigger if this idea of establishing a local army and police force in Iraq to take over the front line duties of American occupation troops is going to work.

Meanwhile, the slaughter of the Fallujah cops provides a grim window on the way this occupation is really operating.

Here in America, we supposedly read about every American soldier's death. But reports from Iraq make it clear that we aren't getting the full story about the Iraqi deaths. Military authorities in Iraq, Kuwait and the Pentagon don't report on Iraqis killed unless specific incidents are brought to their attention. That is, if reporters learn about an incident in which Iraqi civilians have been slain, and ask the military about it, they may get an answer as to what happened and how many were killed, though there are no guarantees. The occupation authority and the Pentagon don't simply issue reports of such killings.

So when something like this happens, where it involves the killing of Iraqi uniformed police, and it is necessarily reported, it lets us see just how quick to resort to massive deadly force U.S. troops really are. In this incident, Iraqi police were pursuing a white Mercedes that they suspected was carrying "bad guys"—either criminals or perhaps guerrilla troops. During that chase, they inadvertently found themselves headed towards a group of American soldiers. The Americans, thinking they were under attack by armed Iraqis, opened fire. Though the police drove off into a field and were reportedly shouting "We're police, we're police," the Americans kept firing, with grim results for the police.

One has to ask, if the police were not firing back—and there is no indication that they did—why did the U.S. troops continue to unleash their deadly fusillade?

The answer is that these are dangerous times for American soldiers. Waiting could mean death. Not waiting, however, means death—lots of death—for the Iraqis.

We have to wonder how many such massacres of Iraqis are occurring in the midst of this madness and chaos.

Unless the Pentagon starts giving an honest, up-to-date accounting of all incidents in which weapons are fired in Iraq, we in the U.S. won't know.

Iraqis will know, however. Every time an Iraqi civilian is mowed down by an American soldier, the family and neighbors of that victim of the occupation know what happened and whom to blame.

Little wonder then, that the longer this goes on, the worse it seems to get.

Every such "friendly fire" incident, every killing of a civilian, deepens and further muddies that water in which the guerrilla forces are swimming.

—CounterPunch.org, Sept. 18, 2003

Hiding the Dead Babies: Infanticide as Liberation

The Bush Administration has become notorious for hiding information—even ceasing to collect it. Now that policy of obsessive secrecy is being applied to the so-called war on terror.

The latest effort to bury bad news comes from the puppet Iraqi "government" in Baghdad, where the so-called Health Minister Khodeir Abbas has issued orders to hospitals and other agencies to cease collecting data on civilians killed by occupation forces. The Health Ministry, it must be noted, is run under the direct supervision and authority of L. Paul Bremer's Coalition Provisional Authority, Iraq's real government.

The count of civilian dead, which was being directed by Nagham Mohsen, the head of the ministry's statistics department, was proceeding well, and according to Mohsen, who was interviewed by the Associated Press, could have been accurately completed. Nonetheless, it was summarily halted, with no reason given.

The reason is pretty obvious, though.

Just as the Bush administration has been cutting health statistics gathered by the U.S. Department of Health, and jobless statistics gath ered by the Department of Labor, just as it has hidden the returning dead and wounded from Iraq and Afghanistan from the media and the public, it wants to hide the horrors that the U.S. military is inflicting on the civilian populations of Iraq and Afghanistan—particularly now that the brutality and aggressiveness of the counter-insurgency campaigns in both those countries is being stepped up.

I suspect that the "collateral damage" slayings of 15 children in two separate U.S. operations in Afghanistan over the last several days has a lot to do with this decision to hide Iraqi civilian deaths.

Needless to say, the dead civilians are not being hidden from the Iraqis, or the Afghans. The families get to bury their dead, and the grapevine which has long served as the news media in such societies will not just spread the word, but may even amplify the horrors in the passing. So who is the Bush Administration really hiding these atrocities from?

Why, us of course.

Who knows how Americans would react at seeing babies and little children, or pieces of children, strewn around battle sites, or at hearing that hundred of kids are being killed by U.S. troops and bombs? My guess is not very well.

The American media has done a great job of turning American wars into bloodless video games, a deception which has produced a widespread macho attitude of "bomb the hell out of 'em" as the initial response to perceived affronts to America. The harsh reality, though, is that when American planes drop a 2000-lb bomb on some suspected terrorist "target"—usually a house of some kind—not only does it destroy everything in it, including whatever family members may be there, but it usually levels or seriously damages many surrounding buildings, and of course the people in them. The military used to call smaller versions of such bombs "blockbusters" in the good old days of World War II, a term which gives a much better description of how inaccurate—and how destructive—these devices are than the modern term "precision guided munition".

The Bush Administration knows that it was pictures of dead babies and napalm-scarred children in Vietnam, as much as anything else, that turned many Americans against that war. They know that the dead babies of Afghanistan, and the slain and crippled children of Iraq, if similarly counted and displayed to the American people, would likely have a similar effect.

Hence the new order to cease counting the civilian dead in Iraq.

The whole thing is an outrage. The first thing reporters ask when they go out to cover an earthquake, a plane crash, a house fire or a car wreck is, "How many people died?" Think about the incredible amount of ink and videotape that was expended covering the issue of exactly how many people actually died in the World Trade Center attacks.

But a war? Heck, who cares how many civilians died?

Journalists in Iraq should insist on answers to this question and if they can't get one, they should do as the Associated Press did in the April-June period, surveying Iraqi hospitals and morgues on their own.

An adapted version of the chant that anti-war marchers used to taunt Lyndon Johnson during the 1960s needs to be a reporters' refrain in Baghdad and Washington today:

Bush's war, Bush's war, How many kids has he killed so far?

—*CounterPunch.org, Dec. 12, 2003*

Speaking of killing kids, on my way to Taiwan in late January 2004, I met a young kid, a Marine, on his way to the Iraqi killing fields. He seemed confident and ready to do his duty, but he offered up a pretty good analysis of why the war was going so badly for the U.S. in Iraq. Sadly, his prediction that his branch of the service, slated to take over from the Army in the so-called Sunni Triangle, would be more sensitive to local concerns and cautious in its use of heavy weapons was shown to be wrong during the April siege of Fallujah, when Marine fire terminated the lives of hundreds of innocent women and children.

A Marine in Transit: "Spray and Pray" in Iraq

While flying off to Taiwan for a residency, I found myself sitting next to a young Latino man with a fresh buzzcut. Somewhere south of Anchorage, I asked him where he was going and he said, "Okinawa."

"Are you in the service?" I asked.

He answered that he was a U.S. Marine.

"Have you been to Iraq yet?" I asked him.

"No," he replied, "but I'm being sent there in a couple of weeks."

The thought of this healthy young Californian walking into that mess disturbed me, but he seemed completely at ease about it.

"I'm not worried," he said, without any bravado. "We can handle whatever they throw at us."

It wasn't the kind of bluster you get from Bush, the AWOL

Guardsman with the fake—and poorly delivered—"Bring 'em on" John Wayne lines. This was the real thing: a quiet confidence in his, and his unit's abilities.

I asked this young man what he thought about the whole Iraq adventure.

"Well, the problem is that the Army's made a mess of it," he said. "They haven't handled the occupation right. We in the Marines say that the Army has a policy of 'spray and pray.' If they take a shot from somewhere, they fire off everything they've got in every direction. When you do that, you kill lots of innocent people, and then you get a whole lot more people mad at you. It's stupid, but that's what they do."

Asked how the Marines would handle things differently, he said they had been trained to be careful, to only shoot at legitimate targets, and to use minimal force.

It sounds nice in the abstract, but I wonder how well this theory of occupation will work in practice. I'm no veteran but conversations with veterans of wars from World War I through the first Iraq war have led me to believe that soldiers, however they're trained, and whatever side they're fighting for, tend to develop an attitude of dehumanizing the guys on the other side—an attitude that tends to carry over rather easily to the entire population of the enemy side, making the slaying of civilian innocents much easier, at least in the moment. It's a transition that is hard to resist, and which later can lead to psychological trauma.

The aging bastards in Washington—most of them arm-chair chickenhawks and the major domo among them, the commander in chief, a duty-ducking AWOL— who have dragged this nation into war in Iraq, have much to answer for already. One of those things is the innocent American lives they have wantonly destroyed by sending them off to become hired killers.

The young man sitting next to me certainly didn't look like a hardened killer. I found it easy to picture him playing with a younger sister and her friends on the floor of a living room, and very difficult to imagine him pumping M-16 rounds into an Iraqi teenager or old woman. I sincerely hope he never has to do that—I hope he doesn't have to kill anybody—and that even if he does, he comes home himself physically whole and looking as innocent and optimistic as I found him on the plane.

—CounterPunch.org, Feb. 7, 2004

Dumb and Dumber in Iraq:
Human Trophies on the White House Wall

Embattled President Bush got the break he wanted with the dramatic execution by missile barrage of Saddam Hussein's universally reviled sons Udai and Qusai—a chance to strut in the Rose Garden and talk tough about getting rid of the bad guys in Iraq—but did this television moment make sense?

The two bad boys were trapped in a building in Mosul, surrounded by several hundred heavily armed U.S. soldiers. The U.S. military, at that point, held all the cards. It could have waited as long as necessary until the people trapped inside gave up, at which point army interrogators would have had a potential goldmine of information, not just about the possible location of daddy Saddam, but also about those purported weapons of mass destruction about which Bush and his warmongering advisors supposedly care so much. They might also have learned important details about the guerrillas who are popping off American GI's at a rate of more than one a day.

Who, after all, would have known more about the whereabouts of Saddam Hussein than his two sons?

Who would more likely have known any other secrets of the fallen regime than Hussein's most trusted compatriots—his two sons?

Who would have known more about guerrilla operations than the founders and leaders of the Special Republican Guard and the Fedayeen irregular forces?

You have to wonder, given the potential trove of information potentially represented by these two trapped men (and the two others killed with them, one of whom was a 14-year-old grandson of Hussein's), why the military was so quick to blow them away with a blitzkrieg assault of at least ten TOW anti-tank missiles.

Clearly, with that kind of an assault, there was no chance of their surviving.

But what was the hurry in offing them?

They were trapped and had no possibility of escaping (apparently in the house of the man who tipped off U.S. authorities, who had a vested interest in making sure they couldn't get away and lose him his $30 million reward).

Could it be Bush wanted something dramatic to deflect all the increasingly embarrassing and potentially dangerous media queries about his and his advisers lies leading up to the invasion of Iraq?

Could it be that he didn't want to have to confront the possibility that even these two closest Hussein confidants would have no information about hidden weapons of mass destruction?

Could it be that he didn't want to have to confront evidence Osai and Qusai would almost certainly have offered, if captured, of U.S. complicity in the rise of their father to power, and in his vicious war against Iran?

These are new questions that should be posed by the media, and by what passes for a Democratic opposition, to Bush, Rumsfeld, Powell, Rice and Cheney.

Bush now has a couple of trophies to add to the Oval Office wall (is that why the bodies have been spirited out of Iraq instead of being mounted on stakes outside the gates to Baghdad?), but the inexplicably idiotic decision to kill Udai and Qusai, instead of trying to take them alive, has deprived the U.S. of potentially invaluable evidence regarding Hussein's whereabouts, about the possible location of any of those incredibly elusive and as yet only alleged WMD's, and about the operations of Iraqi guerrillas.

—CounterPunch.org, July 24, 2003

Now What?: The Saddam Dilemma

The capture of Saddam Hussein poses some interesting dilemmas, not just for the Bush administration, but for Democratic presidential candidates, the Democratic congressional delegation, and for ordinary Iraqis.

For Bush, the dilemma will be how to deal with Hussein. Captured by the Americans, he could be treated as a U.S. prisoner of war and held under U.S. jurisdiction. If that were done, he'd probably eventually have to end up in a cell beside Yugoslavia's deposed dictator Slobodan Milosevic facing war crimes charges at The Hague. Alternatively, the White House could decide to hand Hussein over to the puppet Iraqi government. If that were to happen, Hussein would probably be executed in fairly short order. No Iraqis would want him hanging around for long.

The advantage of having Hussein in U.S. custody is that he would be humiliated in public over a long period of time, giving the Bush administration plenty of great publicity heading into the November presidential election—a kind of living trophy on the White House wall that Bush could point to even when things were going badly in Iraq. The disadvantage would be that Hussein would be able to talk himself, and might embarrass the administration by revealing the many links and deals he had with current Bush administration figures like Vice President Dick Cheney and Secretary of Defense Donald Rumsfeld.

Perhaps the best solution for the Bush administration, which is anxious to get clear of Iraq before next fall, when the presidential campaign will be in full swing, would be to toss Hussein to the Iraqis, and to walk out of Iraq, saying "mission accomplished" yet again. The country could still fall apart into civil war and anarchy, but if Bush waited until say, September or early October to release Hussein from U.S. custody, not much could happen before Election Day, and afterwards, it wouldn't matter.

Turning Hussein over to Iraqis sooner than that would pose serious problems though. If he were summarily executed, it would make a joke out of claims that a new democratic system was being established in Iraq. If he were to linger in custody, he'd likely become a focal point for some Baathist guerrillas, who could be expected to try to spring him or at least wreak revenge for his capture and captivity.

Meanwhile, the capture of Hussein itself will put several theories to the test. According to the White House (though not to many military sources on the ground in Iraq), the militant opposition to U.S. and other occupation forces in Iraq has primarily been coming from Hussein loyalists, and has been funded, directly or indirectly, by Hussein. With Hussein out of the picture, this theory predicts that violent resistance to the occupation and to the U.S. should quickly peter out. In the unlikely event that this happens—and the blast at the Palestine Hotel within hours of Hussein's capture is clear sign that it won't—Bush has essentially been handed a second term in the White House. If it does not, then the whole theory of who's behind the resistance has to be rethought.

According to a counter theory, the resistance to occupation forces could now actually increase dramatically. This theory goes that many Iraqis resent and oppose the occupation of their country by western forces, but have shied away from joining the guerrilla insurgency because they also hated Hussein and didn't want to contribute to his possible return to power. With Hussein removed as a threat, these Iraqi nationalists are now free to join in what could quickly become much more of a genuine national liberation movement.

Add to this the fact that the Shiite/Sunni rivalry does not go away with the capture and removal of Hussein. To the extent that Sunni Iraqis fear and will resist formation of a government run by Shiite Iraqis, it might be expected that with Hussein out of the way, there will be a surge in the number of Sunni fighters, who no longer have to worry that they might be helping to bring back Hussein.

As for the Democrats back home, they now have a problem. Do they sit on their hands and let Bush wallow in the media adoration that will inevitably follow this capture of one of the "evil ones"? While Hussein's capture is a bit of luck for the Administration, its handling of the broader so-called War on Terror hasn't been going so well. Reports suggest that efforts to shut down the funding of Al Qaeda have failed, the U.S. is no closer to catching Osama Bin Laden than it ever was, Afghanistan is collapsing into warlordism and the Taliban is resurgent, and Americans are growing increasingly uneasy about the war in Iraq and its cost in lives and money.

It's long past time for the Democrats in Congress to call for an end to the U.S. occupation. Such a move, even if it failed to win a majority, would serve notice that at least henceforth Iraq is a Republican war.

Dennis Kucinich, the strongest and most consistent opponent of the war among the Democratic presidential hopefuls, was quick to nail down a position. Hussein is captured, he said. Now the U.S. can pack up and go home, turning over Iraq to the Iraqis and the U.N. and letting Iraq and the U.N. deal with Hussein.

It will be interesting to see how many other of the candidates will sign on to this unambiguous position.*

—*CounterPunch.org*, Dec. 15, 2003

Recalling LBJ in Vietnam: Bush's Baghdad Pit Stop

The corporate media are in a predictable paroxysm of praise and admiration for President Bush's furtive and carefully televised and photographed quickie visit to wartime Baghdad—or at least to the airport—and his faux turkey dinner with some selected troops there.

"A tough act to follow" crowed the *Philadelphia Inquirer* in a front-page second-day banner headline that justified itself by the circular

---

*Sadly, none did.

logic that the trip would be tough on the Democratic opposition because editors would be giving it front-page play in the media.

But before too much is read into this second attempt by our duty-dodging former National Guardsman turned commander-in-chief to bask in the reflected glory of America's soldiers, it might be worth reflecting on prior trips to the front by American presidents.

It was on Oct. 26, 1966, that Lyndon Johnson made his then celebrated trip to Vietnam to visit the troops. The administration at that time was busily touting the line—generally parroted by the American media—that the war was going well, and that there was a "light at the end of the tunnel." Johnson had ramped up U.S. troop levels from 185,000 in 1965 to 385,000, and had increased the size of the U.S. military overall by 1.5 million. North Vietnam was being bombed relentlessly by B-52s.

But, as Johnson's advisers well knew, the war wasn't going well—at least for the U.S. The number of U.S. soldiers killed in action by the time of his "morale-boosting" visit was approaching the 10,000 per year mark, and would reach over 16,000 in one year in 1968, when over half a million American soldiers would be in Vietnam.

By that time, Johnson's political career had been destroyed by the war, and he had been replaced by Richard Nixon, in no small part because Nixon had promised the electorate that he had a "secret plan" to end the war.

Nixon too, made a surprise wartime visit to Vietnam, on July 30, 1969. Again there was a lot of positive spin coming from the White House about light at the end of the proverbial tunnel, about winning the war, and about Americans coming home. In fact, by that point, American troop levels were at their peak of 540,000, and the Vietnamese were still winning. (By that time, too, an equal number of protesters could be counted on to turn out at the increasingly frequent demonstrations against the war, and the media were beginning to question the wisdom of continued fighting.) While Nixon spoke of "Vietnamization," that is, of turning the war over to the South Vietnamese Army, nearly as many American GIs were killed during his two terms of office—25,000—as during the entire rest of the war. A total of 58,000 Americans—and three million Indochinese people—died.

It was a bit over a year after Nixon's visit to Vietnam that he actually expanded the war, first "secretly" carpet bombing (secretly from Americans, that is) Cambodia and Laos, and then sending an invading army of American troops into neutral Cambodia, in a disastrous move that, combined with a CIA-backed coup overthrowing the government of Cambodia, led to the ultimate victory of Pol Pot's Khmer Rouge guerrillas in Cambodia and the descent of that once peaceful land into a nightmare of genocidal killing and civil war.

Again, that presidential visit was hardly a positive indicator for either the people of Indochina or for the American troops who had to greet and cheer their commander in chief.

It's worth remembering both of these two past trips—and the thumb-sucking, patriotic manner in which they were covered by the media—as we view the puerile PR photos of a smiling Bush passing a plastic turkey to the soldiers stuck, thanks to Bush's ill-conceived invasion, in the sands of Iraq over Thanksgiving.

Again we're hearing the groundless claims by White House and Pentagon officials that the war in Iraq is going well, the latest spin being that the "rate of attacks" on American troops has declined. What these government propagandists carefully ignore is that while the frequency of those attacks has dropped over the past few weeks from over 50 a week to closer to 25 per week, the lethality of the remaining attacks has increased dramatically. In November a record 104 American and allied troops were killed in attacks, which included rocket assaults on helicopters, a truck bombing of Italian military headquarters, and the forced downing of a DHL cargo Airbus. All this has made November hands down the deadliest month of the war since May 1, 2003, when Bush donned a flight suit and somewhat prematurely announced the "end of major combat." Worse yet, there are reports that members of the much touted American-trained Iraqi security forces were instrumental in organizing some of the more successful guerrilla attacks against occupation forces—a bad sign for the Bush administration's Nixonian "Iraqization" scheme for getting the U.S. out of the Iraq war "with honor."

No, I'm afraid there's no light at the end of this tunnel any more than there was at the time of Johnson's and Nixon's visits to Vietnam, and the likelihood is that this latest presidential war-zone junket will someday be seen as a precursor not of victory, but of increased bloodshed, a wider war, and quite possibly, of another humiliating defeat for American forces.*

—*CounterPunch.org, Dec. 1, 2003*

Good Morning, Vietnam!
A Strategic Rhetorical Retreat

As the American Democratic primary campaign heats up with the addition of a general and second Vietnam veteran, retired Gen. Wesley Clark, it is perhaps appropriate, and certainly no surprise, that the situation facing the American invaders and occupiers in Iraq would start to truly resemble that earlier disastrous conflict.

It was only a few days ago that newscasters were reporting that things had been "calmer" in Iraq, with attacks seeming to let up. That, however, proved to be like the calm along the North Carolina coast just before the arrival of Hurricane Isabel. A day later, on Thursday, that deceptive calm in Iraq was broken by an unusually heavy attack on an American military convoy, which may have left as many as eight American soldiers dead and more gravely wounded. A few hours later, there was another attack, in which three more Americans were killed and several wounded. (The U.S. has been unusually cagey about the casualties in the first, larger attack. Eyewitnesses had reported eight-10 dead, while an AP reporter trying to get to the scene was, suspiciously, fired upon by an American tank guarding the site of the attack. Meanwhile the American military has not confirmed any deaths, suggesting that a cover-up may be underway, in which, as in Vietnam, casualties might be "moved" to later dates and attributed to other incidents so as to avoid evidence of a calamity.)

The Bush administration, clearly rattled now, both by the deepening quagmire it finds itself facing in Iraq, and by the prospect (now that there's a general among Democratic ranks making some of the charges), of increasingly forceful political attacks on its military and foreign policy fiascoes, has begun a strategic rhetorical retreat. All key administration officials, from the president on down to Deputy Secretary of Defense Paul Wolfowitz, have begun backing off earlier assertions about weapons of mass destruction and links between Saddam Hussein and Osama Bin Laden. Caught in a lie, they are hoping now that the notoriously ill-informed and short-attention-span-plagued American public will forget what they were saying earlier.

They may be right in guessing that many people will just hear what they're now saying, but certainly some key people won't prove so

---

* In fact, scarcely four months after Bush's turkey visit, and after the writing of this column, it was clear that the U.S. occupation was in trouble, and the Pentagon was asking for more troops—20,000 to start with.

easy to befuddle. You have to wonder, for instance, what American soldiers, who had gone to Iraq pumped full of adrenaline-inducing propaganda about Saddam's complicity in the 9/11 attacks and his alleged preparations to nuke or poison America, are making of word from the president, the vice president and the secretary of defense that, well, they never really did expect to find those WMD's and that well, they never did really say that Saddam was involved in 9/11. What, many of them must be wondering, including the over 100,000 now dodging RPGs and mortars in Iraq, and the thousands now hospitalized with missing eyes, legs or arms, what, the family members of the several hundred dead soldiers must be wondering, have they been fighting for?

If it was not for post-9/11 vengeance and to prevent a WMD attack on America that they have been sweating, fighting and dying, then what? It couldn't have just been to overthrow an evil tyrant, or why would Iraqis be so angry at them?

And what about the rest of us? Now that Bush and his war cabinet are admitting that they snookered us into supporting a war under false pretenses, what are we to think? Do we go with the idea that, well, mistakes were made, lies and exaggerations were fed to us, but now there's this big mess in Iraq, and we can't leave, we just have to keep paying through the nose and watching our soldiers get picked off—seemingly in bigger and bigger numbers?

That's kind of what happened in Nam, remember? By 1968, when Nixon came in with his "secret plan" to end the conflict in Indochina, it was clear that the reason given for the war—fighting the spread of Communism—was a fraud or, if true, a failure. The war, if anything, was spreading the fires of Communism and anti-imperialist nationalism through Laos and Cambodia, and South Vietnam itself was a lost cause. Under Nixon, the refrain became not defeating the Communist insurgency, but "peace with honor."

Actually, what "peace with honor" meant was giving Nixon some kind of a fig leaf to hide his shame when America finally pulled up stakes and gave up the fight. Providing Nixon with that little bit of greenery ended up costing an extra 20,000 American and perhaps up to a million extra Vietnamese, Khmer and Lao lives. Honor?

Now the situation in Iraq is starting to look the same, even if the numbers of dead, so far, are mercifully much lower on both sides.

It is becoming increasingly clear that the longer the U.S. stays in Iraq, the bigger the insurgency against the occupation will become, and the higher the casualty figures will mount.

Bush's plan has to be to keep those casualties down, while tamping down the insurgency temporarily, with increased firepower, through the November '04 presidential election. Like Nixon before him, he cannot give up now, because the American public would then hold him responsible for the pointless deaths of its soldiers and for the incredible waste of over $200 billion in taxpayer money.

Definition of "quagmire": a swamp from which there is no escape, because the more you struggle, the deeper you sink into the muck.

So once again, we pursue a bloody strategy of "peace with honor," this time euphemistically called "the rebuilding of Iraq." We'll pursue this criminal strategy not because it has a chance of working, but because our unelected president doesn't have the *huevos* to tell the American people that he and his neo-con advisers made a colossal mistake.

It is then up to the public, and to the Democratic presidential candidates, to put a halt to this criminal madness. Don't expect too much from the Democratic presidential candidates—at least not from the so-called front-runners. They may blast Bush for starting the war, but except for the likes of Kucinich, Sharpton and Moseley-Braun, they won't be calling for an immediate end to the occupation. Before any of them develops the spine to issue such a call, they'll need to hear a public outcry.

That makes the coming October 25 march on Washington, so reminiscent of the 1967 march on the Pentagon (something I remember well, having been arrested and beaten by Federal marshals on the mall of the Pentagon, and locked up in Occoquan Federal Detention Center on that former occasion), so important. Coming as it does on the run-up to the first presidential primaries, a big turnout should give those timid Democratic presidential wannabes some more spine, while boosting the chances of those candidates who are willing to come out more strongly, demanding an end to the war and occupation.

Unless we want another president to drag on the occupation through another four- year-term looking for "peace with honor," unless we want to wake up for four more years to "Good morning, Iraq!", the Democratic 2004 campaign battle cry needs to become the slogan of the October march: "Bring the troops home!"

—*CounterPunch.org, Sept. 20, 2003*

The Bush Speech: Spinning a Fiasco

Listening to President Bush's address last night, which—despite not a single line of contrition—was clear proof that the Bush/Cheney/Rumsfeld strategy in Iraq has been a fiasco, I was stumped trying to locate a policy disaster of similar scale in recent American history with which to compare it.

Certainly the Vietnam War offers some parallels, built as it was on similar hubris and lying to the public. But Vietnam was a disaster that was at least five presidents in the making, beginning with President Truman's morally reprehensible decision to endorse a return of French colonial authority in Indochina following the end of World War II, and ending with President Nixon's criminal expansion of the war into Cambodia and Laos. This disaster in Iraq is wholly of the Bush Administration's making.

No, to locate parallels on a scale equal to this historic idiocy one has to look beyond the U.S. In terms of foolishness and failure, the French Maginot Line strategy during the years before World War II, or perhaps the Great Wall of China, could compare. But of course while in the end these two costly failed strategies, by diverting policy makers and resources from sounder approaches, proved disastrous to the survival of those two nations, neither began as an act of belligerence. Rather, they were ill-conceived defensive measures.

That said, the current Iraq policy—which Bush and his handlers have disingenuously tried to present as a kind of offensive defense (we act pre-emptively to destroy an alleged threat)—resembles those two infamous failed policies in one way. Like them, the consigning of over half the U.S. military's available manpower to Iraq, where they are now tied down indefinitely, and the down payment of an already admitted $166 billion (a figure that only runs through October 2004, and which will surely prove too low), on a winless war and occupation, effectively guts American defenses and makes it impossible to finance alternative defensive strategies, from strengthening port security and domestic fire and emergency rescue services, to bolstering the economy.

The administration clearly knows it has screwed up badly. Hence last night's televised speech.

The president, during his delivery, was a far cry from the strutting cock of the Abraham Lincoln V-I Day photo-op. He looked rather as if someone had just given him a wedgie on his way into the Cabinet Room, and stumbled nervously several times while reading his allegedly "vetted and revetted" speech on the teleprompter.

The president's efforts to dredge up that now grizzled canard, those infamous and apparently non-existent "weapons of mass destruction," were less than half-hearted. Even his efforts to link the Saddam Hussein regime to Al Qaeda seemed dispirited and perfunctory. Instead, Bush and his speechwriters tried, vainly I suspect, to bolster support for this war by claiming that even if those links can't be proven, Iraq is now a "central front" in the war on terror. Putting aside for a moment the question of whether or not that is true, the obvious question is: Why is Iraq, which previously was not in any way linked to global terror or Al Qaeda, now a "terrorism magnet?"

The answer—that the U.S. invasion and occupation, by destroying a central government and by antagonizing Arab nationalists and Muslim fundamentalists everywhere, has made it a cause—is not something that the Bush team wants Americans to think too hard about.

If last night's speech is the best this administration can do to make its case for the War in Iraq, it is in deep trouble. To me, this was the Bush version of President Carter's disastrous "malaise" speech.

Polls show Bush's popularity is plummeting, with his approval rating now down to pre-9/11 levels—a time when he was being dismissed widely as a one-term president. The flags aren't waving on the TV screen during news reports any more. Martial music doesn't introduce the president on the news. And even the timid corporate news media are taking cracks at this president following what was supposed to be a rousing new call to arms to support U.S. policy. (CNN's reporter in Baghdad even went so far as to debunk the claim that the invasion had been to fight terror, saying that this part of the president's speech was sure to anger Iraqis, who say their country was never in support of global terrorism.) After cheerleading the invasion of Iraq, the theme of CNN's post-address report this time around was that the president would face tough questioning in Congress, and that he had not spelled out an exit strategy for American involvement and American troops

And indeed he didn't do that, because for him, there is no exit.

Of course, Bush could in practice simply declare victory, turn over the reins of power to the Iraqi people, and bring the troops home tomorrow, but if that were done, Iraq would dissolve quickly into civil war and chaos, and he would have to admit to defeat—and answer for all of America's lost blood and treasure. For the Bush administration, then, the only course is continuation of a clearly doomed strategy that will mean more slaughter and misery in Iraq, more Americans in body bags or crippled and maimed, and a budget deficit that defies description.

Eventually, Americans will get around to assigning blame for this unprecedented screw up. When they do—and it's looking increasingly as if that day will come in November 2004— it could be a political earthquake.

—*CounterPunch.org, Sept. 8, 2003*

One consequence of the disastrous course of the Bush war in Iraq was that by the fall of 2003, it was becoming apparent that the U.S. was going to run out of troops to do its dirty work. With the insurgency growing in strength and tenacity, and the long-suffering American Guard and Reservists watching their families, jobs and businesses disappear back home, and with re-enlistments and new recruitments starting to decline, it seemed evident to me that the people with clearer heads in the Pentagon had to be thinking about how to scare up some new bodies. A little checking around produced the evidence. The draft machinery was being pulled out of the Pentagon attic. My story in *CounterPunch*, and another I did for *Salon* magazine around the same time, caught the attention of a number of papers, and of CNN, which had me on to discuss the issue. While there was still considerable skepticism in the mainstream media, by early 2004, even the Pentagon itself admitted that because of troop shortages it was considering a limited draft of people with "special skills." If the Iraqi resistance continues to grow in strength, clearly the special skills qualifier will be deleted.

A Draft in the Forecast?
The Pentagon Puts Out the Help Wanted Sign

With winter approaching, it appears the White House may start feeling a bit drafty. It's not a matter of poor insulation, but rather the result of mounting evidence that the Bush/Cheney/Rumsfeld war plan in Iraq is not going well, and there may well need to be more U.S. troops sent to Iraq.

The shoot-down of a Chinook helicopter earlier this week, causing the death of 15 soldiers and the wounding of another 21, is a good example of the problem. It turns out this military disaster was, in large part, the direct result of a shortage of troops on the ground. With the military's 134,000 troops in Iraq spread so thin, there was nobody available to secure the area around the helicopter landing zone in what is acknowledged to be a high-risk area. Because helicopters are particularly vulnerable to attack during their slow landings and ascents, it is standard procedure to secure the perimeter of landing areas, but in this instance, the military had to abandon standard practice and take a chance. There were no soldiers available to protect the area.

A *New York Times* column following the shoulder-fired missile attack notes, correctly, that because of the high numbers of personnel required for support, maintenance and high-tech "back-office" functions in Rumsfeld's "lean and mean" military, actually only some 56,000 of the 134,000 U.S. troops in country are available to carry guns. Since these guys need to eat and sleep, at best there are then only 28,000 U.S. troops available to patrol all of Iraq, a hostile country the size of California with 24 million people, at any given time.

There were hopes at the White House and in the Pentagon that Turkey would ride to the rescue with an influx of armed troops, but, like India and Pakistan before it, Turkey has thought better of this incredibly bad idea, and now says it will not participate in the U.S. war and occupation. That announcement assures that the U.S. will at a minimum have to call up more reservists and National Guard soldiers for Iraq duty during this election year.

But besides the political problems of calling up more weekend soldiers for active duty overseas, the reality is that there simply are not enough Americans in uniform to handle a bigger war in Iraq.

It should come as no surprise then, even as the president and his advisers continue to claim that everything is going well and according to plan, that saner heads at the Pentagon are taking steps to prepare for return to the draft.

As I reported on Monday in *Salon Magazine*,[3] using a Defense Department news website called DefendAmerica that provides Pentagon reports about the so-called "War on Terrorism" to "military communities," the government put out a call for volunteers to help fill the hundreds of vacancies in over 2000 local draft boards and draft appeals boards. Current draft board members also report that last summer, they were urged to go out and recommend people to fill those vacancies, which currently run at about 16 percent nationwide.

The goal, according to a Selective Service spokesman, is to have the draft machinery ready to go "at the click of a finger."

Of course, the time between that "click" and the delivery of the first cannon fodder to Army boot camps for training would not be such a smooth or quick process. First, Congress would have to pass a bill authorizing a draft. Then it would have to be signed by the president. At that point, the Selective Service law says the Selective Service System has 193 days to deliver the first draftees to the tender mercies of the military.

A draft would be a political disaster for the president, so most military experts say it is unlikely that a return to conscription would occur before the November 2004 presidential election, but if the guerrilla war in Iraq continues to get worse, the day after that election, the president could well be forced to decide on either a phased withdrawal or escalation—and a national call-up. Faced with the same choices in Southeast Asia, Presidents Lyndon Johnson and Richard Nixon both chose escalation over withdrawal. What Bush or a Democratic successor would do faced with that choice is anybody's guess.

Rep. Charles Rangel (D-NY) and the retiring Sen. Fritz Hollings (D-SC) have companion draft authorization bills in the House and Senate. Rangle, for his part argues that a universal draft based upon a lottery would be fairer than the present system, which he calls an "economic draft," which forces low-income people without job prospects into military service. So far their bills have languished for lack of Republican support, but as the rosy assumptions of the war advocates in the Bush administration continue to be disproven, Republican hawks in Congress and the White House could well begin pushing for more troops to "do the job right."

According to Charles Peña, director of defense studies at the libertarian Cato Institute, the closest model to the current Iraq occupation is Northern Ireland. There, he says, British "pacification" efforts required a force ratio of 10 soldiers to every 1000 citizens, and at the height of the Northern Ireland conflict, a ratio of 20 soldiers to every 1000 people. "If you transfer that to Iraq, it would mean you'd need at least 240,000 troops and maybe as many as 480,000, says Peña. The U.S. military, with a total of 1.4 million in uniform, would have to strip every fighting unit domestically and around the globe to come up with such numbers—an impossible move that would leave the U.S. and many of its overseas strategic interests completely unguarded.

Recall that during the Vietnam War, when the U.S. had a military about twice as large as today, fielding a force of 500,000 soldiers required a major conscription program.

Clearly, if the war keeps getting worse, there is a draft in the forecast.

—*CounterPunch.org, Nov. 5, 2003*

While the Pentagon is having trouble finding cannon fodder for President Bush's wonderful desert adventure, the Bush administration, unbelievably, has been sticking it to current men and women in uniform, certainly contributing to an exodus of skilled fighters, not to mention to the slump in morale at the front. I'm at a loss to explain this stabbing of one's own side in the back, but perhaps it has to do with the even more unbelievable deficits that the Bush budget and tax cuts for the wealthy have created. It may be that there just is no more money to be had for those heroes in uniform that the president is so fond of getting photographed among.

Bush's War on Veterans: The White House Attack on the Troops

Veterans' Day is traditionally a grand opportunity for members of the nation's political class to wrap themselves in Old Glory and bask in the patriotic aura of soldiers from the last century's wars.

You probably won't see our duty ducking president or his gopher-like, hideaway vice president marching in any parades though. It's not so much that they have to worry about an attack by terrorists, as that they might get hit with raspberries from the old vets and young soldiers in the parades.

Conservatives have been quick to cry "Support the troops!" at anti-war demonstrators, but the Bush administration and its supporters in the Republican-dominated Congress have meanwhile been busy screwing both veterans and active duty troops with a vengeance this year.

The hypocrisy of this administration, when it comes to veterans and active duty military, is truly staggering.

Thanks to the Bush Administration's and Republican Congress's refusal to approve increases in the budget for the Veterans Administration, veterans now have to wait an average of six months to be seen. In fact VA spending per patient today is an average of $624 *less* than it was seven years ago. To add insult to lack of treatment for injury, the administration also is proposing levying a $250 charge on all veterans receiving treatment in VA facilities, and to end access for vets suffering from service-related problems who earn more than $26,000 a year.

The Bush administration has also sought this year, even as soldiers are risking their lives in the Iraqi desert, to cut "imminent danger" pay by $75 per month, and to also cut a family separation allowance of $150.

Even more miserly, until the media made it an issue, the government was actually charging injured GI's from Iraq $8 per day for their meals at the Ft. Stewart, Georgia base where most are brought to await treatment for their war injuries.

That's not all, though, This president, who came to office with the help of bushels of military absentee ballots—ballots which tipped the election to Bush in Florida's disputed presidential election in 2000*—and who loudly proclaimed to the armed forces during his campaign that "help is on the way," has proceeded to close dozens of Department of Defense-run schools for military dependents, and has shuttered 56 commissaries relied upon by military families to help them buy food and supplies on their limited incomes.

The callous disregard and disrespect for older veterans and for those now on active duty in Iraq and elsewhere in the U.S. and around the globe has extended to the petty. For example, when a Green Beret, confronted with the horror of combat for the first time (he witnessed an Iraqi cut in half by machine gun fire), froze in a panic attack and asked his commanding officer for help, he was court-martialed and charged with "cowardice." Only when his case was publicized did the army back down and lower the charge to "dereliction of duty."

Worse was the case of a woman in the National Guard, who was serving in Iraq along with her active-duty husband. She returned home on leave and decided to stay with her two small children rather than return to Iraq, because she was in danger of having them taken away by the state (her mother-in-law had been caring for her kids in the parents' absence, but could no longer do so when her own husband became ill). Instead of responding to her family crisis humanely, the Pentagon court-martialed her, only backing down after media attention and a nationwide public outcry.

Meanwhile, the Bush Administration has gone to court seeking to block a federal judge's award of damages to a group of mostly black servicemen who had successfully sued the Iraq government for their having been captured and tortured by Iraq during the 1991 Gulf War. The government's argument: damn the torture claims, the money is needed now for Iraq reconstruction.

---

* Many of those military ballots were technically invalid, as they were stamped after the date of the election, but Democrat Al Gore, afraid to look like he was anti-military, declined to challenge any of them—a huge mistake.

At least one presidential candidate has loudly protested the White House's attack on vets and soldiers. "The Administration has made a mockery of the treatment of our veterans; ignoring their needs and slashing the Department of Veteran Affairs budget by 27 percent," says Rep. Dennis Kucinich (D-Ohio). "While thousands of men and women stood risking their lives in the Middle East early last month, the Bush administration cut their combat pay by one-third. Although this reduction is built into the $87.5 billion President Bush has just received [for Iraq and Afghanistan operations], Halliburton and Bechtel have not been asked to reduce any of their enormous profits. The members of the Guard and Reserve units that are in Iraq are finding out that the separation pay which they have received for their families is also being reduced. This is a shameful dishonor and it must be stopped. We must support our troops by bringing them home and by providing them with health coverage and adequate compensation."

"This president lied us into an illegal war and glorified it with TV specials," says Woody Powell, executive director of Veterans for Peace. "Yet he won't show up at a funeral" for any of the Iraq War dead. Of the Bush Administration's and Congressional Republicans' astonishing trashing of vets and active duty soldiers, Powell, a Korean War veteran, says, "I don't think they see it as attacking them. They see it as saving money. But it's the wrong thing to be cutting, just like cutting education is a bad thing."

—*CounterPunch.org, Nov. 11, 2003*

Misers of War:
Troop Strength and Chintzy Bonuses

The desperation move by the Pentagon to try and maintain U.S. troop strength by offering soldiers a re-up bonus of $10,000 gives the lie to earlier assertions that were made to me by Pentagon officials last fall when I was writing about contingency planning for a return to the draft.

At that time, Army manpower officials assured me that they were having no problem with reenlistments and recruitment.

What a difference a few hundred dead soldiers, a few downed choppers, and a few months make!

A bigger lie is that if the Bush administration had had its way, that bonus being offered to soldiers to reenlist and risk their lives for another year or more in the Iraqi desert—a bonus that works out to about

$3350 a year or $280 a month—would be just about the amount they would have lost in reduced combat pay. And in fact, they may still lose that much and more next year.

As I reported in In These Times[4] and CounterPunch last November, the Bush Administration, having nuked the American budget with tax giveaways to the rich, tried to cut some of its costs by eliminating $150 a month in combat pay for the 130,000 soldiers in Iraq. That adds up to about $1800 a year. They also tried to eliminate another $75 per month in family allowance money paid to troops who are separated from spouses or children. If they'd gotten their way, this would have represented a $225/month pay cut for married troops in the battle zone—about $2700 a year in lost pay.

Luckily, when Congress got wind of the pay cut for the troops doing Bush's dirty work in the desert, they nixed the deal—for this year. But the Pentagon has promised to come back with the proposed combat pay cut plan next year.

If the Bush administration were to get its way, soldiers signing up for another tour of battle duty, after collecting their bonuses, would be netting a whopping $1950 for their three-year tour of duty—less than $55 a month to put their lives on the line for Uncle George.

No wonder reports from the field say the grunts are laughing at the offer—and turning it down.

Paying the workers and grunts fairly has never been a strong point with this crew in Washington. These are the same folks who recently pushed through a rule change at the Department of Labor that will strip some 8 million workers of eligibility for overtime pay when they are asked to put in more than the standard 40-hour week. The same administration that also has been offering employers tips on how to avoid having to pay overtime pay to some 1.3 million lower paid workers who the same new rules were supposed to be making eligible for overtime for the first time.

It would seem to be all of a piece. President Bush, the prep school boy who grew up in a blue blood family where servants are the norm, seems to take the view that average Americans should be glad just to have a job. They should not expect to get extra pay if they have to work long hours, or get shot at.

He's willing to use market incentives, like the re-up bonus, to get people to work for him when he has to, but he obviously is ready to take that money back out of their pockets when they're not looking if he gets the chance. It's a little like that plastic turkey the Commander-in-

Chief carried around during his photo-op quickie visit to the airport near Baghdad at Thanksgiving—it looks good but you can't eat it.

I don't know about the grunts in Iraq, but if I were over there getting close to the end of my tour, and contemplating that re-up bonus, even if I were willing to put my life on the line again for the benefit of Halliburton and Exxon/Mobil, I'd still want it in writing from the brass that they wouldn't be turning around next year and taking away my combat pay and family separation allowance.

With this administration, you really need an enforceable contract.

—*CounterPunch.org, Jan. 9, 2004*

I know it's hard to believe that 30 years after our disaster in Vietnam, here we are again in a pointless, endless war. But when it comes to things that are really hard to believe, the hunt for those so-called weapons of mass destruction really wins the prize. We even had the president trying to make fun of the whole thing himself, in a tasteless presentation he did before the Washington press corps which had him looking under tables and chairs for the elusive weapons—a pretty sick joke given that people in Iraq were dying over that fraud even as he kibitzed around. The truth is, the whole weapons of mass destruction story has been a sick joke. After all, when it comes to killing large numbers of people indiscriminately, the U.S. is the undisputed champion.

Weapons in Search of a Name: Let's Reserve WMD for the Really Big Ones. You Know, Those Made-in-America Bombs

We need a new name for WMDs.

I for one am sick of hearing about Weapons of Mass Destruction—those alleged chemical, biological and dirty nuke bombs that the likes of Saddam Hussein and Osama Bin Laden are supposed to covet for use against us innocent Americans. I'm especially sick of hearing about them from President Bush, who has a way of slurring the words together into a kind of single noun.

What is the real definition of a weapon of mass destruction, anyhow?

Presumably it's a weapon that kills a whole lot of people indiscriminately. More people than a land mine or a typical bomb, I suppose.

Okay, top of the list would have to be a nuclear bomb, then. That's clearly a WMD. No contest. And who's got those? Not Saddam, and not Osama. We do. Britain does. So do China, Russia, India, Pakistan, Israel and (or so it and the White House claim) North Korea.

How about cluster bombs? Some of those things, dropped in an urban area or in the midst of an encampment of troops, could easily kill hundreds of people—maybe thousands. Ditto that new weapon built by the U.S. for use in Iraq, fortunately too late to be used: the MOAB (Mother of All Bombs), a 16-ton monster bomb so big it has to be pushed out the back of a transport plane. That sucker could kill tens of thousands of people if dropped in a populated area. Clearly both these are WMDs.

Likewise the propane bomb that was first used in the first Gulf War, and later in Afghanistan, and probably in the latest war in Iraq. This baby releases a giant cloud of propane, which spreads over acres of land before being ignited in an enormous flash fire. Again, clearly a WMD. Note that these—up to and including nukes—are all weapons that are owned and used not by terrorists or even Saddam Hussein, but by the U.S. military.

We might well also consider inadvertent WMDs—the mines sown by U.S. forces that kill and maim thousands of innocents for years after a war ends, and the depleted uranium bombs and shells, thousands of tons of which were used in the recent invasion of Iraq, which incinerate their targets causing, sometimes, massive loss of life, but which also poison the environment with radioactive dust that will hang around causing untold numbers of cancer cases, many of them fatal, for a million years to come.

Clearly, if the words Weapons of Mass Destruction are to mean anything, all the above weapons are WMDs. But when the White House or Downing Street or the Pentagon talk about WMDs, they aren't talking about any of those things. They're talking about germ weapons, about toxic chemical weapons, or about so-called "dirty bombs."

Thing is, most of those weapons are virtual—nobody's ever used one or seen one—and moreover, if they were used, their kill potential would probably be pretty small—a lot smaller than some of the weapons that are now routinely used by the U.S. military.

Take dirty nuke bombs. Most experts say that these would be made of ordinary explosives embedded in some kind of nuclear waste products, such as uranium dust, cadmium, radioactive iodine or some other nasty chemical. The idea would be to blow the bomb, and spread the fall-out as widely as possible. But experts also say that the likely number of deaths from such a weapon, even if exploded in an urban center, would be small —perhaps at most a few hundred. More would probably die of the actual detonator explosion, if it were set off in a crowded spot, than from any fallout. This is because in a developed country like the U.S., there would be treatments available for those who suffered contamination.

The biggest threat from such a bomb would be panic, and the commercial losses to properties that would have to be decontaminated before they could be used again. A dirty nuke then, far from being a WMD, is probably more of an ACW (anti-capitalism weapon).

Chemical weapons are even less scary. As a group of self-styled millenialist terrorists in Japan who tried deploying a Sarin WMD, killing only a handful of subway riders, discovered, it's not that easy to make chemical weapons kill a lot of people. You need luck, because the weather has to cooperate, and a lot of control over the situation. Saddam Hussein was able to kill a lot of his own people and a lot of Iranians back during the Iran-Iraq war because he had control over the skies, and was able to drop numbers of poison gas bombs in towns or over battlefields at the time of his choosing. Terrorists would have a hard time replicating this. More likely would be a single bomb, and again, in a country like the U.S., should such an attack happen, the resources are there to minimize the impact, as was the case in Tokyo. Once again, it's a stretch calling such weapons, especially the home-made weapons terrorists would likely use, WMDs.

Germ weapons are even more problematic. Again experts say that most germs that could cause disease are not that easy to disseminate. Some, like Anthrax, can be very dangerous, but don't spread beyond those initially exposed (look at the anthrax attack that did occur in September, 2001, which caused enormous economic losses, but only five deaths, making it not a WMD, but just another ACW). Others, like Smallpox, can spread as an epidemic after release, but are hard to disseminate initially—and devilishly hard to work with without becoming exposed oneself. In any event, in a modern society with an ample healthcare infrastructure, such bombs would again likely cause few deaths, at least compared to the genuine WMD's filling in the Pentagon's arsenal.

The main function of the weapons that terrorists might use (assuming they don't get ahold of one of the Pentagon's nastier toys) is really to sow fear and panic, and in that respect, any of the big three—dirty bombs, germ weapons or chemical weapons—could be highly effective. A dirty bomb detonated in Manhattan would probably kill far more people by trampling and car collisions than by actually exposing them to radiation. Ditto for a germ or chemical weapon.

So, with that in mind, it's time to rename these things. Let's save WMD for weapons that really do kill, or have the potential to kill, thousands of humans. That would mean things like nuclear bombs, cluster bombs, MOABs, propane bombs and the like. Good old American weapons, that is.

As for the terrorist weapons, let's call them WMH for Weapons of Mass Hysteria.

Once we start recognizing them for what they are, maybe people will start asking why the Bush Administration keeps harping on these things as a threat to America's way of life. You really do have to wonder what the hell these guys are really trying to do when they keep going around trying to scare the living shit out of the American public. If the purpose of terrorist terror weapons is to sow terror, why is the Administration so busy priming the pump?

After all, remember back during the dark days of the Cold War, when U.S. and Soviet bombers and missiles stood poised and ready to initiate mutual annihilation on 15 minutes' notice? Back then, the guys in the Pentagon and the White House didn't tell us to panic. On the contrary, they routinely used to assure us that we didn't have to worry. We'd survive an attack and go on to win.

It was a ridiculous lie, but the point is, they didn't try to scare us into simpering passivity. Rather, they tried to get us to buck up and stick with the program, which was building more and more of these genuine WMDs.

These days, when America is the preeminent superpower in the globe, they seem bent on scaring us, the citizenry, out of our wits.

Why? On the evidence of the past two years, it looks like the goal is to get us to acquiesce in the evisceration of our Constitution and Bill of Rights, and in the administration's bloody imperial adventure.

So maybe WMH is the wrong term. Maybe we should call these virtual terrorists' weapons WCEs—for Weapons of Constitutional Eradication.

—*CounterPunch.org, July 1, 2003*

Coronado in Iraq: Laughter in the Dark

The Bush administration's fiasco in Iraq is now reaching the point where, if it weren't for the thousands of dead and maimed Iraqi's and Americans, if it weren't for the hundreds of thousands of American military families whose lives have been turned upside down, if it weren't for the millions of Iraqi's living under the gun, if it weren't for the millions of Americans paying through the nose for it, this would be the stuff of comedy.

Take David Kay, the earnest leader of the massive 1400-member Iraq Survey Group. Like a modern-day Coronado searching the American southwest for his fabled lost city of gold, Kay, after scouring the Iraqi countryside unimpeded for three months and blowing a reported $300 million in a vain search for those elusive Weapons of Mass Destruction, returns to Washington empty-handed, with a report saying that he can't find anything.

What does the administration then do? It asks for more time—three times more—and more money—twice as much again—to keep looking.

CNN, meanwhile, invites Kay's biggest cheerleader in the media, N.Y *Times* reporter Judith Miller, on to the Aaron Brown News Hour to comment on Kay's report, without mentioning to viewers that she herself has a book out all about those dangerous WMDs—a book will be filling the $1 remainder sale bins at Barnes&Noble if Kay turns up nothing. Miller, predictably, suggests that what Kay has provided is merely a "snapshot in time" (never mind that the exposure time for the snapshot was three months). If we keep looking, she suggests with a bright smile, though on the basis of no evidence, we'll find those elusive weapons.

As for the attacks on American troops, which are growing more frequent, more lethal and more professional as each week goes by, the Pentagon, in a marvelously clever maneuver, offers up the theory that this is because the American military's attacks are succeeding. "The resistance forces are getting whittled down to the leadership, the professional military people who have been organizing the attacks, who are now having to go out on their own," they say—again with no evidence to support this idea. Never mind that this rationale flies in the face of countless reports from Iraq suggesting the opposite—that the ranks of the resistance guerrilla movement are swelling as the occupation goes on.

Bush himself goes to the U.N. to beg for military and financial help cleaning up his mess in Iraq, but because he's afraid to look weak at home, he offers no apologies for his abuse of the international institution or of the Security Council members who had sagely opposed America's war adventure last spring. Meanwhile, by his very appeal to the U.N., an institution reviled by American conservatives, he risks being viewed as a spineless wimp by those very Americans he wanted to impress with his toughness.

Even the president's vaunted staged aircraft carrier victory landing last May, which was once supposed to be the centerpiece of the ad campaign in his re-election bid— is now the butt of jokes by Democrats, who are at this point feeling comfortable enough about the Bush Administration's weakness to joke about the president's fondness for playing "dress up."

Karl Rove, once the dreaded force behind the throne, the bane of a Democratic resurgence, is now the subject of a felony investigation for the outing of an undercover CIA agent and is at risk of being led out of the White House in cuffs and leg irons, unless he can manage to get some underling to take the fall for him.

As for Iraq's oil, which the Bush warmongers long promised would be up and flowing after the war and able to finance the country's reconstruction, it is still just trickling out of the country, at perhaps a fourth of pre-war export volume. It turns out American military planners— while investing enormous military assets in protecting the refineries and oil fields from the earliest days of the invasion, forgot about the ease with which pipelines can be sabotaged. So now the Administration, which has already run the U.S. budget off a cliff with a mind-boggling $500-billion deficit, has been forced to ask Congress for another $87 billion for Iraq—a staggering figure that everyone knows is just a fraction of what will actually be needed.

If we as an American electorate had partied all night on election eve in November 2000, and then gone out the next day and deliberately tried to vote in a collection of clowns and know-nothings in a perverse effort to see how badly they could screw up the country in just four years, we couldn't have come up with an Administration more inept and bungling than this one.

Is anyone laughing?

I don't hear anyone laughing.

—*CounterPunch.org*, Oct. 7, 2003

Will He Replace Ari?:
The Catch and Release of "Comical Ali"

According to a report in the London's *Daily Mirror*, American military forces captured, and arrested, interrogated, and finally released Iraq's famed information minister, Mohammed Saeed al-Sahaf.

Saeed al-Sahaf, you may recall, provided a much-needed element of comic relief during the televised U.S. invasion of Iraq, repeatedly denying U.S. and British military advances, and even denying that U.S. forces had entered Baghdad when reporters were already seeing American military vehicles driving on local streets and when the sounds of battle could be heard from the hotel where press conferences were being held.

In the U.S. media, he had even earned the nickname "Comical Ali," a take-off on the nickname of another Iraqi official in charge of Iraq's purported (but never actually located) unconventional weapons program dubbed "Chemical Ali."

The question puzzling me, however, is what exactly the U.S. occupying authority intended to charge poor Comical Ali with when they first picked him up. He was, after all, not torturing anybody— except with laughter.

The guy was a flak. His job wasn't to tell the truth. It was to tell reporters whatever his bosses wanted him to tell them about the course of the invasion.

Sort of like his White House counterpart Ari Fleischer.

So was Viceroy Bremer planning on charging Saeed al-Sahaf with lying?

That would be a good one, given what we know about the lies we were all told leading up to this war by British P.M. Tony Blair, President George Bush, V.P. Dick Cheney, Secretary of State Colin Powell, Secretary of Defense Donald Rumsfeld, et al.

There are two ways of approaching at this situation.

Maybe we should encourage the military to go ahead and prosecute Saeed al-Sahaf for public lying. Then we could bring that concept home to the U.S. and bring similar charges against the whole Bush administration, using the legal concept of reciprocity. That would get a jump on Comical Ali, who could be counted on otherwise to adopt the defense of lying raised last Sunday in Bush's defense by the *New York Times*: "They all did it."

And why stop there? We could go after the corporate flaks who routinely deny that their companies have engaged in malfeasance, corruption, pollution, labor law violations, safety violations, etc. Just going after the flaks for the tobacco, power and automotive industries alone for lying in public could keep an army of prosecutors busy for years.

Alternatively, maybe it would be just as well to let U.S. authorities hypocritically go after Saeed al-Sahaf alone. The spectacle of watching someone be prosecuted and jailed just for telling whoppers might conceivably jar some jaded Americans into contemplating the state of affairs we've arrived at here at home, where lying by White House officials has become so routine that it no longer merits any notice or comment in the media or any condemnation by the public

Sadly, it looks like Bremer and the Pentagon have realized that holding poor Saeed al-Sahaf was a no-win situation, and two days after picking him up, they've let him go, just another benched spinmeister.

Keep an eye on this guy, though. He had what it takes, and when Iraq's quisling regime of compradores and U.S. lackeys is up and running, it will need someone who, with a straight face, can call a dictatorship a democracy, a colony an independent state, war an occupation and exploitation productive investment. If anyone can do that, it's the guy who insisted Iraq was winning the war even after American tanks were at his doorstep.

—*CounterPunch.org, June 27, 2003*

The New White House Slogan: "Case Closed. Just Move On"

So President Bush considers the issue of his lying to the American people about Iraq's possessing or trying to possess nuclear weapons to be "closed." Now that CIA Director George Tenet has admitted he "should have" noticed this whopper and complained about its inclusion in Bush's speech explaining his reason for attacking Iraq, the president says we can just stop bugging him about it. So what if Iraq is now a huge mess requiring the indefinite stationing of 145,000-150,000 or more soldiers for years to come at a cost of $4-5 billion a month? So what if hundreds of GIs and thousands of Iraqis, including women and children, have died? So what if one or two U.S. soldiers are being killed and more wounded every day there?

Our president has "moved on."

Some nit-picking Democrats are complaining that the president needs to come clean; that there should be an independent commission to investigate this whole thing. Nonsense! Do we want our commander-in-chief and his staff badgered for the rest of this term and through the 2004 election campaign by a bunch of congressional investigators and would-be chief executives? Not me. I think the president's attitude is salutary, and suggest that we all ought to adopt his stalwart approach to life's little annoyances.

Think about it.

If you cheated on your spouse and now she or he is nagging you about it, tell her or him to stop complaining. You've "moved on." The issue is closed.

Did you get one of those annoying notices from the IRS questioning your deduction for a non-existent home office or your claim of a child tax credit when you don't have a kid? Send them a note telling them to get a life.

You've "moved on." The issue is closed.

How about that fender-bender you caused when you were gabbing on your cell phone and didn't notice that the light ahead had turned red? Now the schmuck who got his bumper dented and his taillight broken is harassing you about paying for it, after you convinced him to let you handle it without reporting the accident. Heck. It's history. Tell the guy you've "moved on" next time he calls. The issue is closed.

Same thing for all those noisome bill collectors who keep calling you at dinner or bedtime, haranguing you to pay those old debts for appliances and furniture you bought on time. Tell them to take a hike. You've "moved on."

Don't take any more guff. The issue is closed.

As for that resume you padded. Okay, so you included a degree in history you never got and pumped up your GPA by a grade. Big deal. Now your boss is saying you should get the sack because you lied? Just tell the guy to stop complaining. You've "moved on." The issue is closed.

Same thing for those 20 parking tickets you never paid. You say the court has issued a warrant? Just send it back with a note saying you've "moved on." The issue is closed.

If anyone complains to you about your unwillingness to respond to all their annoying fussing and complaining, just tell them you're "pulling a Bush."

Okay, I'll concede it may not be easy for everyone to just brush off their actions and decisions with a blithe comment and a wave of the hand. But we can learn from our president, who has had a lot of practice. He has, after all, already had to tell us he's "moved on" regarding his going AWOL for the last year of his tour as a National Guardsman. He's "moved on" about his college-age cocaine use, and his years of alcoholism. He's "moved on" regarding the financial chicanery that enabled political backers to enrich him at the expense of ordinary citizens and investors. He's "moved on" after every execution he approved as governor in Texas, whether or not there were questions raised about the condemned individuals' guilt. He's "moved on" about his becoming president despite having lost the election to Al Gore and about having had to rely on partisan Supreme Court judges to prevent an honest recount in Florida.

We should all take heart from this man's remarkable ability to just move right on without troubling pangs of guilt or conscience.

So let's all admit it. America would be a much nicer place if everyone would just stop getting so worked up about stuff. All that needless angst and anxiety over silly issues like parking tickets or war. Everyone should just start telling each other to get over it. Move on. The issue is closed.

See how much smoother things are already? You're sleeping better. You're enjoying your meals more.

Just move on. The issue is closed.

—CounterPunch.org, July 12, 2003

One big difference between this war and the one in Indochina is that, despite the best efforts of the right-wing, and of officials in the Bush administration, to make opposition to the war equivalent to treason, there hasn't been much animosity by those who support the war effort against those of us who oppose it. This is actually quite astonishing, given that American troops are fighting and dying, and it suggests that even the support of the war is pretty tepid at best. I've never been big on polls as a measure of public opinion, but I have inadvertently been conducting one for the past year, and it says that this war is hugely unpopular.

The Poll of the Shirt: Bush Isn't Wearing Well

The polls are saying President Bush is in trouble. His approval rating, by most accounts, is currently somewhere around 50 percent, down from a high of 90 percent right after the 2001 attack on the World

Trade Center and Pentagon, and down 10 points just over the past month. Now 50 percent may sound high, but apparently you have to factor into that the fact that many Americans automatically give the benefit of the doubt to any president because of the office, not the man in it, and a 50 percent rating is pretty darned low speaking historically. It's also a figure that's been dropping like a stone off a cliff.

But I have my own poll, and it says Bush is in even bigger trouble than the official polls might indicate.

My poll is my favorite T-shirt—a plain white thing with a peace sign on the back and "No War in Iraq" printed in huge brown block letters on the front. I purchased this piece of clothing on the eve of the war while speaking at the Socialist Scholars Conference in Manhattan last spring.

When I first began wearing it around the mostly Republican suburb where I live, just north of Philadelphia, as the war was underway, I got some scowls in the supermarket and the gym. Nobody verbally chewed me out or swung a punch, but there were quite a few definite grimaces and unmistakably angry glares. At the same time, I also got a lot of thumbs-up gestures while jogging in the park, and some favorable comments about the sentiment in the checkout line at the local market and at the post office. In general, though, I'd say that back then in March and April of 2003, there was enough of a level of discomfort associated with displaying this shirt that I'd always kind of brace myself when I went out wearing it.

No longer. Now when I sport this shirt in public, whether it's to take my car to the body shop for a fender repair, go running in the park or go grocery shopping, there's not an unfriendly face to be seen. And plenty of the good Republican citizenry of my community offer friendly encouragement, even if they seem slightly bemused that someone would actually go around wearing such a charged political statement.

I contrast this to my experience as a long-haired collegiate anti-war activist back in 1968 or 1970, and am stunned at the lack of criticism I'm getting today.

In 1968, it was enough to simply sport a beard and longish hair, as I did at the time, to find myself hauled aside by a bunch of pro-war barstool cowboys in a small town in Nevada and be roughly shorn with a pair of scissors.

Wearing an anti-war T-shirt in a Republican or even a blue-collar Democratic neighborhood even in 1970 was to court catcalls or worse.

Even in 1991, at the start of Bush Pere's Gulf War adventure, when

I was living up in Ithaca, New York (an island of leftish politics in a sea of conservative upstate Republicans), there was at one point a throng of aggressive, angry, shouting frat boys and ROTC types who tried to attack a peace vigil in the downtown pedestrian mall. They had to be kept at bay by local police. My wife, Joyce, who had to drive through a long stretch of upstate New York and central Pennsylvania one day while Desert Storm was underway, actually had to stop her car and remove a sign we'd made with masking tape on the back window of our hatchback saying "No War," because she was having other drivers blare their horns at her and even try to run her off the road as she was driving along.

These days I ride my bike down the main road in town, wearing my shirt, and haven't heard one horn honk, and no one has tried to run me into a ditch.

This is all very bad news for the president and his war-mongering advisers.

Americans tend to be a jingoistic lot, and if this war is not rousing those demons in the public, it must mean that there's a lot of antipathy towards this Iraq war, even among those who voted for Bush in 2000.

If this keeps up, I may even get tempted to start selling copies of my polling shirt.*

—CounterPunch.org, Sept. 30, 2003

For me the most amazing and downright shocking thing about this war, to someone who lived through the whole Vietnam War era, is how quickly this one went to hell. Back in the 1960s it took smart and dedicated opponents of the war years to start to convince significant numbers of average Americans that the war was a doomed enterprise and that it had to be ended. This time, we weren't even a year into the thing and already half the country was convinced the war was wrong and nearly that many thought we should get out.

But the death knell of the war this time, as in Vietnam, can be pinpointed. In the Vietnam, it was the 1968 Tet Offensive, which showed both the Vietnamese and the Americans that, although at great cost in lives, the American military machine could be beaten, and the massacre at My Lai a month later, which convinced many Americans that, with its soldiers wantonly raping women and killing babies, the

---

* In fact, by May 2004, I was having people—including some of my middle-aged, middle-class Republican neighbors—come up to me to ask where they could buy a shirt like mine.

U.S. was on the wrong side.

In Iraq, the siege of Fallujah and the uprisings in Baghdad's Sadr City and the southern Shi'ia cities of Najaf and Karbalah, which saw poorly equipped Iraqi guerrillas beat the cream of America's troops to a standstill, and ultimately to a humiliating withdrawal, was the equivalent to Tet. Across Iraq and the Arab world, the message was clear: the U.S. can be beaten.

This was followed by the Abu Ghraib prison torture scandal, which dealt a fatal blow to the Bush administration's pretense of "bringing freedom and democracy" to Iraq.

The graphic pictures—some secreted out of Saddam Hussein's former hall of torture by disgusted American soldiers, some actually taken by sadistic U.S. soldier-torturers themselves as souvenirs—circulated widely through the Arab media and the internet, were the moral and practical equivalent of those earlier gruesome images of My Lai.

The president, a the-buck-stops-there leader if there ever was one, didn't help his doomed cause by initially trying to block news reports of the ongoing atrocity, then by feigning ignorance, and finally by trying to limit the damage. The truth: the White House, the Pentagon and the CIA had consciously turned to general use of torture on prisoners in 2001 as a tool in its new "War on Terror."

Bush's Torturous Logic:
Shocked, Shocked, Shocked

George Bush is shocked, shocked that there is torture being used by U.S. forces on Iraqi prisoners of war, in direct violation not only of basic human rights but of the Geneva Convention on Treatment of Prisoners of War of which the United States is not only a signatory, but a founding writer.

So shocked that he had his Pentagon try to get CBS not to show the pictures of the shocking behavior.

The truth is that if the commander-in-chief—remember him? He's the guy in charge of the military that was running the Abu Ghraib detention facility in Baghdad—really did feel the "deep disgust" he claims he feels, and that such treatment is "not the way we do things in America," heads would be rolling at very high levels of the military.

Instead what we see is a handful of very low-level soldiers facing possible court martials and seven higher-ups at the prison, as well as Brig. Gen. Janis Karpinski, commander of the 800th Military Police

Brigade which was in charge of running Abu Ghraib, being removed from their duties there.

You can always tell whether prosecutors are serious about a case by whether they go after the little guys with the big guns, or whether they start cutting plea bargains with the small fry, in order to get them to rat on the higher-ups. If they go after the little guys, like they did in the My Lai Massacre case in Vietnam, you can bet that will be the end of it. No senior commanders will be called to account.

And so it appears to be going this time. So far the "punishments," such as they are, are being strictly limited to the prison command structure, not to the officers above. This is exactly what was done with the My Lai case. No one responsible for the policies that led to that sickening massacre, or the countless others like it that went unpunished, was ever sanctioned.*

Obviously everyone from General John Abezaid, and probably from Defense Secretary Donald Rumsfeld (who actually visited the prison), on down knew what was going on, not only in Abu Ghraib, but in the other less publicly known prison camps where captured Iraqi insurgents are taken to be softened up for information. There have been enough reports leaking out about torture not only in Iraq but also in Afghanistan and in Guantanamo, for us to know that torture is not an aberration but rather is the policy.

It is in fact very much "the way we do things," both at home in America (where brutality and torture are routine in police stations and especially in the nation's prisons), and wherever American soldiers fight the empire's battles.

If anything, what sets America apart from some of its client states and from Saddam Hussein's regime is not torture itself, which the CIA has long endorsed and practiced and taught to client states' police, and which U.S. soldiers do at least as capably as the next centurion. It's that some American soldiers actually believe strongly enough in the notional values of the American Constitution they ostensibly are fighting to protect to actually report such evil, even at the risk of personal loss or punishment. What sets America apart is that its mainstream media, as compromised and timid as they have become, will still occasionally, as CBS's "60 Minutes" has done here, blow the whistle on such criminality and barbarism.

---

* Interestingly, and perhaps significantly, the current secretary of state, Colin Powell, who has expressed such dismay and regret about the current POW atrocities, was a key figure in the cover-up and containment of the My Lai scandal.

I suppose President Bush might be forgiven for saying that torture is not something American soldiers engage in. He wasn't in Vietnam, or anywhere more dangerous than a rowdy bar back in the '60s, and probably the guys in his National Guard unit, at least on those days when he chose to show up for duty, weren't into torturing the locals in Texas or Alabama. Democratic presidential candidate John Kerry, of course, would know better. Though he seems to deny having said it these days, he once admitted to committing atrocities in Vietnam, which he said was something everyone was doing over there.

Still, if Bush were genuinely distressed at the images broadcast by CBS over his Pentagon's objections, he would be demanding the stripes and stars of every ranking officer in the chain of command who either knew what was going on, or should have known and allowed it to happen on their watch.

Don't hold your breath.

—*CounterPunch.org, May 1, 2004*

With all the war mongering of this administration, and the glorification of our uniformed imperial enforcers, I was struck by a little service that was held on Memorial Day 2003 that hit pretty close to home.

My Grandfather's Medal:
A Final Memorial Day Thought

My father, a World War II Marine veteran, stood in this past Memorial Day for a re-awarding of a Silver Star to my grandfather at a ceremony hosted by the local American Legion in a small town in northeastern Connecticut. My grandfather died half a century ago, and over the years, the family had lost the medal, which my grandfather had received for bravery under fire during World War I, when he had served as an unarmed ambulance driver on the front lines in France.

It was, my father says, a moving service. My grandfather, William Lindorff, had never said much about his war experience or his obvious heroism. He had been an Army ambulance driver not because of some affinity for helping the wounded but because the xenophobic military brass didn't trust him with a weapon: he'd been born in Germany and brought to America as an infant, making his loyalty suspect.

At any rate, he had earned that star back in a time when they weren't just handing those things out to everybody and his brother who saw some kind of battle. He earned it in a genuine war, when the enemy was at least as powerful and well equipped as were the Allies.

These days, everybody in a uniform is being called a hero. Every cop, every firefighter, every soldier. Even the kids who panic in Iraq and blow away whole families trying to flee the fighting, who shoot up ambulances like the one my grandfather drove, even the cops who chase down African immigrants and shoot them in the back, or who toss concussion grenades at old ladies in Harlem. No distinctions are made. They're all heroes today. Talk about turning noble metal into dross.

The somber service at which my grandfather's lost silver star was replaced stands in marked contrast to the cheap theatrics of President Bush at Arlington Cemetery that same day, where this AWOL National Guard drunkard once again, vampire like, tried, with the help of a complicit media, to suck some second-hand glory from the congealed veins of young men whose needless deaths he caused by his unprovoked assault on Iraq.

My great grandmother may have been a lifelong Eugene Debs-style socialist, but my grandfather was not a political guy. If he had been, he might have been one of those tens of thousands of desperate Bonus Marchers who, in the waning days of the Hoover administration, were teargassed and brutally attacked by U.S. troops led by Douglas McArthur, simply for trying to get the government to make good on promises made to veterans. Instead, he docilely lost his house during the Great Depression, a victim of the same kind of feed-the-rich politics that are now gutting social programs and wrecking the economy once again.

There has always been jingoism, and there certainly were politicians in the years following World War I who tried to win votes by claiming to be friends of veterans like my grandfather, but nothing like we see today.

Now we have members of Congress singing "God Bless America" in their seats as they vote to strip funds from Veterans Administration programs and kill off VA hospitals. And we have a president who ducked his duty and avoided combat in Vietnam strutting around as if he were a genuine war veteran.

My grandfather wasn't political, but I wonder if today, looking at the brazen, flag-waving hypocrisy in Washington, he wouldn't just turn in his medal, the way a number of Vietnam veterans did in the latter days of that war. Maybe not. My dad says he was quiet about it, but I'm sure he was proud of that medal, too.

Meanwhile, I suspect some of the soldiers now busy occupying Iraq will be ready for their own Bonus March after a few years have passed and they realize that the flag-waving politicians in Washington have gutted their retirement program, slashed their veterans benefits, and driven all their jobs south to Mexico and west to Asia.

If they do march again, this time they'll be called terrorists, of course.

Even if they are wearing their medals.

—*CounterPunch.org, May 28, 2003*

Chapter 3

Bush and Hitler:
Gleich oder Änlich?

Few things I've written about over the past few years—even including my breaking of the story about Attorney General John Ashcroft's mad scheme of assembling a national network of community spies and having them turn their reports over to Fox Television's "America's Most Wanted" program—have gotten such attention, or aroused such a furor, as a couple of pieces published in *CounterPunch* drawing some disturbing parallels between the Bush administration and the early years of the Nazi movement in Germany. Now, over the years I've learned that when a story hits close to the mark, that's when you can expect the most rabid attacks from the targets of a piece. If that's true, I must have really hit home with this one!

Consider the attacks quoted here, that followed an initial article I did in February, 2003 in *CounterPunch* pointing out a few parallels between Bush and his partisans on the one hand, and Hitler and his early Nazi movement on the other:

> A staple of Bush-hating is the portrayal of the president as a Nazi. That has, of course, been a prominent part of other attacks against other presidents, but today it seems to be deployed with particular aggressiveness against Bush. There are thousands of references, across the vastness of the Internet, linking Bush to Adolf Hitler and the Third Reich. ...
>
> And it's not just doctored photos..."It's going a bit far to compare the Bush of 2003 to the Hitler of 1933," writes Dave Lindorff in "Bush and Hitler: The Strategy of Fear," which appeared in February on the far-left site CounterPunch.org. "Bush simply is not the orator that Hitler was. But comparisons of the Bush administration's fear-mongering tactics to those practiced so successfully and with such terrible results by Hitler and Goebbels...are not at all out of line."
>
> Lindorff is not an obscure, solitary blogger. The author of *Killing Time: An Investigation into the Death Row Case of Mumia Abu-Jamal,* he has contributed to The Nation and Salon, and has appeared on National Public Radio. And CounterPunch is not an obscure website. It is edited by the leftist journalist Alexander Cockburn, features writing by Edward Said and Philip Agee, and claims to attract 60,000 visitors each day....

> Perhaps it will all somehow remain confined to the Internet. But experience tells us it probably won't, and, sooner or later, the ideas of CounterPunch and Bushbodycount and Presidentmoron will find their way into the political debate of 2004.
>
> —Byron York, Washington correspondent for the
> *National Review,* September 2003

> *CounterPunch* (run by Alexander Cockburn, the *Nation* columnist), an outfit whose staple is stuff comparing Bush to Hitler.
>
> —James Taranto, columnist,
> *The Wall Street Journal,* July 16, 2003

But conservatives weren't the only ones who were offended by this analogy. When Cockburn wrote a piece on the topic of Bush-Hitler comparisons in his regular column in the *Nation* magazine (the lineage of which he traced to my *CounterPunch* articles), editor Katrina vanden Heuvel felt obliged to insert a box into the magazine disassociating herself and the publication from both Cockburn and me. I'm not sure whether that was because vanden Heuvel wants to preserve Der Führer's unique spot in mankind's pantheon of evil-doers (in which case she should have been running such boxes every time there was a reference in the magazine to the Bush gang's comparisons of Saddam Hussein to Hitler), or because she feels such maligning of the president is somehow unworthy of the magazine (in which case she should move over to the prissy *New York Times*).

The point is that one doesn't need to suggest—and I don't—that Bush and the Republicans are neo-Nazis, to see certain disquieting parallels. For example, consider the similarity between this administration's power grab, its war-mongering, its nativist, anti-foreign flag-waving, and its domestic assault on civil liberties, and what German democracy experienced at the hands of Hitler's National Socialists in the late 1920s and early 1930s. Nor does drawing such parallels mean that we should expect to see African-Americans being herded off to concentration camps in the Nevada desert a few years hence (though it's a fair bet there are within the Republican electorate, and perhaps even in the Republican congressional delegation and the White House, a fair number of unreconstructed racists who wouldn't be upset if such an ethnic cleansing campaign were mounted).

The point of drawing the controversial analogy between the Nazi rise to power and the Bush II rise to power is that both groups resorted to war, the Big Lie, xenophobic scare tactics and increased police-state powers to gain control. And in both cases, the media, the mainstream opposition, and the public at large were slow in realizing the democratic coup d'etat that was slowly taking place around them, until it was too late.

Every presidential administration, regardless of party, has used the powers available to it—control of foreign policy, the military, the federal law-enforcement system, the intelligence services, and to as great an extent as possible the media—to aggrandize and preserve control. Some, most notably the Nixon Administration, but also the administrations of John Kennedy and Lyndon Johnson before him, were more aggressive and less principled than others. But the administration of George W. Bush has set a new standard in its disdain for the Bill of Rights, its dismissing of Congress, and its willful deception and manipulation of the public, particularly in the matter of putting the country at war. These are dangerous times, and it is important to point out what happened the last time a Western democracy was so subverted.

It's worth recalling that during Hitler's rise to power, far from being considered a racist madman and a scourge to humanity, he was praised not just within Germany, but abroad in France, the U.K. and the United States, as a man of principle and as a strong leader for troubled times. Just as one example of how Hitler was being portrayed as late as 1938 within nations that were soon to be his bitter enemy, consider an article that ran that year in a popular British tea table magazine. Swooning over the German chancellor's sumptuous alpine chalet, the magazine wrote:

> It is over 12 years since Herr Hitler fixed on the site of his one and only home. It had to be close to the Austrian border, barely ten miles from Mozart's own medieval Salzburg...Here, in the early days, Hitler's widowed sister, Frau Angele Rauhal, kept house for him on a 'peasant' scale. Then, as his famous book, Mein Kampf, became a best-seller of astonishing power (4,500.000 copies of it have been sold), Hitler began to think of replacing that humble shack by a house and garden of suitable scope....
>
> It is a mistake to suppose that week-end guests are all, or even mainly, State officials. Hitler delights in the society of brilliant foreigners, especially painters, singers and musicians. As host he is a droll raconteur.
>
> —Homes & Gardens, November 1938

Reading this passage, you almost expect Frau Laura Bush or someone like her to glide into the gathering, tray of pralines in her hands. And indeed in the U.S. today, even as a war based upon lies and deceit ravages families in both Iraq and the U.S., we can find just such dippy feature articles playing in the domestic media, purporting to depict the Bush family at home and at play.

Take this one from an article in *USA Today* just two months after the 9/11 attacks, at a time that American soldiers were already fighting and dying (and killing thousands of innocent civilians) in Afghanistan, and that the Bush Administration was preparing to send hundreds of thousands of American men and women into Iraq, and when he was signing the USA PATRIOT Act into law and gutting the Bill of Rights:

> On Thanksgiving mornings, the Bush family kitchen traditionally gets busy at dawn to prepare the 1 p.m. holiday meal. The familiar scents of dressing, giblet gravy and pecan and pumpkin pies warm the family's souls.
>
> This year, given the events of Sept. 11 and the resulting war on terrorism, those holiday routines are more cherished than ever, says first lady Laura Bush. It's unclear where the Bushes will enjoy this Thanksgiving meal—possibly not at the White House, for security reasons—but they'll relish the occasion, she promises.
>
> Wherever the turkey roasts, it will have just the right touch of Texas twang: The family dressing is one-third corn bread, one-third rice and one-third white bread, sometimes with a sprinkling of jalapeño peppers. The gravy, a family favorite, is laced with liver and gizzards.
>
> It's comfort food indeed. In what she senses will be one of the most important Thanksgivings in our history, the first lady says the meal should be a time to appreciate time-tested values, communal ties and lasting relationships.
>
> "The tradition of Thanksgiving this year will be particularly affirming—to have your family around you, share meals with loved ones, have the fireplace going," Mrs. Bush says...

The article concludes:

> Marriage and motherhood brought new traditions. Daughter Jenna started making the holiday pumpkin pie at age 7. Her sister, Barbara, makes the pecan pie. This year, if tradition holds, they'll take a family walk in the afternoon to savor the crisp November air. "That's really a Bush tradition," the first lady says, laughing. It's "a great way to get extra exercise and walk off a few of the calories."[5]

Looking at this kind of publicity, and at what the Bush administration has done so far, my feeling is, it's better to note what's happening now than to be caught by surprise later.

As I wrote in a letter to the *Nation*, following that publication's public disassociation of itself from Cockburn's column and my work on the subject:

> No doubt the leftist fringe critics who in the 1930s were writing alarmist pieces drawing comparisons of Hitler to Attila the Hun or Ivan the Terrible were, like today's Bush critics, being disavowed by more "responsible" editors. I suspect that the fear engendered by the kinds of analogies drawn by Alex and me is that they might offend those who want to hold the Holocaust out as a singular evil in history, and Hitler as a uniquely evil leader. Sadly, he is not unique, except in the scale of his crimes. Recall that in the early days of the massacre of two million Cambodians by Pol Pot and his gang of mad Communists, those who began referring to that genocide as a holocaust were criticized by the guardians of the Holocaust. Eventually, as the numbers of dead soared past the first million mark, the atrocity that devoured a third of a nation was permitted to bear that badge of distinction.
>
> Remember, analogies are used all the time—as they should be—and as anyone with a high school math background should know, "analogous to" ought not be confused with and an equals sign. There are very troubling goings-on in Washington—a campaign of war without end, the termination of the sanctity of citizenship, a return to Cointelpro, corruption of the very process of counting votes, the equating of political opposition with support for terrorism. In such scary times, it is not at all unreasonable to look back to the last time such tactics were employed, to see what they produced.[6]

Bush and Hitler: The Strategy of Fear

It's time to stop trying to explain why a war on Iraq is a bad idea.

The logic, of course, is clear. The administration has no evidence that Saddam Hussein has weapons of destruction. If it did, it would have shown it to the American public and the U.N. long ago. It has no evidence that Iraq is in league with Al Qaeda for the same reason. And it's obvious that even if—a big if according to General Norman Schwarzkopf—a U.S. invasion does succeed in easily toppling Hussein, the result of that unprovoked assault, especially if it is carried out by the U.S. without a U.N. endorsement, will be a wave of terror against

Americans and American interests that will dwarf anything seen in the past.

This is all self-evident, and even the Bush Administration has tacitly admitted that increased terrorism will be the result of an attack on Iraq: it has had the State Department issue a warning to Americans overseas and to Americans planning to travel that they should be prepared to be terrorist targets.

The point, however, is that this is precisely what the Bush Administration wants to happen.

A permanent state of American panic, fortified by regular doses of terror attacks, hijackings and building demolitions by crazed Muslim fanatics, is exactly what Bush needs to stay in power, win re-election in 2004, stack the federal courts, gut the Bill of Rights, and enrich its corporate sponsors.

Don't hold your breath waiting for some politician on the Democratic side of the aisle to stand up and confront the administration about this treasonous plan.*

That means it is urgent for the left to address the issue—to insert it into the public debate.

If Bush truly wanted to reduce the threat of terror against Americans, he would not be harassing Arab-Americans and Muslims at random and deporting people for minor alleged visa violations after secret hearings and detentions (a terrific way to create blood enemies!). He would not be using cowboy rhetoric and threatening to invade Iraq all on his own, knowing that one result will be the political undermining of a whole series of repressive secular Arab regimes, and their replacement by fundamentalist Islamic governments. He would not be holding back funds for legitimate homeland defense efforts, such as bolstering fire departments and police departments. And if he were really trying to steel America for a battle against the "forces of evil" in Iraq and the rest of the world, he'd be using Churchillian language, talking about mutual sacrifice and of fortitude under fire. Instead he calls up dire warnings of fanciful nuclear or germ attacks against urban centers, and the specter of unimaginable horrors—things that can only induce a cowering response.

---

* I was wrong about this. Sen. Robert Byrd (D-West Virginia) has repeatedly distinguished himself by calling the Bush invasion just what it is—an unjustified and illegal war of aggression that was the product of administration manipulation and deceit. Several other members of congress have been equally outspoken, most notably Rep. Dennis Kucinich (D-Ohio).

The sad thing is that Americans, fattened up and soft of muscle from their diet of McDonald's Whoppers and dim-witted from an overdose of "reality" TV shows and entertainment programs posing as news, suck up this kind of fear-mongering (all of which is eagerly played up by ratings-hungry media executives). If one plane gets hijacked, plane travel plummets. If a few letters are found to be contaminated with anthrax spores, people across the land stop opening their mail, or start zapping it first in their microwaves. If a child is reported missing in Arizona, parents across the land clutch their children to their bosoms and begin lecturing them about the evils of talking to "strangers," forgetting that this is exactly what a child ought to do if she gets lost.

In Europe, Asia, Africa or South America, where wars and terrorism, not to mention natural disasters, have been a way of life, the loss of a few hundred, or even a few thousand people, to a bomb, an earthquake, a flood or a civil war, does not induce a national catatonia. People clean up the mess as best they can, count their losses, and go on with their lives.

The other sad thing about us Americans is that we have no notion of the horrors of war, and yet are quick to wish it on others (Native Americans, Tulsa African-Americans and the MOVE and Branch Davidian organizations aside, the last war on American soil was fought nearly a century and a half ago). It's no wonder those people of "Old Europe," as our combat-avoiding Defense Secretary Donald Rumsfeld disparagingly referred to Germany and France, are more reluctant about going to war in Iraq. They know that dropping bombs from B-52s all across the country and fighting door-to-door in Baghdad will produce horrific casualties and create destruction that will take years to repair (There are still several mountains on the outskirts of Darmstadt, Germany—where I spent a year as a high school student—the stacked rubble, including many human remains, of a city of 200,000 destroyed in one night by a British fire-bombing. Similar man-made mountains can also be spotted around Berlin.) Europeans also know that if terrorism on a wider scale is the result, in the U.S. and in Europe, it will be a grisly affair.

Americans have only the WTC to look at when they try to contemplate the effects of war, and all in all, that was a pretty antiseptic affair. One second you saw the towers, another second, they were gone, and within a year or so, the site was all cleaned up and ready for a nifty new building. Indeed, the only institutional memory left of that atrocity is the unseemly battle by survivors of the once high-flying investment banker victims of the attack to get better reimbursements from the government for their unfortunate loss of those six-figure incomes, and the equally distressing struggle of survivors of low-income victims to get a decent amount of compensation.

The naiveté of Americans about the reality of war was brought home to me years ago, when as a young journalism student, I found myself working on a story about a truck accident and ended up in a local firehouse in Middletown, CT. It was 1970, at the height of the Cold War, and the fireman on duty asked me if I'd like to see the bomb-proof back-up government offices that had been built under the new station thanks to some federal disaster funding. We walked down a stairwell through three feet of casehardened concrete, and through a blast door, into a spare-looking room filled with desks. On each desk was an etched nameplate, identifying the government bureau that would be represented by the official seated there. I saw a sign for "Mayor," another for "Police," and a third for "Fire," but there were also desks for "Welfare," "Assessor" and "Tax Collector," as though, after a nuclear holocaust there would be need for these worthy bureaucrats!

That, of course, is not how wars look—especially modern wars where military planners don't bother distinguishing between civilian and military targets. Vietnam is still recovering from its having been the target of all those bombs, napalm and Agent Orange attacks, not to mention the loss of a generation of its young men and women. Afghanistan may never recover from the relatively minor recent war America has been fighting there.

If we Americans value our society, our polity, our rights and liberties, and our security, we must begin exposing George W. Bush and his War Party for what they are: craven usurpers aiming at nothing less than the undermining of all those things that most of us hold dear.

It's going a bit far to compare the Bush of 2003 to the Hitler of 1933. Bush simply is not the orator that Hitler was. But comparisons of the 9/11 attack to the Reichstag Fire, or of the Bush Administration's fear-mongering tactics to those practiced so successfully and with such terrible results by Hitler and Goebbels on the German people and their Weimar Republic, are not at all out of line.

—*CounterPunch.org, Feb. 1, 2003*

As mentioned earlier, this initial article—my first column in *CounterPunch*—caused such a stir in the publications of the right, that I followed up with a second column. In this one, the analogies between Bush and his handlers and Hitler and his early rise to power were drawn more explicitly (though I hope with a certain degree of tongue-in-cheek).

Bush and Hitler...Compare and Contrast: A Response to the WSJ's James Taranto

Is George W. Bush another Hitler?

James Taranto, writing in the Wall Street Journal, offered up an offhand dismissal of *CounterPunch* as "an outfit whose staple is stuff comparing Bush to Hitler," which seems to suggest he thinks the very notion is beyond the pale of civil discourse.

But stay. As one of the first to point out some similarities between Bush II and the early Hitler, I didn't actually say that George and Adolf were joined at the hip. Indeed, I suggested in my *CounterPunch* article back on Feb. 1, during the high-pressure White House drive to war in Iraq, that our unelected president was surely no Hitler, since "Bush simply is not the orator that Hitler was." More importantly, I didn't equate Bush with Hitler because there are some other big differences between the two.

So far, for example, while he has rounded up some Arab and Muslim men purely because of their ethnicity or religion, Bush has not started gassing them—at least not yet.** What I did say, however (and I think subsequent events have proven me even more correct than did the events that had occurred prior to Feb.1), is that some of the tactics of the Bush administration resemble those of Hitler and his Brownshirts. I would go further and add that Bush's attorney general, John Ashcroft, a man who has pointedly praised the old Confederacy, would probably feel quite comfortable in brown with a *hakenkreuz* tacked to his sleeve.

What are some of the Nazi-like tactics of the Bush administration? Let's start with war mongering. The *American Heritage Dictionary*,

---

** Subsequent to my having published this column, of course, there have been well-documented reports that Bush's minions at Guantanamo, Abu Ghraib, and other unnamed detention centers in remote parts of the empire did in fact terrorize, rape, piss on, electroshock, chemically burn, humiliate and even kill countless suspected and captured "terrorists" and "enemy combatants." There were reports of summary executions in Afghanistan and Iraq as well. Thousands of American Muslims were also subjected to arrest, detention and secret deportation in the U.S. Our troops, that is, acted like the SS.

no bastion of leftism, defines fascism as "a system of government that exercises a dictatorship of the extreme right, typically through the merging of state and business leadership, together with belligerent nationalism."

Now we may not yet have a dictatorship, but we do have the extreme right with a solid grip on power in Washington today, and a glance at the top echelon of the Bush administration makes it clear that there is not just a merger, there's a thorough melding of state and business leadership in this administration. As for belligerent nationalism, what else is one to call a war of aggression like the one against Iraq, especially now that it's clear what most thinking people realized before the war even started—that Iraq had no significant offensive military capability, much less weapons of mass destruction—was correct. It was all a massive lie deliberately designed to scare the living crap out of an already nervous American public, so that we would accept the ongoing assault on the Bill of Rights being masterminded by Ashcroft. That strategy was vintage Goebbels.

Then there's the suspension of habeas corpus, right to counsel, and a host of other civil liberties. When American citizens like Jose Padilla can be clapped into prison—a military prison at that—with no charges filed, no access to friends or relatives, and no right to talk to a lawyer, we have crossed a line into fascist territory. Maybe we haven't reached the point of wholesale mass arrests and concentration camps (though even that, reportedly, is being contemplated by the proto-fascist Ashcroft, and we know who appointed that right-wing religious zealot and racist to his post), but once the principle of arrest without charge or trial is accepted by the courts, the move to camps is a quantitative, not a qualitative step. I would note that Guantanamo, where hundreds of Afghan and other foreign combatants have been languishing for nearly two years in horrific conditions, is being turned into a concentration camp, and Bush has ordered the establishment of a kangaroo-court military tribunal assemblyline that ends with a gas chamber and execution, so maybe even that parallel will prove prescient.

What is particularly troubling about the Bush administration's enthusiastic foray into preventative detention and arrest without charge is that it is also appointing wholesale a group of federal judges at all levels who have little or no respect for such niceties as habeas corpus or the right to face one's accuser. Eventually, if this process continues, victims of Ashcroft's mad vendetta against civil rights and liberties will have no one to turn to but equally rightwing and perverse jurists like Antonin Scalia (a man with so little respect for the First Amendment that he countenances the forced erasure of reporters' tape recordings of his public speeches) and his adoring acolyte Clarence Thomas.

It's worth pointing out too that Hitler was not the monster of 1939 when he took power in 1933. Indeed, when he first came to power, in the wake of the Reichstag fire, a traumatized nation saw him as a savior of the German government, which at the time was a parliamentary democracy. Even as he began ratcheting down the rights of the citizenry, and as his brownshirted minions and his Gestapo began oppressing certain unpopular minorities and political enemies on the left, there were many, including in the United States, who saw Der Führer positively (Henry Ford and Charles Lindbergh spring immediately to mind). So the fact that the Bush administration is not at this point a fascist government should not preclude or deter us from examining its behavior for evidence of fascist-like behavior.

The fundamental difference I see between the Germany of the middle 1930s and the America of today is that, even as many Americans sit on their sofas and absorb the propaganda that passes for news on their TV sets,*** there remains a vestigial notion of democracy and civil liberties, the legacy of over two centuries of American civil society. A significant percentage of Americans—certainly far greater than in Hitler's Germany in the years before World War II—are troubled by the current trampling of democracy and the Bill of Rights, as attested by the wave of towns and cities and even state governments which have passed statutes protecting the Bill of Rights against the Ashcroft-inspired onslaught of the Patriot Act.****

So let's make ourselves clear here. George Bush is not Hitler. Yet. America is not a fascist state. Yet. John Ashcroft is—well, let's not go there. The attorney general, a man whose claim to fame is having lost an election to a dead man, is perhaps the leading edge of a drive in that direction.

Wall Street Journal commentator Taranto may mock *CounterPunch* and other publications that point to fascist tendencies in the current administration, but he had his forebears aplenty in 1930s Germany, where the newspapers of the day were awash in apologists for

***Like the week-long homage to Ronald Reagan that dominated the airwaves following his death—a propaganda blitz worthy of Leni Riefenstahl.
**** 298 cities and the states of Hawaii and Alaska by May 1, 2004

Chancellor Hitler's gradual assumption of dictatorial powers. These pundits, like Taranto and his ilk, failed or were unwilling to see where things were heading, and justified the obvious erosion of freedom and democracy in the name of combating the scourge of terrorism and revolution, as well as the threat of the "other" posed by such undesirables as the Jews and the Gypsies. Today's American counterparts of these apologists, like Taranto, justify the setting aside of long-standing civil liberties in the name of combating terror and dealing with such undesirables as the Middle Eastern immigrants in our midst.

Calling attention to the parallels with the demise of Weimar Germany and the rise of Hitler is hardly out of line.

It is what we should be seeing more of in the "respectable" media.

        —CounterPunch, July 18, 2003

Taranto responded to this column with one of his own in the *Wall Street Journal*. In it, he clearly missed the tongue-in-cheek, and took the whole thing as being dead serious. His response: "Yeah, OK, big deal, another left-wing nutjob, who cares? But it's rather stunning to contemplate that this is the kind of thing these people say when they're *trying to sound reasonable*."[7]

Reasonable or not, it was becoming increasingly clear as 2003 progressed, that the Bush re-election campaign would be heavily dependent upon a fear factor for success. With the economy failing to perk up, and with the Iraq war becoming increasingly the disaster that many of us "nutjobs" on the left had predicted it would be, more and more Bush's campaign strategists were realizing that their best bet was getting Americans so scared that they'd want a tough guy—or at least somebody who affects a cowboy image and talks with a carefully cultivated drawl—to protect them.

The Bush Election Strategy: The Politics of Fear and Blood

The broad outlines of the Bush re-election campaign strategy have begun to appear, and they present an ugly picture.

From now until November 2004, we can expect to have a series of dramatically named military actions in Iraq—and occasionally in Afghanistan perhaps—which will each be described as striking a "crippling blow" against the enemy (how many times can you cripple someone?).

We will have a raising and lowering of the color-coded terror alerts, designed to keep voters on edge.

And we will perhaps even have a conveniently spaced-out series of arrests of key leaders of the terrorist movement, who will be trotted out (or whose dead bodies will be laid out) for the cameras, to be followed on each such occasion by a strutting, smirking President Bush, saying that the War on Terror is succeeding.

All this will be accomplished with the willing and able assistance of the media, which is hungry for ratings, and which, in order to get the dramatic scoops it wants, complete with visuals, will continue to avoid covering the war's real stories—the SS-like assaults on Iraqi and Afghan civilians by U.S. troops, the wholesale violations of the Geneva Conventions for prisoners of war, the mounting anger at the occupation among ordinary Iraqis, and the deepening demoralization of American troops.

The capture of Saddam Hussein, coming so suspiciously as it did at a point where Bush's own poll numbers were hitting their post 9-11 nadir, may have been the kick-off of this campaign. It has already been suggested by some, including Congressman Jim McDermott (D-Wash.), that the capture of Iraq's fallen dictator may have been orchestrated—that in fact U.S. military leaders knew exactly where Hussein was for some time and were just waiting for the order to go pick him up when it would do Bush the most good politically.

Certainly it defies belief that with over a hundred fifty thousand US and British troops in the country, with a $30-million ransom out there looking for a stoolie, and with hundreds of thousands, maybe millions of Iraqis having a personal desire for revenge against him, that Hussein could have hidden successfully in the country for almost a year.

Yet even if this conspiracy theory isn't correct (and it would be hard to prove), it certainly appears that Hussein's televised capture has provided the kickoff to this new campaign.

Next we have the latest highly touted crackdown in the so-called Sunni Triangle, which features shoot-to-kill orders against unarmed demonstrators, Vietnam War-style assassination squads and fenced-in "strategic hamlets," as well as Israeli-style bulldozings of the homes of suspected guerrillas.

If the conspiracy theory of Hussein's arrest proves correct, we can expect more public arrests, perhaps leading up to the October Surprise—the capture or killing of Osama Bin Laden.

Along the way, we can expect to see six to 10 more get-tough military campaigns which will kill and round up several hundred "suspected terrorists" in Iraq each time, and as well a series of heightened domestic alerts, perhaps culminating in a top-level red alert just before Election Day, a move which would allow the government to set up M-16-toting National Guard soldiers at voting booths—a wonderful way to remind the electorate to vote Republican.

It won't matter that none of this will really affect what is actually happening in Iraq, where we can expect to see continued rebellion and chaos, and probably eventually civil war, and certainly increasing opposition to U.S. occupation. That will be a problem for the next administration, whoever it is. From this point on, the Bush administration will be focused mightily on November '04.

A group of Democratic presidential candidates played right into this trap with a concerted attack on frontrunner Howard Dean, who was portrayed by his opponents and their establishment backers as the reincarnation of both George McGovern and Michael Dukakis.

But explain why anyone, faced with Republican scare tactics, would vote for someone like John Kerry, Dick Gephardt or Joe Lieberman—the unsung authors of this attack—if their main argument is, "We need to fight the war in Iraq and the War on Terror just like George Bush is doing, but we can do it better."

The only way to combat the Republican "Reichstag Fire" campaign strategy of terrorizing the electorate is to challenge it frontally, as Dennis Kucinich and, to a lesser extent, Howard Dean have done, calling the administration's bluff, explaining that the War in Iraq is a diversion and that a War on Terror is counterproductive and is about as likely to be successful at making the world or the U.S. a safer place as the War on Drugs was at making America drug-free.

Meanwhile, playing by Bush's rules makes the Democrats, and indeed American democracy itself, particularly vulnerable to the possibility of another Al Qaeda attack on American soil. General Tommy Franks has warned recently that such an attack, if it were even partially successful, could spell the end of the Bill of Rights and of a 228-year-old experiment in American Democracy. Yet that dire prophesy, while quite credible, is only possible if the political leadership continues in advance to scare the American public into a quivering mass of irrationally spineless cowards ready to retreat into their bunkers at the first sound of a firecracker.

If Democratic leaders would instead start talking about the strength of the Constitution, the inviolability of the Bill of Rights, and the need to stand together in defense of American freedom and democracy in the face of those who oppose these traditions, any attack, should one come, would not be seen as reason to give it all up, but rather as a reason to rally to the defense of freedom.

For the sake of the '04 election, but more importantly for the sake of American democracy, the Bush campaign of fear, deception and manipulation needs to be challenged directly. No Democrat who plays along with that game should be given a chance in the primaries.

—*CounterPunch.org., Dec. 29, 2003*

Unfortunately, the anti-war candidate Howard Dean was brutally trashed by the establishment media, and with the help of some bad campaign strategy on the part of his own campaign, he self-destructed in the first event of the primary season in Iowa. That handed the Democratic nomination to John Kerry, who offers little by way of substantive choice on the key issues of the war and protecting civil liberties. Kerry, remember, voted for both the war and for the so-called Patriot Act.

Meanwhile, the next opportunity to highlight some of the Bush campaign's adoption of Nazi techniques and policies came in the form of a defense of several clever entries in a contest sponsored by the organization MoveOn.org, for ads in support of the coming Democratic presidential campaign. The ads in question, which explicitly compared Bush to Hitler, had aroused a firestorm of criticism not just from Republicans, but also from the Anti-Defamation League.

For the record, I thought the ads were quite good, myself.

RNC Plays the Hitler Card:
MoveOn.org Shouldn't Apologize for Those Ads

You can tell that the Republican Party is more worried than it lets on about November. Today's shrill attack on the MoveOn.org organization, which the Republican National Committee is accusing—incorrectly and dishonestly—of endorsing two sample political ads which draw comparisons between Hitler and George Bush, demonstrates how much the Bush braintrust fears this remarkably successful populist internet-based organization—and the analogy itself.

The two ads were actually among some 1000 that were submitted as part of a contest established by MoveOn to come up with strong ads for the 2004 Democratic campaign. The organization put them all on its website and allowed members to vote for the best. A group of fifteen 30-second submissions which received the most votes were then posted as finalists.

Sadly, neither of the controversial Hitler/Bush ads made that cut, but the RNC went ahead and issued press releases, as well as sending RNC Chairman Ed Gillespie rushing over to Fox TV, to denounce MoveOn for presumably insulting Bush and American Jews.

MoveOn's Eli Pariser has responded to this GOP assault explaining that clearly the organization never endorsed those ads, and that its membership obviously rejected them. Further, he says MoveOn "regrets the appearance" of the two ads on the MoveOn website, where they were briefly available for viewing along with all the other submissions initially (they've been removed now). Interestingly, now that those ads have been pulled by MoveOn, the only place the scripts can be read is on the RNC website.

But Pariser shouldn't be so quick to express his regrets. The truth is that the two ads are pretty darned good. The first shows Hitler in a parade and speaking, followed by scenes of German troops attacking, planes bombing, tanks firing, and victorious troops goose-stepping into occupied territory, as a voiceover says "A nation warped by lies—lies fuel fear—fear fuels aggression—invasion—occupation." As the scene fades from Hitler giving a raised-arm salute to Bush with his hand raised at his inauguration, the voiceover says, "What were war crimes in 1945 is foreign policy in 2003."

And the truth: The Bush administration deliberately stoked public fears after 9/11—just as the Nazi's used the Reichstag Fire—to win support for an illegal, unprovoked invasion of Iraq, an act of aggression which, at the Nuremberg Trials, was specifically determined to be a war crime. The ad might have added that the "shock and awe" terror campaign that was the centerpiece of the U.S. invasion of Iraq was also by definition a war crime, since its target was the Iraqi public.

As for the second controversial ad, it features first a picture of Hitler, speaking in German, with a voiceover translating the lines as "We have taken new measures to protect our homeland…I believe I am acting in accordance with the will of the Almighty Creator." Then, as Hitler continues to speak, the voiceover says, "God told me to strike Al-Qaeda, and I struck him." As the picture morphs into George Bush, the voiceover continues, "And then He instructed me to strike at Saddam, which I did." With a picture of cheering Germans in the background, the voiceover concludes, "Sound familiar?"

And the truth here? President Bush did in fact publicly claim divine instruction to have been behind his decisions to invade Afghanistan and later Iraq—a rather scary example, if he is being sincere, of the very kind of megalomania that characterized Hitler.

Were these two ads unfair to either Bush or to the memory of the Holocaust? Hardly.

They were legitimate warnings that the American public is being manipulated by demagoguery, jingoism and the worst kind of lies.

Are they saying that Bush is Hitler? Only to the most simplistic or willfully unimaginative of viewers—that is to say the RNC poobahs. What the ads are saying is that the same technique used by Hitler and his National Socialist brownshirts to whip up nationalist fervor in Germany in the early and mid 1930s is being employed today by the Bush Administration and the Republican Party, and to the same end— to get the American public to acquiesce in surrendering its democratic rights, to accept one-party rule, and to agree to a national policy of permanent war.

The MoveOn crowd was apparently repelled by the bluntness of the two ads, and rejected them, but Pariser needn't apologize for inspiring their creation.

Both, in their way, are sadly prophetic.

Pariser and MoveOn should be proud that they were produced, happy that the RNC is helping to circulate them, and encouraged that the Republicans are making such a fuss about the whole thing.

—*CounterPunch.org., Dec. 29, 2003*

My last foray into this particular rhetorical swamp came in early 2004. That's when the Spanish government of Jose Maria Aznar, a staunch backer of the Bush war in Iraq, tried using the Goebbels scaremongering strategy on the Spanish electorate, only to have it blow up in his face.

Scare Tactics and Elections: A Spanish Parallel

There is an interesting parallel between the dramatic events in Spain earlier this month and the dramatic weeks that followed the attack on the Pentagon and the World Trade Center in 2001, but it's not the one most pundits and politicians have been making.

In Spain, there was a terrorist attack on the Madrid train station, which the government of the country then went to great lengths to pretend, in the face of evidence which it apparently withheld, had been perpetrated by the Basque Liberation Front, or ETA. In fact, the conservative Popular Party of Jose Maria Aznar well knew that the killers were Islamic fanatics, and that the ETA had nothing to do with the attack.

When this deception began to unravel, so did support for the conservative ruling party. In the end, angry voters turned out the ruling party and handed an upset win to the opposition Socialist Workers. They in turn promptly made it clear that they attributed the attack to the former government's slavish support for the U.S. invasion of Iraq, and—consistent with their long-held opposition to that war—have pledged to quickly withdraw Spanish troops from that country.

The parallel to this Spanish drama is not with the airplane attacks on the Pentagon and the Twin Towers, though; it is with the other terror attack that dated from that horrible day: the anthrax letters.

From day one, when the germ scare began, the Bush Administration and its Justice Department insisted, despite no evidence to support them, that the anthrax attack had been linked to Al Qaeda. They pushed this line early and hard, because it fit with the Karl Rove's Reichstag Fire strategy for ensuring Republican electoral hegemony: scare the crap out of the public with stories about chemical, biological and nuclear terrorism weapons, and the public will willingly surrender their rights, their common sense and their votes.

They did the same thing with poor Jose Padilla, the young Latino-American who was arrested a few months after the bombing on a flight into Chicago. Charged with plotting to build and explode a so-called dirty nuke, Padilla was then "disappeared" into the bowls of the American military, where for two years now he has been held without charge in solitary confinement and barred from meeting anyone from the outside—no family, no lawyer.

Note that no evidence has ever been made public to prove that Padilla, a minimally educated former Puerto Rican gang member, ever so much as looked at a nuclear bomb plan, saw a grain of nuclear material, or in fact did anything to promote or initiate such a scheme. We're just told that this was something he had been "sent" to do by Al Qaeda.

It was around the same time that the Bush Administration was hyping these alleged threats by "international terrorists" to poison us, infect us, or nuke us, that they pushed the wacko idea of everyone buying sheets of plastic and duct tape to construct "safe rooms" in homes in case of attack. There was a run on duct tape that must have made 3M shareholders happy, but that has mainly left a lot of embarrassed suburban homeowners with drawers full of the stuff.

In Spain, the people figured out what was going on. They called the government's bluff. Instead of cowering in safe rooms, they took to the streets by the millions, demanding an end to Spain's participation in America's war against Iraq. And within days of the Madrid bombings, they ousted that government.

Here in the U.S. it has become increasingly clear that the Bush Administration has been playing the same cynical and manipulative game as the Aznar government in Madrid. There were no "weapons of mass destruction" in Iraq, much less a way to deliver such mythical weaponry to the U.S., and the government knew this even as it beat the drums of war. Nor were Arab terrorists behind the Anthrax attacks, which in any event were rather minor in scope. As for Padilla, he is at worst a poor misguided young man caught at an opportune moment by a rabid attorney general out to make a point at his expense. He is clearly not the person anyone would turn to in order to make a sophisticated nuclear weapon, even if he might have wanted to do such a thing.

We know all this, but with no clear alternative like that which the Socialist Workers Party provided Spanish voters, we Americans don't quite know what to do.

We have a cynical bunch of liars running the country, wreaking death and havoc abroad and attacking the foundations of democratic government at home, but our alternative is a man who cannot bring himself to call for an end to the war in Iraq, who cannot even bring himself to condemn the basis for that war—the Bush doctrine of peremptory war. Centrist Democrat John Kerry is not a man who could bring millions into the street. Indeed, he has even condemned the new Spanish government for honoring its campaign pledge and vowing to remove Spanish troops from Iraq and to pull Spain out of Bush's comically misnamed "Coalition of the Willing."

If the public fails to rally to his lackluster Gore-like candidacy, Kerry could be forced to take a stronger stand against Bush and the new American Imperialism. If he does, Bush could end up going the way of Spain's Aznar.

Meanwhile, don't be surprised to see the Bush administration come up with another scare story for the public before election time.

Before they do that, though, Rove & Co. should meditate on what just happened in Taiwan. There, only a day before a tight election

March 20, which the massively corrupt and pro-business Kuomintang was expected to win, someone attempted to assassinate the country's president and vice president. Both candidates, members of the pro-independence Democratic Progressive Party, were injured in the shooting, but instead of the public rallying to the opposition Kuomintang candidates in the wake of this attempted act of terror, they handed the DPP a narrow victory.

It could well be that further scare-mongering by the Bush administration, or even an attack on Americans by Al Qaeda supporters, could backfire, leading Americans, like Spaniards, to decide to reject Bush's failed War on Terror, and his messy imperial adventure in Iraq.

—*CounterPunch.org, March 24, 2004*

Chapter 4

The Assault on Civil Liberties

It is common knowledge that the administration of George W. Bush and Dick Cheney, which slipped into power courtesy of a politically stacked Supreme Court and with a friendly assist from a Bush family political machine in Florida, always had a secret agenda. Despite having campaigned on the themes of "compassionate conservatism" and "uniting" the country at home and of "non-intervention" overseas, that secret agenda was to mount an aggressive two-front war—one against Iraq and the other on the Constitution. The new White House, staffed with neo-cons full of grandiose ideas of empire, corporate welfare and one-party rule, wanted only a pretext to begin this campaign. The 9/11 attacks on the World Trade Center and the Pentagon provided it.

In short order after that terror attack we had the start of preparations for an Iraq invasion, and we had the Patriot Act, a collection of police-state laws and regulations that was really a long-standing wish-list of right-wing politicians and law-enforcement authorities, and that was presented to Congress as a complete package with suspicious dispatch scarcely a month after the attacks. This cleverly if cynically named law was passed without debate and almost without opposition by both houses in late October, 2001.

The thing is, these Bush guys are like kids the morning after Halloween. Once they've cadged that shopping bag full of candy, they can't stop stuffing it down by the fistful.

And so, not long afterwards, in early 2002, Attorney General John Ashcroft, a man for whom the only sacred and inviolate amendment in the Bill of Rights is the Second—the right to bear arms—took things a giant step further towards remaking America into the land of the once free and once brave by announcing plans to establish a nationwide network of neighborhood spies. It was an idea that was both stunning in its simplicity, and mind-boggling in its audacity: sign up millions of ordinary Americans to spy on their neighbors, collect the data and log it all into government computers, and bingo! Terrorists, deviants, criminals and undesirables would be located, monitored and removed from society.

Like many Americans of all political stripes, I found this scheme, which Ashcroft dubbed Operation TIPS (for Terrorism Information and Prevention System), to be much like its author—both laughable and frightening at the same time. Unlike most Americans, though, I have had some knowledge of and experience with similar operations in other countries. As a reporter, I had visited East Germany, the German Democratic Republic, just before the demise of that most advanced of totalitarian Stalinist states, and had been shown examples of how far-reaching the Stasi's TIPS-like neighborhood spy network had been. In the GDR, with virtually every third or fourth person spying on family, friends and neighbors, there were so many files generated that the actual intelligence officials had no time to examine or even catalog them anymore, so they were just piling up in warehouses and on computer tapes. In China, where I lived and worked for several years, the system was far less technologically advanced than in East Germany, but was also both more pervasive and more deep-rooted. Chinese citizens, after three generations of this kind of neighborhood spying, had developed a culture of secrecy in which everyone knew what could or could not be said in any particular social setting. Even as recently as 1996, children as young as six or seven still already knew what kinds of things said at home were meant for public consumption and what things were to be kept within the family. Students in high school and college knew what questions it was okay to ask a teacher and what things were dangerous. (Actually, looking at these two systems—both a kind of Neighborhood Watch gone mad—you could sort of guess where Ashcroft lifted his ideas from.)

Knowing how dangerous, and stultifying, such a system could be, I decided to explore Ashcroft's creation from the inside. I went to the TIPS page on the website of Citizen Corps, an organization founded by President Bush to promote volunteerism, and signed myself up as a TIPS volunteer. I fraudulently listed my occupation as "teacher," on the assumption that "journalist" might have led to my being disqualified (it was only a white lie, since I was a former teacher, having taught journalism for several years). In short order, I got an email message thanking me for joining in the fight on terrorism, asking me for the names of other people who might be recruited for the cause, and telling me I'd be hearing more later.

That was an understatement, as the following story I did for *Salon Magazine* explains.

When Neighbors Attack!

Volunteers for Operation TIPS, John Ashcroft's citizen spy army, are being steered to the Fox crime show "America's Most Wanted." Is the merger of tabloid TV with the federal snooping operation funny or scary or both?

Aug. 6, 2002 | When Attorney General John Ashcroft announced the formation of Operation TIPS, a planned army of tens of millions of American volunteers charged with ferreting out terrorists in their neighborhoods, plenty of pundits questioned whether Americans spying on Americans was a good thing. Very few people asked exactly how it would work, and the Justice Department didn't offer any clues.

To find out, I went to the Citizen Corps web site, then to the Terrorism Information and Prevention System (TIPS) page, and signed up as a volunteer. I quickly discovered that TIPS is having a devilish time getting off the ground. After an initial welcome from the Justice Department, I heard nothing for a month. When I finally called two weeks ago to ask what citizens were supposed to do if they had a terror tip, I was given a phone number I was told had been set up by the FBI.

But instead of getting a hardened G-person when I called, a mellifluous receptionist's voice answered, "America's Most Wanted." A little flummoxed, I said I was expecting to reach the FBI. "Aren't you familiar with the TV program 'America's Most Wanted'?" she asked patiently. "We've been asked to take the FBI's TIPS calls for them."

Has Ashcroft turned his embattled volunteer citizen spy program—which has been blasted by left and right alike—over to Fox Broadcasting's "America's Most Wanted"? If so, the connection shouldn't be all that surprising. Ashcroft's Justice Department and John Walsh's popular crime-busters show have been a mutual-admiration society for some time now. Walsh started coaxing ratings out of the 9/11 disaster for Fox TV while the dust was still settling from the twin towers' collapse. Only two days after the attack, Walsh loaded his whole production team onto a bus in Indiana and drove the show to ground zero, where, he claimed, government officials had told him to "help us catch these bastards."

But it's still hard to nail down the exact nature of the relationship between TIPS and "America's Most Wanted." Officials at the Justice Department and Fox Television denied reports of a formal link—even though their switchboard operators last week were working happily in concert. "TIPS doesn't exist yet," said Linda Monsour, a spokeswoman for the attorney general's Office of Justice Programs, which will oversee

Operation TIPS if it gets going this fall as planned. Then Monsour conceded that the Justice Department, which has an $8 million start-up budget for TIPS, had already begun signing up individual volunteers, in advance of the program's ratification by Congress. She wasn't exactly sure how those calls were being handled. But she denied knowing anything about a hotline to the Fox show. "It's probably something I should explore," she said.

"America's Most Wanted" publicist Kim Newport also denied knowing about a formal link between the Justice Department and the TIPS program when interviewed last Friday, but she did acknowledge that the show regularly takes tips from callers about possible terror threats. "We have been taking calls on terrorism," she said. Noting that TIPS is not officially running yet, she mused, "Maybe the Justice Department just turned to us because that's how our program works." Newport says the show turns over all of its terrorism tip calls to the FBI, or to the Postal Inspector's Office if they relate to anthrax threats.

Clearly, someone in the Justice Department decided to enlist the show in processing TIPS calls, and civil libertarians aren't sure whether the Fox-TIPS synergy is funny or scary or both. "On a certain level, it's laughable—a Keystone Kops kind of thing," says Bill Goodman, legal director at the Center for Constitutional Rights. "But the frightening thing about it is, what if someone actually did find evidence of a real terrorist ring, and they brought it to a TV station instead of the FBI?"

"This is really, really bad judgment on the part of the administration," says Rachel King, lobbyist for the American Civil Liberties Union, who was "stunned" when I told her TIPS calls were being directed to the Fox show.

"TIPS was supposed to be about reporting suspicious behavior, which would then be interpreted by the FBI or local law enforcement. Now it turns out the information is being handed to a TV program that encourages vigilantism. What will 'America's Most Wanted' do with the information? It's kind of mind-blowing. It was bad enough when the reports were going to be filed with the Justice Department or the FBI. With this information in private hands, who's going to protect people from malicious complaints?"

A spokeswoman for Sen. Joe Lieberman, D-Conn., whose Governmental Affairs Committee is handling the Senate's version of the Homeland Security bill that would include TIPS, said, "It's inappropriate for a TV program to be taking these kinds of calls. That is certainly not what Sen. Lieberman has in mind."

Observers on all sides of the debate are still trying to figure out what Ashcroft has in mind.

The goal of TIPS, for those who missed the initial surge of coverage, was to enlist patriotic Americans in the hunt for the terrorists in our midst—much the way, it should be said, "America's Most Wanted" enlists ordinary TV viewers in catching bad guys. Ashcroft's vision was that millions of TIPSters would volunteer to look for the odd, the unusual, the suspicious among us, and would report them to the Justice Department, which would then evaluate our evidence and decide what to do with it.

When first announced as part of President George W. Bush's Citizens Corps volunteerism initiative during his State of the Union address, TIPS was billed as "a national system for reporting suspicious and potentially terrorist-related activity," which would "involve the millions of American workers who, in the daily course of their work, are in a unique position to see potentially unusual or suspicious activity in public places." The plan initially called for a million volunteers in 10 urban trial centers, which were to begin operations this month.

But when Congress and the public began to imagine phone repairmen, maids, postal workers and cable guys nosing around people's houses and reporting on whatever struck them as suspicious, an uproar ensued. Critics noted the parallels between TIPS and life behind the Iron Curtain, where neighbors spied on neighbors, and Ashcroft seemed to retreat, canceling the 10-city trial (but not the online call for individual volunteers). He delayed the official kickoff of the program until autumn and said that, instead of millions of citizen volunteers, he would aim the program at truckers, postal workers and others in particular industries who would be well positioned to notice unusual activities. The Postal Service immediately said it would not cooperate.

TIPS ran into political fire especially on the right. House Majority Leader Dick Armey, R-Texas, has attached a measure to the House version of the Homeland Security Bill barring any government program from having citizens spy on other citizens. The bill has 295 sponsors, according to Armey spokesman Richard Diamond, who predicts, "TIPS is going to die." He says that although the Senate version of the bill does not address the program, Armey, one of the most powerful members of the Republican-dominated House, has determined that his measure "will stay in the bill in conference" when the two chambers' versions of the bill are reconciled.

But he may not get his way: Lieberman considers Armey's opposition to TIPS to be "too broad," according to one source. The Connecticut Democrat and former Gore vice-presidential running mate is said to think that modeling a program on the Neighborhood Watch idea and enlisting the help of workers in certain industries "makes sense." Civil rights groups are said to be livid at Lieberman's reported waffling on TIPS.

But whatever Lieberman decides, congressional opposition to TIPS is strong. So is Ashcroft rethinking his plan to establish a sprawling team of feds to oversee the operation? Is he planning on turning it into a television program, where people will rat on their neighbors, and John Walsh and his "America's Most Wanted" TV crew will come banging on the doors of the suspected terrorists, demanding that they come clean? It could be novel way of getting around congressional reservations and restrictions. Armey's measure, for example, would bar only "the government" from running any program having citizens spying on citizens—but it might not apply to a Fox-run effort.

Certainly it wouldn't be the first time Walsh and the feds have cooperated. On the 30-day anniversary of the Sept. 11 attack, Fox, at the administration's request, preempted its Friday evening schedule to air a special Walsh production called "America's Most Wanted: Terrorists—A Special Edition." Fox Entertainment Group president Sandy Grushow told *Daily Variety*, an industry newspaper, "This is something we wish we had more time to put together, but it seemed quite important to the FBI and White House that we do this as soon as possible." Walsh claimed later that the program netted 1,500 call-in tips, compared with the program's usual 200 to 300 phone tips following a show. Clearly the administration needed the help: Even today, the FBI doesn't have a dedicated line to handle terrorism tips. People are expected to contact their local FBI office. The New York office reports that it was overwhelmed last fall with more than 100,000 calls per month. Now it no longer bothers to separate terror tips from regular crime tips.

It's still next to impossible to get firm answers about any aspect of TIPS. After my conversation with Justice Department spokeswoman Monsour last Friday, operators at the attorney general's office have apparently begun sending callers to a number that really is the FBI, not the "America's Most Wanted" switchboard. "We are now being told to refer TIPS calls to the FBI," an operator told me. But when I phoned the number (which proved to be the FBI's main Washington switchboard), I got little help. After an interminable period of mind-numbing

Muzak, an operator said she couldn't help me. "You should probably call your local FBI office to report any suspicious activity," she said. An FBI spokeswoman then told me that the bureau is not fielding any calls from TIPS volunteers. "That's being handled by the Justice Department," she said. I'd finally come full circle with my questions about where TIPS calls should go. Additional calls to Monsour's office to clarify the relationship went unreturned.

I tried the "America's Most Wanted" hotline one last time. And once again I was told that the show was "helping with the TIPS calls" and that any information about suspicious terrorist activity would be "forwarded to the FBI."

Even if the TIPS-Fox connection is just a stopgap measure while the Justice Department tries to figure out what to do with a program nobody but the president and the attorney general seems to support, the solution shows Ashcroft's tin ear when it comes to privacy rights. The idea of privatizing a citizen spy operation is alarming to many civil libertarians, not reassuring.

"This is all very, very disturbing," says the ACLU's King.

—Salon.com, Aug. 6, 2002

CBS Evening News picked up my *Salon* piece (actually dispatching a camera crew and van all the way from New York headquarters to my home near Philadelphia to do an interview) as did a number of newspapers around the country, and people in Congress, where Ashcroft's plan was already raising eyebrows, went ballistic. In the end, OperationTIPS died unmourned for lack of funding. Congress, reflecting the fears of the American public at its intrusiveness, killed it off as Rep. Armey's office predicted. Poor Ashcroft, thwarted in his plans to take volunteerism to Alpine heights, has had to turn to the far costlier paid services of the FBI, ATF, DEA, CIA, NSA and state and local law enforcement authorities to do his dirty work for him of spying on the American public. Fortunately for our gospel-singing, office-prayer-session promoting attorney general, he has the Patriot Act and a whole lot of financial backing from Congress to assist him in this Herculean effort.

Meanwhile, not content to monitor Americans on the ground, Ashcroft came up with another scheme, this time in the air.

Since 9/11, a growing number of people have found themselves being harassed repeatedly as they tried to fly. Some have been pulled aside and strip-searched every time they approach a boarding gate. Some have been taken to small rooms to be interrogated by local police or federal officials. Some are simply denied the right to board a plane. It seemed there was some kind of a list at the airline check-in counters, but no one in government or the airline industry would comment. What was going on?

In an investigation for *Salon* magazine, I discovered that there was indeed a list. Two actually. One was a list of people, considered a "threat to aviation," who were barred from flying. The other, much longer, just seemed to be a list of political dissidents, no threat to planes, but targeted for harassment.*

Grounded

A federal agency confirms that it maintains an air-travel blacklist of 1,000 people. Peace activists and civil libertarians fear they're on it.

Nov. 15, 2002 | Barbara Olshansky was at a Newark International Airport departure gate last May when an airline agent at the counter checking her boarding pass called airport security. Olshansky was subjected to a close search and then, though she was in view of other travelers, was ordered to pull her pants down. The Sept. 11 terrorist attacks may have created a new era in airport security, but even so, she was embarrassed and annoyed.

Perhaps one such incident might've been forgotten, but Olshansky, the assistant legal director for the left-leaning Center for Constitutional Rights, was pulled out of line for special attention the next time she flew. And the next time. And the next time. On one flight this past September from Newark to Washington, six members of

---

* I finally made my way onto this second list in April 2004, something I discovered when I was flying to Taiwan with my 11-year-old son Jed in April, 2004. We were at New York's JFK Airport in a line of people who were punching in information from our E-tickets for a Northwest Airlines Flight to Hong Kong via Tokyo, when an airport security worker from the Transportation Security Administration pulled us aside. We hadn't even checked our bags in yet when she asked for my boarding pass. When I handed them to her, she perused them quickly and then penned an "S" on both my and my son's passes. At the metal detector, we were pulled aside and subjected to a much stricter inspection—our carry-on luggage was rifled through, our clothes were checked, and when we arrived in Hong Kong, I learned that our checked baggage had also been thoroughly rifled through. We were also electronically tagged, because the same procedure was applied to us when we changed planes at Narita Airport in Tokyo, even though we'd never left the secure flight transfer area and thus didn't need a second check.

the center's staff, including Olshansky, were stopped and subjected to intense scrutiny, even though they had purchased their tickets independently and had not checked in as a group. On that occasion, Olshansky got angry and demanded to know why she had been singled out.

"The computer spit you out," she recalls the agent saying. "I don't know why, and I don't have time to talk to you about it."

Olshansky and her colleagues are apparently not alone. For months, rumors and anecdotes have circulated among left-wing and other activist groups about people who have been barred from flying or delayed at security gates because they are "on a list."

But now, a spokesman for the new Transportation Security Administration has acknowledged for the first time that the government has a list of about 1,000 people who are deemed "threats to aviation" and not allowed on airplanes under any circumstances. And in an interview with *Salon*, the official suggested that Olshansky and other political activists may be on a separate list that subjects them to strict scrutiny but allows them to fly.

"We have a list of about 1,000 people," said David Steigman, the TSA spokesman. The agency was created a year ago by Congress to handle transportation safety during the war on terror. "This list is composed of names that are provided to us by various government organizations like the FBI, CIA and INS...We don't ask how they decide who to list. Each agency decides on its own who is a 'threat to aviation.'"

The agency has no guidelines to determine who gets on the list, Steigman says, and no procedures for getting off the list if someone is wrongfully on it.

Meanwhile, airport security personnel, citing lists that are provided by the agency and that appear to be on airline ticketing and check-in computers, seem to be netting mostly priests, elderly nuns, Green Party campaign operatives, left-wing journalists, right-wing activists and people affiliated with Arab or Arab-American groups.

- Virgine Lawinger, a 71-year-old nun in Milwaukee and an activist with Peace Action, a well-known grassroots advocacy group, was stopped from boarding a flight last spring to Washington, where she and 20 young students were planning to lobby the Wisconsin congressional delegation against U.S. military aid to the Colombian government. "We were all prevented from boarding, and some of us were taken to another room and questioned by airport security personnel and local sheriff's deputies," says Lawinger.

In that incident, an airline employee with Midwest Air and a local sheriff's deputy who had been called in during the incident to help airport security personnel detain and question the group, told some of them that their names were "on a list," and that they were being kept off their plane on instructions from the Transportation Security Administration in Washington. Lawinger has filed a freedom-of-information request with the Transportation Security Administration seeking to learn if she is on a "threat to aviation" list.

- Last month, Rebecca Gordon and Jan Adams, two journalists with a San Francisco-based antiwar magazine called *War Times* were stopped at the check-in counter of ATA Airlines, where an airline clerk told them that her computer showed they were on "the FBI No Fly list." The airline called the FBI, and local police held them for a while before telling them there had been a mistake and that they were free to go. The two made their plane, but not before the counter attendant placed a large S, presumably for "search" but perhaps for "security risk," on their baggage, assuring that they got more close scrutiny at the boarding gate.

- Art dealer Doug Stuber, who ran Ralph Nader's Green Party presidential campaign in North Carolina in 2000, was barred last month from getting on a flight to Hamburg, Germany, where he was going on business, after he got engaged in a loud, though friendly, discussion with two other passengers in a security line. During the course of the debate, he shouted that "George Bush is as dumb as a rock," an unfortunate comment that (however accurate) provoked the Raleigh-Durham Airport security staff to call the local Secret Service bureau, which sent out two agents to interrogate Stuber.

"They took me into a room and questioned me all about my politics," Stuber recalls. "They were very up on Green Party politics, too." They fingerprinted him and took a digital eye scan. Particularly ominous, he says, was a loose-leaf binder held by the Secret Service agents. "It was open, and while they were questioning me, I discreetly looked at it," he says. "It had a long list of organizations, and I was able to recognize the Green Party, Greenpeace, EarthFirst and Amnesty International." Stuber was eventually released, but because he missed his flight, he had to pay almost $2,000 more for a full-fare ticket to Hamburg so that he would not miss his business engagement. In the end, however, after trying several airports in the North Carolina area, he found he was barred from boarding any flights, and had to turn in his ticket and cancel his business trip.

A Secret Service agent at the agency's Washington headquarters confirmed that his agency had been called in to question Stuber. "We're not normally a part of the airport security operation," Agent Mark Connelly told *Salon*. "That's the FBI's job. But when one of our protection subjects gets threatened, we check it out." Asked about the list of organizations observed by Stuber, the Secret Service source speculated that those organizations might be on a list of organizations that the service, which is assigned the task of protecting the president, might need to monitor as part of its security responsibility.

Additional evidence suggests that Olshansky, Stuber and other left-leaning activists are also seen as a threat to aviation, though perhaps of a different grade. A top official for the Eagle Forum, an old-line conservative group led by anti-feminist icon Phyllis Schlafly, said several of the group's members have been delayed at security checkpoints for so long that they missed their flights. According to Pax Christi, a venerable Catholic peace organization, an American member of the Falun Gong Chinese religious group was barred from getting back on a plane that had stopped in Iceland, reportedly based on information supplied to Icelandic customs by U.S. authorities. The person was reportedly permitted to fly onward on a later flight.

Hussein Ibish, communications director of the American Arab Anti-Discrimination Committee, says his group has documented over 80 cases—involving 200 people—in which fliers with Arabic names have been delayed at the airport, or barred altogether from flying. Some, he says, appear to involve people who have no political involvement at all, and he speculated that they suffered the misfortune of having the same name as someone "on the list" for legitimate security reasons.

Until Steigman's confirmation of the no-fly list, the government had never even admitted its existence. While FBI spokesman Paul Bresson confirmed existence of the list, officials at the CIA and U.S. Immigration and Naturalization Service declined to comment and referred inquiries back to the TSA. Details of how it was assembled and how it is being used by the government, airports and airlines are largely kept secret.

A security officer at United Airlines, speaking on condition of anonymity, confirmed that the airlines receive no-fly lists from the Transportation Security Administration but declined further comment, saying it was a security matter. A USAir spokeswoman, however, declined to comment, saying that the airline's security relationship with the federal transit agency was a security matter and that discussing it could "jeopardize passenger safety."

Steigman declined to say who was on the no-fly list, but he conceded that people like Lawinger, Stuber, Gordon, Adams and Olshansky were not "threats to aviation," because they were being allowed to fly after being interrogated and searched. But then, in a Byzantine twist, he raised the possibility that the security agency might have more than one list. "I checked with our security people," he said, "and they said there is no [second] list," he said. "Of course, that could mean one of two things: Either there is no second list, or there is a list and they're not going to talk about it for security reasons."

In fact, most of those who have been stopped from boarding flights (like Lawinger, Stuber, Gordon and Adams) were able to fly later. Obviously, if the TSA thought someone was a genuine "threat to aviation"—like those on the 1,000-name no-fly list— they would simply be barred from flying. So does the agency have more than one list perhaps—one for people who are totally barred from flying and another for people who are simply harassed and delayed?

Asked why the TSA would be barring a 74-year-old nun from flying, Steigman said: "I don't know. You could get on the list if you were arrested for a federal felony."

Sister Lawinger says she was arrested only once, back in the 1980s, for sitting down and refusing to leave the district office of a local congressman. And even then, she says, she was never officially charged or fined. But another person who was in the Peace Action delegation that day, Judith Williams, says she was arrested and spent three days in jail for a protest at the White House back in 1991. In that protest, Williams and other Catholic peace activists had scaled the White House perimeter fence and scattered baby dolls around the lawn to protest the bombing of Iraq. She says that the charge from that incident was a misdemeanor, an infraction that would not seem enough to establish her as a threat to aviation.

Inevitably, such questions about how one gets on a federal no-fly list creates questions about how to get off it. It is a classic—and unnerving—Catch-22: Because the Transportation Security Administration says it compiles the list from names provided by other agencies, it has no procedure for correcting a problem. Aggrieved parties would have to go to the agency that first reported their names, but for security reasons, the TSA won't disclose which agency put someone on the list.

Bresson, the FBI spokesperson, would not explain the criteria for classifying someone as a threat to aviation, but suggests that fliers who believe they're on the list improperly should "report to airport security and they should be able to contact the TSA or us and get it cleared up." He concedes that might mean missed flights or other inconveniences. His explanation: "Airline security has gotten very complicated."

Many critics of the security agency's methods accept the need for heightened air security, but remain troubled by the more Kafka-esque traits of the system. Waters, at the Eagle Forum, worries that the government has offered no explanation for how a "threat to aviation" is determined. "Maybe the people being stopped are already being profiled," she says. "If they're profiling people, what kind of things are they looking for? Whether you fit in in your neighborhood?"

"I agree that the government should be keeping known 'threats to aviation' off of planes," Ibish says. "I certainly don't want those people on my plane! But there has to be a procedure for appealing this, and there isn't. There are no safeguards and there is no recourse."

Meanwhile, nobody in the federal government has explained why so many law-abiding but mostly left-leaning political activists and antiwar activists are being harassed at check-in time at airports. "This all raises serious concerns about whether the government has made a decision to target Americans based on their political beliefs," says Katie Corrigan, an ACLU official. The ACLU has set up a No Fly List Complaint Form on its website.

One particular concern about the government's threat to aviation list and any other possible lists of people to be subjected to extra security investigation at airports is that names are being made available to private companies—the airlines and airport authorities—charged with alerting security personnel. Unlike most other law-enforcement watch lists, these lists are not being closely held within the national security or law-enforcement files and computers, but are apparently being widely dispersed.

"It's bad enough when the federal government has lists like this with no guidelines on how they're compiled or how to use them," says

Olshansky at the Center for Constitutional Rights. "But when these lists are then given to the private sector, there are even less controls over how they are used or misused." Noting that airlines have "a free hand" to decide whether someone can board a plane or not, she says the result is a "tremendous chilling of the First Amendment right to travel and speak freely."

But Olshansky, alarmed by her own experience and the number of others reporting apparent political harassment, is fighting back. She says now that the government has confirmed the existence of a black-list, her center is planning a First Amendment lawsuit against the federal government. CCR has already signed up Lawinger, Stuber, and several others from Milwaukee's Peace Action group.

—*Salon.com, Nov. 15, 2002*

Half a year later, in a second article for *Salon*, I got solid confirmation from the FBI that the TSA was working with two lists—a "no-fly" list of "threats to aviation" and a "selectee" list (Ahah! So that's what that "S" on the boarding pass stands for!) of people who were marked for special searches and interrogations when they tried to fly, but who would be permitted onto planes (if the process didn't cause them to miss their flights, that is).[8] The ACLU has filed a class action suit against the TSA over the lists, claiming that they violate constitutionally protected freedom of travel, and that they are compiled without any standards or any mechanism for challenging one's inclusion on them.

The most disturbing thing about all this domestic spying activity being conducted by the Bush administration and the Ashcroft "Justice" Department is how little the public, and members of Congress, seem to care. With the media nightly dishing out breathless tales of terror threats and with the Department of Homeland Security raising and lowering its color- coded warning flags, the public is in a fear-addled tizzy. And if you're wondering whether the Bush administration might like it this way, just look at this annual festivity that the government is sponsoring these days. So much for the old community picnic!

Snoops' Night Out: FEMA's Paranoid Communities

Leave it to FEMA (the Federal Emergency Management Agency) to take a good tradition and turn it to crap.

If there is one thing missing in America these days, it's a sense of community. I remember a few years ago my kindergarten-aged son missed his bus to school. My car was in the garage, and my wife had already driven off to work with the other vehicle, leaving me stranded. This was in mid-December and bitter cold (about 15° Fahrenheit, with a ripping wind blowing, and making it feel like –10° F). The school was a straight shot two miles down a rush-hour artery. I figured anyone would pick up a father (even a hirsute one) and his small boy in this weather, but to make doubly sure, I lettered a large cardboard sign saying "Missed the schoolbus!"

For longer than I want to admit (for fear of being charged with child abuse), my son and I huddled on the corner, watching car after car drive by us, eyes guiltily averted. Many of the drivers—most of them male—actually looked familiar; they were people I'd seen many times in the local stores. But no one stopped. Finally, mercifully, a woman in a van, going the other way, who had already passed us once, turned around, picked us up, and, nervously confessing that she had done so against her better judgment, delivered us to my son's school.

Welcome to suburban America, where almost nobody will go an inch out of her or his way for anyone unless it's a relative or a close friend.

Logically, our civic institutions, beginning with government, should be trying to combat this modern day curse of fragmentation and atomization, this profound loss of communal consciousness.

So what does FEMA do? This haven for right-wing zealots and martial law planners has brought us the National Night Out program, an annual law-enforcement extravaganza which, in FEMA's words, is part of "a year-long community-building campaign" designed to:

(1) heighten crime prevention awareness;
(2) generate support for, and participation in, local anticrime programs;
(3) strengthen neighborhood spirit and police-community partnerships; and
(4) send a message to criminals letting them know that neighborhoods are organized and fighting back.

Building better communities by fighting crime.
Did anyone hear the words "getting to know one another"?
At National Night Out festivities across the country this Friday evening, local police will show off their S.W.A.T. gear, let kids try on handcuffs and learn how to dial 911—all kinds of good stuff designed

to make everyone…

What? Feel good and neighborly about the strangers in their midst? I don't think so.

A real community-building program should be teaching people in a neighborhood to get to know one another, to learn each others' cultures and needs, to find common interests, and to figure out ways to work together to improve the life of the whole community. It should, in short, be trying to reduce fears, suspicions and hostilities. A real community-building program might, for example, organize a community ride-sharing program, so people with cars could volunteer to help housebound neighbors (or parents stuck with a car in the shop) to get to work or school. Or it might just host get-to-know-your-neighbors block parties. It might even include a meeting to look into the causes of crime in the community.

National Night Out, which does none of these things, appropriately is part of the Bush/Ashcroft Citizen Corps—the folks who tried to bring us TIPS, the Terrorist Information and Prevention System which, until cancelled by an outraged Congress last summer, was hoping to enlist millions of Americans to spy on their neighbors. It's also sponsored by the National Association of Town Watch, a mini version of the aborted TIPS concept.

I'm not saying getting a community involved in crime stopping is a bad idea per se. Watching out for your neighbors' house when they're away on vacation is a community-spirited thing to do. But centering a so-called "community building" program around crime fighting and crime prevention is exactly the wrong way to go about building a community.

FEMA has always had a police-state mentality. But the Bush administration seems to have a one-note song. With these guys everything is about crime, terror and paralyzing fear.

National Night Out is playing right into this theme.

—*CounterPunch.org, Aug. 8, 2003*

Spying on the public and making everyone suspicious of neighbors is not the only thing the Bush administration has decided is what we need in the New American Century. The other necessity is to put a lid on dissent—especially dissent that might embarrass the president or vice president. Image is everything with this gang in Washington, and crowds of angry people holding off-message signs can't be allowed to intrude. Ever wonder where the crowds of protesters are when you see the wildly unpopular Dubya in his trademark starched black suit addressing handpicked crowds of supporters on military bases or in other controlled settings? They're out there, but to see, or even to hear them, you have to check out the cages where they're being held. Those would be the "free speech zones."

Keeping Dissent Invisible:
How the Secret Service and the White House keep protesters safely out of Bush's sight—and off TV

When Bill Neel learned that President George W. Bush was making a Labor Day campaign visit to Pittsburgh back in 2002 to support local congressional candidates, the retired Pittsburgh steelworker decided that he would be on hand to protest the president's economic policies. Neel and his sister made a hand-lettered sign reading "The Bushes must love the poor—they've made so many of us," and headed for a road where the motorcade would pass on the way from the airport to a Carpenters' Union training center.

He never got to display his sign for President Bush to see, though. As he stood among milling groups of Bush supporters, he was approached by a local police detective, who told him and his sister that because they were protesting, they had to move to a "free speech area," on orders of the U.S. Secret Service.

"He pointed out a relatively remote baseball diamond that was enclosed in a chain-link fence," Neel recalled in an interview with *Salon*. "I could see these people behind the fence, with their faces up against it, and their hands on the wire." (The ACLU posted photos of the demonstrators and supporters at that event on its web site.) "It looked more like a concentration camp than a free speech area to me, so I said, 'I'm not going in there. I thought the whole country was a free speech area.'" The detective asked Neel, 66, to go to the area six or eight times, and when he politely refused, he handcuffed and arrested the retired steelworker on a charge of disorderly conduct. When Neel's sister argued against his arrest, she was cuffed and hauled off as well. The two spent the president's visit in a firehouse that was serving as Secret Service and police headquarters for the event.

It appears that the Neels' experience is not unique. Late last month, on Sept. 23, the American Civil Liberties Union filed a lawsuit in a federal court in Philadelphia against the Secret Service, alleging that the agency, a unit of the new Homeland Security Department charged with protecting the president, vice president and other key government officials, instituted a policy in the months even before the Sept. 11 terrorist attacks of instructing local police to cordon off protesters from the president and vice president. Plaintiffs include the National Organization for Women, ACORN, USA Action and United for Justice, and groups and individuals who have been penned up during presidential visits, or arrested for refusing to go into a "free speech area," in places ranging from California to New Mexico, Missouri, Connecticut, New Jersey, South Carolina and elsewhere in Pennsylvania.

The ACLU, which began investigating Secret Service practices following Neel's arrest, has identified 17 separate incidents where protesters were segregated or removed during presidential or vice-presidential events, and Pittsburgh ACLU legal director Witold Walczak says, "I wouldn't be surprised if this is just the tip of the iceberg. We don't have the resources to follow Bush and Cheney everywhere they go." The suit also comes at a time of mounting charges by many civil libertarians on both the left and the right that the Bush Administration and Attorney General John Ashcroft's Justice Department are trampling on civil liberties.

"There is some history supporting the notion that all presidents dislike people who don't like them," says Stefan Presser, head of the ACLU of Philadelphia ACLU chapter and another lead attorney in the suit the Secret Service. "But this approach of fencing protesters in and removing them from view is unprecedented, and it's gotten worse over the past two years."

Well, maybe not exactly unprecedented. Pittsburgh's Walczak notes that during Nixon administration, especially during his second term, police "made quite a practice" of tearing up protest signs and confining protesters, and at least in one case that went to court, the Secret Service admitted being behind the actions. He says there were some isolated instances of interference with protesters during the Reagan administration, and even at President Clinton's inauguration, an attempt was made (unsuccessfully, thanks to ACLU intervention) to bar anti-abortion protesters from the inaugural march.

In its complaint, the ACLU cites nine cases since March 2001 in which protesters were quarantined. And it alleges that the Secret Service, with the assistance of state and local police, is systematically violating protesters' First Amendment rights via two methods. "Under the first form," the suit says, " the protesters are moved further away from the location of the official and/or the event, allowing people who express views that support the government to remain closer. Under the second form, everyone expressing a view—either critical or supportive of the government—is moved further away, leaving people who merely observe, but publicly express no view, to remain closer."

In either case, the complaint adds, "protesters are typically segregated into what are commonly referred to as 'protest zones.'"

In the ACLU's view, the strategy, besides violating a fundamental right of free speech and assembly, is damaging in two ways. "It insulates the government officials from seeing or hearing the protesters and vice-versa, and it gives to the media and the American public the appearance that there exists less dissent than there really is."

Certainly, as television cameras follow a presidential motorcade lined with cheering supporters, the image on the tube will be distorted if protesters have all been spirited away around a corner somewhere, fenced in for the duration.

Contacted by *Salon*, the Secret Service denied that it discriminates against protesters. "The Secret Service is message-neutral," said spokesman John Gill. "We make no distinction on the basis of the purposes or intent of any group or the content of signs."

Further, Gill insisted that the establishment and oversight of local viewing areas during a presidential or vice presidential visit "is the responsibility of state and local law enforcement." In practice, it's apparently not that simple, though. Nor is the Secret Service's carefully worded denial of responsibility as definitive as it might appear. The "establishment of viewing areas" is indeed a local law enforcement responsibility, but local law enforcement officials say that the Secret Service has in some cases all but ordered them to pen in protesters. And it appears that the Secret Service is making recommendations about how that should be done.

Paul Wolf is an assistant supervisor in charge of operations at the Allegheny County Police Department and was involved in planning for the presidential visit to Pittsburgh last fall. He told *Salon* that the decision to pen in Bush critics like Neel originated with the Secret Service. "Generally, we don't put protesters inside enclosures," he said. "The only time I remember us doing that was a Ku Klux Klan rally, where there was an opposing rally, and we had to put up a fence to separate them.

"What the Secret Service does," he explained, "is they come in and do a site survey, and say, 'Here's a place where the people can be, and we'd like to have any protesters be put in a place that is able to be secured.' Someone, say our police chief, may have suggested the place, but the request to fence them in comes from the Secret Service. They run the show."

The statement by Wolf, who ranks just below the Allegheny County police chief, is backed up by the sworn testimony of the detective who arrested Neel. At a hearing in county court, Det. John Ianachione, testifying under oath, said that the Secret Service had instructed local police to herd into the enclosed so-called free-speech area "people that were there making a statement pretty much against the president and his views." Explaining further, he added: "If they were exhibiting themselves as a protester, they were to go in that area."

Asked to respond to the accounts of Wolf and Ianachione about the Secret Service's role in handling of protesters, spokesman Gill said only, "No comment." Asked pointedly whether Wolf's account was incorrect, Gill again said, "No comment."

Wolf also raises the possibility that White House operatives may be behind the moves to isolate and remove protesters from presidential events. He cannot recall specifically whether they were present with the Secret Service advance team before last year's presidential Labor Day visit, but says "I think they are sometimes part of" the planning process. The Secret Service declined to comment on this assertion, saying it would not discuss "security arrangements." The White House declined to comment on what role the White House staff plays in deciding how protesters at presidential events should be handled, referring all calls to the Secret Service.

Asked specifically whether White House officials have been behind requests to have protesters segregated and removed from the vicinity of presidential events, White House spokesman Allen Abney said, "No comment." But he added, "The White House staff and the Secret Service work together on a lot of things." (While the Secret Service won't confirm that it is behind the pattern of tight constraints placed on protesters at public appearances by Bush and Cheney, the ACLU claims that mounting evidence suggests that this is exactly what is going on.)

In its lawsuit the ACLU makes this charge. A number of individual plaintiffs in the suit say that when they were directed into remote "free-speech areas," or arrested for refusing to go to such sites, they were informed that the local police were acting "on orders from the Secret Service."

That's the story Bill Ramsey got when he was arrested last Nov. 4 by police in St. Charles, Mo., while attempting to unfurl an antiwar banner amid a group of pro-Bush people during a presidential visit to a local airport. "The police told us if we wanted to show the banner, we'd have to go to a parking lot four-tenths of a mile away and out of sight of the president's motorcade," says Ramsey. "When we attempted to put it up anyway, they arrested us, and said they'd been ordered to by the Secret Service."

But Ramsey says that when his organization, the Instead of War Coalition, has sought to obtain permission to hold its demonstrations during presidential visits, they are told by the Secret Service that such matters are the responsibility of local police. "When we go to the local police, though, they say it's up to the Secret Service."

Efforts to obtain a comment from the St. Charles Police Department were unsuccessful.

Andrew Wimmer, another member of the Instead of War Coalition, says he was offered a similar explanation last January in St. Louis when he attempted to unfurl a sign reading "Instead of War, Invest in People" on a street full of Bush supporters. According to Wimmer, St. Louis police officers told him he'd have to leave a street full of Bush supporters and go to a protest area two blocks from the presidential motorcade route because of his protest sign. He recalls that as crowds of people walked down a thoroughfare toward the trading company that President Bush was slated to visit, "local police were pulling out people carrying protest signs and directing them to the protest area." The 48-year-old IT worker says, "When they got to me, I said no, I'd just as soon stand with the people here. But they said the Secret Service wanted protesters in the protest area."

In the end, Wimmer, like Ramsey and others who have refused to be caged during protests, was arrested. "They charged me with obstructing passage with my sign, which was a 2.5-foot-by-2-foot lawn sign," he says, noting that a woman standing nearby with a similar-size sign saying "We love you Mr. President," was left alone.

"The Secret Service keeps saying that the decision to separate protesters and remove them from view is a local police matter," says Denise Lieberman, legal director of the ACLU of Eastern Missouri, who is representing both Ramsey and Wimmer in their arrest cases. "But these kinds of things only happen when the Secret Service is involved. We've had many visits to St. Louis—by the pope, by candidates, by dignitaries—and it's only when the president or the vice president come to town that this kind of thing happens."

"We expect to see a lot more of this heading into a campaign sea-son," says Chris Hansen, senior staff attorney at the ACLU and one of the lead attorneys handling the suit against the Secret Service.

Presser, the Philadelphia ACLU attorney, traces the tactic to the last Republican National Convention, which nominated Bush for the presidency in August 2000. "The GOP tried to reserve every possible space where a protest group might rally," Presser recalls. "Part of the party's contract with the city of Philadelphia for the convention was that they were given an omnibus permit to use 'all available space' for the two weeks of the convention. They basically privatized the city to block all legal protest."

During that convention, the city attempted to require that all groups seeking to protest during the convention apply for permits to get a 15-minute protest time slot, during which they would be allowed to assemble and make their statement in a sunken "protest pit," remote from the Convention Center. Many groups refused, and the result was a series of conflicts with local police and many arrests, most of which were later tossed out by the courts.

Since then, Presser charges, the Bush administration has contin-ued the strategy of using the Secret Service and cooperative local police departments to keep protesters at bay, and not incidentally, out of easy range of the media. "People used to say that Ronald Reagan's was the most scripted administration we ever had," the attorney says, "but this Bush administration has gone way beyond that." Presser adds that he was told by William Fisher, a senior Philadelphia police captain and head of the department's Civil Affairs Unit, that the tight restrictions and decision to cordon off protesters during presidential visits have come "at the Secret Service's direction." Fisher declined to be inter-viewed for this article, but when asked, did not deny Presser's account of their conversation.

Presser and the ACLU don't question the Secret Service's respon-sibility to protect the president and other key government officials. Even plaintiffs in the case agree that the president must be protected. But "putting protesters behind a fence isn't going to help," says Neel, the former Pittsburgh steelworker. "I mean, somebody who was going to attempt an assassination wouldn't be carrying a protest sign. He'd be carrying a sign saying 'I love George!'"

The ACLU's Presser agrees. "Just as the terrorists who attacked the World Trade Center were careful to blend in and stayed away from mosques," he says, "anyone who had ill will towards the president could just put on a pro-Bush T-shirt and, under this policy, he'd be allowed to move closer to the president by the Secret Service."

He adds, "It seems that these 'security zones' for protesters have very little to do with the president's physical security, and a whole lot to do with his political security." Asked how many times in history an attack had been made on a president or other official under Secret Service protection by someone clearly identifiable as a protester, agency spokesman Gill said, "I'm not going to comment on that." Interestingly, Gill at no point claimed that protesters posed a special threat to the president or vice president.

Whatever the real motives behind it, the Secret Service policy of fencing off protests and protesters during presidential events may be in for a tough challenge. The judge assigned to the case, John Fullam, is an appointee of former President Lyndon B. Johnson, and back in the late 1980s issued a permanent injunction in Philadelphia—still in effect—that bars both the city of Philadelphia and the National Parks Department (the agency in charge of the city's many federal monuments), from treating protesters or people wearing protest paraphernalia any differently from other citizens.

The ACLU, which is seeking an injunction barring the Secret Service and local police from treating protesters differently from other spectators at administration events, is hopeful that the court will act "before the presidential campaign gets into full swing next summer," says Walczak. Meanwhile, Presser says he is optimistic that the lawsuit, simply by being filed, could make things easier for protesters during the coming campaign season." I suspect that this suit may give the Secret Service and local police some pause in how they treat protests," he says.

—Salon.com, Oct. 13, 2003

Dossiers on dissidents, harassment of fliers, caged protesters and picnics with your local SWAT team. The new America is getting to be a fun place to be a citizen. It's even more fun if you're an immigrant. And wait until you see what we've got in store for you if you're a prisoner of war or an enemy combatant (whatever that is). I should add that when I wrote this particular column, in the early days of the Iraq invasion, I had no idea how it would play out a year later, with tales of sodomy, torture, and murder courtesy of the American army of liberation.

Reaping What Has Been Sown:
Prisoners, Torture and Hypocrisy

When I was a journalist working in China back in the early 1990s, I was furious when two administrations in the U.S.—those of both the first Bush and Clinton—condoned executions of American death row prisoners from foreign countries who had been arrested and tried without their home countries' embassies being notified. The current Bush Administration has taken the same cavalier approach to international law also, which clearly requires that an embassy be notified when one of its nationals is arrested in a country, and further, that that embassy be permitted to have access to the detained individual and to provide a lawyer.

I was furious because America's willful and repeated violation of this basic international agreement was a direct threat to my personal health and safety. I was going out into the Chinese countryside as a journalist—often without the benefit of a journalist's visa, which can take weeks to obtain and which often is denied—and was at risk of being arrested by Chinese security forces. In fact, I was brought in and interrogated by the Public Security Bureau twice during such journalistic forays, once to a relatively remote area of Anhui Province and a second time to a rural part of Jiangsu Province, and I can report that the experience was harrowing each time.

How could I hope to have the protection and help of my embassy in China if my own country was thumbing its nose at international law?

Now we see the same thing happening during the war on Iraq, where the implications are even more serious as—predictably—American soldiers begin to be captured by Iraqi forces.

The Bush administration is loudly decrying their use by Iraq as propaganda on Arab television, where they have been shown being questioned about what they were doing in Iraq. It's good domestic PR. After all, their treatment, while so far thankfully not brutal, is in violation of the Geneva Convention on the treatment of POWs. But nobody outside the U.S. is going to take the American protests seriously.

The sad truth is that the U.S. is in no position to make a complaint, for America, too, has been in gross violation of that convention. Iraqi soldiers taken prisoner during this war have been marched before American television cameras, they have been blindfolded and terrorized by U.S. soldiers taking them into custody, and their faces have been displayed on American television—all clear violations of international law.*

But the U.S. is doing even worse with regard to other POWs it has captured in Afghanistan. Along with most international legal scholars, I would argue that anyone fighting U.S. forces in that country is a soldier in a war. Once captured, they should have been held in accordance with the Geneva Convention. They have not been so treated, however. In fact, the Bush administration expressly *exempted* them from Geneva Convention standards.

Certain of those captured have been either turned over to other countries' security forces—for example those of Egypt or Pakistan—where they reportedly have been subjected to torture, or they have been held at a U.S. base in Afghanistan, and also subjected to conditions that can only be described as torture, or in some cases—well over 600—they have been transported, bound and hooded, to a concentration camp at Guantanamo Bay, Cuba, where they are caged in individual pens and held in a legal limbo—not prisoners and not prisoners of war.

Arguably the non-Afghan members of Al Qaeda in Afghanistan might be termed "unlawful combatants" by the U.S., and denied POW status, though this is making a rather fine distinction. Al Qaeda fighters, while they might have originally been in Afghanistan as terrorist trainees, seem to have been acting as a legitimate ally of the government of Afghanistan at the time of their capture, fighting alongside government forces. But even granting that distinction, the U.S. also has taken captured Afghan Taliban fighters, who clearly were the official army of the government of Afghanistan, off to Guantanamo, denying them too, any POW status.

The whole world sees this treatment of captured Afghan fighters as the most outrageous violation of international law and the Geneva Convention, yet the U.S., even knowing it was about to become involved in a war in the Middle East, went ahead with this outlaw behavior.

All it has done in the process is open the door to similar abuse of captured Americans. After all, if the U.S. is seen as fighting an illegal war of aggression, might not Iraq decide that any soldiers it catches are not POWs at all, but rather "unlawful combatants"?

One has to wonder at the hubris of Bush Administration policy-

---

* This column was written more than a year before the breaking of the Abu Ghraib torture scandal, which showed just how completely the U.S. has trashed the Geneva Accords.

makers, who seem to think that they can trample over any international rules and agreements they want, without suffering any consequences.

The same might be said of the charge that Fedayeen irregulars are violating international law by dressing up in civilian clothes and attacking American and British troops in Iraq by deceit. While this standard guerrilla war tactic is a violation of the international rules of war, which are designed to minimize civilian casualties, we know that U.S. special forces, such as the Delta Force troops, have also been dressing as local civilians in the Afghanistan conflict (they were shown doing this in the American media), and it strains belief to think that they are not doing the same thing now in Iraq.

The Bush Administration is counting on the jingoistic American media to ignore its own blatant violations of international law in the Afghanistan and Iraq wars, while it loudly condemns Iraq's violations as evidence of the evil of the enemy. So far their hopes have been largely rewarded domestically. But the rest of the world is seeing this two-faced policy on POWs for what it is.

So we have the pathetic picture of President Bush, with a straight if chronically besmirked face, condemning first Iraq for violating the Geneva Convention on POW treatment and then Russia for "violating U.N. sanctions" against Iraq! This from a commander-in-chief who has condoned and continues to condone the most egregious violations of prisoner of war rules, and who has violated the most basic part of the U.N. charter by initiating an unprovoked war of aggression against a member state without the sanction of the Security Council.

An old adage about war has long been: the winner makes the rules. But a more venerable adage should be on both the mind of this chickenhawk administration and the minds of the soldiers who are being asked to put their lives on the line for its ill-conceived aggressive policies: As ye sow, so shall ye reap.

—CounterPunch.org, March 26, 2003

When I wrote the above column, I was mainly concerned that the blatant abuse of American-held prisoners of war would lead to similar mistreatment of American soldiers. In fact, while mercifully few American GI's have been captured in the Afghan and Iraq wars, the Bush administration's medieval approach to conquest and capture of the enemy has produced an even worse disaster—a culture of torture and abuse of prisoners by U.S. troops, the inevitable exposure of which has doomed any hope the White House and Pentagon ever had of winning over occupied Iraqis to a pro-American regime in Iraq.

Meanwhile, while we're talking about thumbing one's nose at civilized rules of war, how about those kids? At least here is a case where maybe something good can come out of something atrocious: a new model for indigent childcare.

About Those Kids in Camp X-Ray: Day Care in the Name of National Security?

Word that the Bush Administration's goons down in Guantanamo Bay have been detaining children under the age of 16 among the "enemy combatants" that they spirited out of Afghanistan following the rout of the Taliban suggests a new strategy for dealing with America's daycare crisis.

We know that as Bush and the conservative Congress continue to hack away at the nation's already tattered welfare "safety net," increasing numbers of single parents are being forced to abandon their small children at home while they go off to remote minimum-wage jobs or workfare assignments in an effort to make enough money to feed them.

Day care is not an option for these people. The federal government has been slashing daycare funding, while financially strapped states are rushing to exit the child-care subsidy business.

What's a poor mother to do?

Bush, the Pentagon and John Ashcroft's increasingly inappropriately named Justice Department have provided us with the answer: detention in the name of national security.

All these working mothers and fathers need to do is get their little offspring to toddle around carrying small arms (the guns don't have to be loaded, for goodness sake!) while spouting easily taught phrases like "Allah Akhbar!" or "Death to America!" and they'll quickly be picked up and placed in confinement where they'll be watched day and night and fed more or less regularly.

Alternately, if the parents in question are undocumented aliens, they might just claim to the Immigration Department that their kids were born overseas and don't have proper visas. That would lead to their being taken away and put in detention, too.

According to Pentagon officials, the youthful enemy combatants being held at Guantanamo are not being kept in cages like their elders, so presumably they are being treated in a manner more appropriate to their tender years—probably kept in some locked base rec room with a big-screen TV set tuned perpetually to the Cartoon Channel or WB.

Since this is pretty much what unlicensed child care services are doing in low-income neighborhoods anyway, parents can feel confident that their children are getting at least as good care in government custody as they would have been getting in a local child care facility, and at taxpayer expense instead of their own.

The only drawback I can see to this scheme is that under Pentagon and Justice Department rules since 9/11, relatives don't have visitation rights where illegal aliens or enemy combatants are concerned.

We could work on this, though, perhaps getting Congress to amend the rules where minor detainees are involved. Surely the "family friendly" Republican majority would see the logic in such a rule change.

If not, at least poor struggling parents would know that their kids were getting three square meals a day in government custody, even if they couldn't see them.

—CounterPunch.org, April 24, 2003

This next piece, written in the late spring of 2003, scarcely a month and a half after Commander-in-Chief Bush had unilaterally and, as it turns out, prematurely declared the Iraq War over, proved to have been reasonably prescient. The uprisings in Fallujah and Najaf, less than a year hence, have basically demarcated the beginning of the end of the U.S. adventure in Iraq, and perhaps of the whole Bush administration misadventure along with it. I hope, though, that I'm wrong about my second prediction—an Al Qaeda attack within the U.S.

What's Next? You Call This Security?

The last 21 months certainly have been wild and crazy. We've seen the vaporization of the World Trade Center, a successful attack on the Pentagon, the transformation of George Bush from a bumbling laughing stock to an awe-inspiring warlord (and back to bumbling laughing stock), the overnight creation of a mammoth global peace movement, a lightning war of aggression and conquest by the U.S., and the simultaneous shattering of a half-century-old alliance and of the

United Nations.

Now it's time to look ahead at what may be coming, which could prove to be crazier and scarier still.

A lot, I suspect, will depend upon what America's enemies and victims decide to do next, and where they decide to do it.

If Osama Bin Laden and his supporters decide to target the U.S. and manage to pull off another high-casualty terrorist attack within the United States, on the scale of what they did in Lower Manhattan, it could spell the end of democratic government and of our civil liberties tradition. The growing backlash against the government's post 9/11 assault on civil liberties, and the tentative questioning of the integrity and competence of the Bush administration that has begun more recently, would likely be swept away in a wave of new anti-terror fervor and Gestapo-like tactics that would be irresistible.

On the other hand, if the Iraqi resistance, with or without the help of outside organizations like al Qaeda, manages to move from isolated attacks on American soldiers in Iraq to a major massacre of American troops in that country, it could have a reverse effect back in the U.S., much like the Tet Offensive in the Indochina War—leading Americans to demand a pull-back from what will be widely viewed at that point as a hopeless quagmire. With the U.S. having kept its casualties relatively low through the duration of the official war, it might seem hard to imagine Iraq's rag-tag guerrillas pulling off such a feat. Recall, however, that occupation is a lot different from invasion. An attacking army has all the advantages of mobility and surprise—and in America's case, of massive aerial support. An army of occupation, in contrast, is a sitting duck, can make little use of air support, and moreover has to struggle against low morale, boredom and lack of attention. Moreover, the more aggressively the U.S. occupiers employ seek-and-destroy tactics against the Iraqi resistance, the more hostile they are likely to make the populace, thus creating an environment all the more favorable to the guerrillas.

It seems a safe bet that the Iraqi resistance and its allies throughout the Middle East are contemplating just such a major attack on American troops. They have to know that American public opinion has little patience for foreign adventures, that much of the occupying army is composed of reservists with families, jobs and lives that they want to get back to, and that heavy casualties are generally not politically tolerated. Thus, it seems only a matter of time before a Lebanon-style attack occurs.

What about a new major terror attack within the U.S.?

Sadly, it would seem such a terrible event is becoming increasingly likely, too. Even under the best of circumstances, the U.S. invasion of Iraq virtually assured that whatever experimental chemical or biological horrors Saddam Hussein might have been cooking up, if they really did exist, plus the nuclear waste materials in Iraq, would find their way into the hands of terrorists. But beyond that, the incredible ineptness and disinterest demonstrated by the invading U.S. and British armed forces, which waited weeks to try to secure dangerous weapons and waste materials, handed such hostile groups a golden opportunity. Not only were the materials available—there was a broken enemy motivated to sell whatever it could, both to punish the U.S. and to raise cash to escape Iraq.

On top of that, beyond creating a ludicrous color-coded alarm system and arresting, terrorizing and deporting hundreds of hapless Islamic immigrant visa violators, it turns out that the Bush Administration has done almost nothing concrete to protect the U.S. against terrorism. The fraudulently promoted Iraq war was a huge diversion not just of attention, but of domestic security forces and financial resources. Whole state police and urban police departments, as well as fire departments, have been gutted, thanks to a legacy of programs which have encouraged people in those jobs to sign up as reservists or in the National Guard. Moreover, Rand Beers, the top Bush counter-terrorism advisor who resigned in disgust in March, says that the Bush administration has been "making us less secure, not more secure," because of a pattern of neglect and homeland security budget cutting, for example in the area of port security or border security.

A conspiracy theorist could have a heyday speculating on whether it's actually in the Bush administration's interest to have the U.S. suffer an occasional terror hit. Certainly the current resident of the White House—whose claim to the title "President" has always been rather tenuous—was not winning any popularity contests until he was able to start calling himself commander-in-chief instead of chief executive. His whole reelection campaign appears to be premised upon his running dressed in khaki.

Whatever the White House's real motives, we have the ironic situation of a military establishment resorting to all manner of aggressive actions in a desperate bid to avoid a calamitous attack on its troops in Iraq, and an administration at home offering, as Beers puts it, "only a rhetorical policy" for protection against a domestic terror attack.

The near certainty of large-scale, bloody attacks on Americans both in Iraq and in the U.S. presents Democrats, liberals, progressives and the whole opposition movement with a dual challenge: to prepare now for both eventualities.

In the case of domestic terrorism, now is the time to forcefully remind Americans that terror attacks, however awful, do not in themselves threaten America's existence; that it is, rather, the unthinking, panicky and jingoistic response to acts of terror—for example sweeping arrests, detentions without trial, hasty passage of laws like the USA PATRIOT Act, and the like—which pose the real threat. If the news media, political leaders and other opinion makers present that argument powerfully and often now, before terror strikes again, it will be far easier to challenge the inevitable push towards a police state that will follow any major act of terror.

At the same time the peace movement needs to lay the groundwork now for a major campaign to recall American troops from Iraq, in order to be able to capitalize on the inevitable loss of support for the war/occupation that will follow any large-scale attack on American troops in that country.

—CounterPunch.org, June 19, 2003

While we're talking about terror attacks, and how, in the hands of demagogues, they can shred the fabric of a democratic society, it's worth recalling what another 9/11 terror attack—this one set in motion and financed by one of the world's leading state-sponsors of terror—did to another once vibrant democracy some three decades ago.

Expanding Power, Gutting Liberty: The Meaning of September 11

Politics as practiced in America has long been a cynical business, but the Bush administration has dramatically raised the bar for cynicism and manipulation.

In his speech yesterday in Quantico, VA to the FBI and a bunch of Marines bused in for patriotic color and canned applause, our active-duty-dodging, "bring 'em on" threat-making president used the anniversary of the 9/11 terror attacks to call for a further gutting of civil liberties and expansion of the lawless behavior and draconian powers of the Ashcroft Justice Department.

The USA PATRIOT Act, in effect since November 2001, has already been used by the Justice Department for everything from conducting warrantless searches and surveillance to arresting and detaining suspected "terrorists" without charge or even access to a lawyer—including U.S. citizens like Jose Padilla. The expanded powers now being sought by Bush and Attorney General John Ashcroft would include the power to strip even native-born Americans of their citizenship, their very birthright, expanded power for warrantless searches and arrests and other further assaults on the nation's constitutional liberties. Plans are even afoot to use military brigs to confine those whose citizenship has been removed, creating a set of Guantanamo-like Gulags across the domestic U.S.

The irony, of course, is that the Justice Department, with all the new powers it already granted itself since September, 2001, has done little to make the country safer against terrorism threats.

The Bush administration knows that opposition to its ongoing rights assault has been growing, not just among traditional liberals and leftists, but on the right too, where there remain powerful constituencies that support a literal and uncompromising interpretation of the Bill of Rights. Over 160 communities and three states, including many dominated by Republicans, have over the past year or so approved laws and resolutions defending the Bill or Rights and attacking the PATRIOT Act's provisions, such as its giving to federal agents the power to examine the library records of patrons without a warrant and without notice to the subject of the investigation.* Administration sources and congressional supporters have been quoted as saying that the intent of having the president make a personal appeal for expansion of the PATRIOT Act provisions on Sept. 10 was to have it reach the public on the second anniversary of the 9/11 terror attack, in hopes that this would mute opposition to the proposed new measures.

This cynical abuse of the pain and suffering of the relatives of the World Trade Center and Pentagon dead, as appalling as it is, is matched by the president's attempt in his Sunday address to the nation and his Wednesday address to FBI and Marine personnel to also use the same 9/11 tragedy to confuse the public and win support for his continued war policy in Iraq. Conflating the terror attacks with the U.S. military's growing problems in Iraq, Bush has tried to say that what "began in America" is being ended in Iraq, as if by attacking Iraqi guerrilla fight-

---

* The number of such states and communities had passed 300 by May, 2004.

ers, the U.S. military is hitting back at the terror network that was responsible for the 2001 terror attacks on New York and Washington, D.C. Of course nothing could be further from the truth. The war against Iraq, which no intelligence has linked to Al Qaeda, diverted military attention and power away from the search for 9/11 mastermind Osama bin Laden. By destroying the government in Iraq, Bush and his Pentagon warmongers also turned that nation into a lawless breeding ground for anti-American terrorists—one that is awash in weapons and explosives, and with people who know how to use them.

No honest observer of the ongoing war in Iraq would claim that even a thorough U.S. victory there, and establishment of a successful, pro-American Iraqi government—a highly unlikely prospect over the next few years—would end, or even reduce terrorist threats against the U.S. Few terrorists over the past decade have been Iraqi, and the terrorist world could get along fine without Iraqis in the future.

Meanwhile, there is a 9/11 anniversary worth recalling, without any cynicism but with a great deal of irony. That's the anniversary of the 1973 coup that overthrew the elected government of Salvadore Allende Gossens in Chile. America suffered a terrible terror attack on 9/11, but it hardly compares with the many more thousands who were brutally killed in that earlier terrorist action, an event which, as Peter Kornbluh, in his new book, *The Pinochet File: A Declassified Dossier on Atrocity and Accountability*,[9] replete with original documents and CIA and State Department cables, proves was instigated and supported by the U.S. government and specifically by President Richard M. Nixon and his Secretary of State Henry Kissinger. This was state-sponsored terrorism at its worst, and as yet, no one in American government has been brought to justice for it.

As we ponder the meaning of the attacks of Sept. 11, 2001, and of President George Bush's call for yet more unchecked police-state powers, we Americans would do well to also ponder the meaning of September 11,1973. The more recent 9/11 terrorist attack clearly demonstrated what can happen when committed terrorists decide to attack even the world's most powerful nation. Sept. 11, 1973 shows something worse: what happens when the very government of the world's most powerful nation is headed by terrorists—whether a Richard Nixon and a Secretary of State Henry Kissinger, or a George W. Bush and a Defense Secretary Donald Rumsfeld—that is, by people who have no respect for law or for constitutionally protected civil rights and liberties, or for human life itself, and who view democracy as a game to be cynically played and manipulated.

September 11, 1973 showed us in blood just what such enemies of democracy and basic human decency are capable of.

—*CounterPunch.org, Sept. 12, 2003*

It is important to point out that not all the news on the civil liberties front is bad. Some shocking surprises have been good ones, I'm happy to say. One such shock—and after all the java he's made me inhale, I hope it caused our attorney general to snort *his* morning coffee—came in a federal courtroom in New York, just blocks from where the World Trade Center towers once stood.

Ashcroft Rebuked: Lynne Stewart's Big Win

Tuesday, July 22, 2003 marked a big victory against the Bush/Ashcroft assault on civil liberties, with a federal judge in Manhattan tossing out the terrorism charges the Justice Department, and the AG in person, had so theatrically leveled against activist attorney Lynne Stewart back in 2002.

Stewart, a people's lawyer who has made a name for herself defending prominent leftists including black nationalists and members of organizations like the Weather Underground, was arrested in front of TV cameras at her home and charged with helping her client, jailed terrorist bomber Sheik Abdel Rahman, pass messages to his terrorist supporters, known as the Islamist Group, in Egypt. The charges were based upon anti-terrorism laws passed hastily by congress in the wake of the 9/11 attacks.

Attorney General John Ashcroft (after first notifying all the city's media outlets so they'd be on hand outside her building), had personally announced the arrest of Stewart, which many activist and civil liberties lawyers saw as a blatant attempt to intimidate lawyers from defending anti-government clients being prosecuted under the so-called USA PATRIOT ACT. Ashcroft hailed the arrest of Stewart as the first prosecution based upon a new federal policy permitting prison authorities to secretly monitor and tape formerly privileged jailhouse conversations between inmates and their attorneys.

Stewart and her own attorney, Michael E. Tigar, had argued that the statutes being used against her were unconstitutionally vague and a violation of both the first amendment and the long-established fundamental right of confidentiality between attorney and client—one of the basic elements underpinning a free and fair judicial system.

It's hard to be shocked any more by the actions of this administration, but at one early hearing in the case, the government even refused to promise in court, as requested by Tigar, not to monitor his conversations with his own client, Stewart. At the time, Stewart said she had been forced to communicate with her attorney "on the street, at public places like McDonalds, or on payphones."

The government charged that Stewart, who has to communicate with Sheik Rahman through an interpreter, had deliberately diverted the attention of prison guards while Rahman, who is serving a life sentence for plotting to blow up New York landmarks, passed a message to his interpreter telling his minions in Egypt that they should cease adhering to a cease-fire in their fundamentalist terror attacks in that country. The government also alleges that Stewart, who had signed an agreement in 2000 with prison authorities agreeing not to pass information on from Rahman, had violated her agreement.

Stewart denies that she passed such information, and argues that her conversations with her client were protected.

The charges against her, which have now been lifted, carried a possible 15-year sentence.

Several lesser charges remain, including making false statements and conspiring to defraud the government, but these are small beer by comparison to the dropped charges. James B. Comey, the U.S. Attorney prosecuting the case, says he is looking into whether to appeal the district court's decision.

Federal prosecutors, in their complaint against Stewart, had called her "an indispensable and active facilitator of the terrorist communication network" and compared her to a bank robbery accomplice whose job it was to distract security guards while the actual robbers took the money.

Stewart called the rejected charges, "so broad that you can sweep anybody under its rug." She asked, rhetorically, how an attorney could be anything but a "conduit of communication" if you were "taking calls from your client."

Her attorney, Tigar, said he hoped to get the other charges against Stewart lifted by the court after further facts were presented in continuing pretrial hearings.

An obviously relieved Stewart said that the lifting of the anti-terrorism charges by the judge "augurs well for things returning to a normalcy where the judges and courts are able to take a good look at what the government is doing, and consider what it's doing and stand up for the judicial branch and for justice."

While Stewart is entitled to celebrate the decision, her statement may be an overly optimistic view of the current state of affairs. Significantly, her case is being overseen by a jurist, Federal District Judge John G. Koeltl, who was a 1994 Clinton appointee to the bench.

Unfortunately, there are fewer and fewer such judges. The Bush administration, for three years now, has been nominating judges to the federal bench who have a much more pinched and antagonistic view towards constitutional protections and lawyer-client privilege.

As the percentage of judges appointed by the Bush administration to all levels of the federal judiciary, from district court to the Supreme Court, rises, the odds of cases like Stewart's being tossed out summarily on constitutional grounds will plummet.

—*CounterPunch.org, July 23, 2003*

If I were handing out those awards for unsung stories, my pick would be the absolutely incredible grass-roots resistance to the Patriot Act, that vicious assault on the foundations of American freedom and democracy being touted by the Bush Administration and the Ashcroft Justice Department as Exhibit A in its claim to be protecting Americans from terrorism—and themselves. Since passage of the Patriot Act, a steady stream of state and local governments have passed counter-measures condemning the act and ordering state and local government and law-enforcement agencies not to cooperate with its draconian measures and demands for assistance. By May 2004, the number of such communities had passed 300 (including Alaska), three times the number that had passed such legislation at the time the following column was written, meaning that some one in 10 Americans by that point were living in jurisdictions protected at least to some extent from Ashcroft's clutches.

Fighting the Patriot Act:
Alaska turns a cold shoulder

The Bush Administration and Attorney General John Ashcroft may have been able to pull a fast one in the wake of 9/11, winning passage of the draconian and grotesquely named USA PATRIOT Act, but a grass-roots resistance movement is starting to blow up in the administration's face.

As of today, 104 towns, cities and even the state of Hawaii, have passed resolutions in defense of the Bill of Rights which, in often forceful language, instruct state and local law enforcement not to participate in the act's assaults on civil liberties. The latest jurisdiction to consider such fight-back legislation is the state of Alaska, a bastion of conservative libertarianism. The city of Fairbanks has already passed its own resolution, and another is being considered in Anchorage, where key sponsors are representatives of the NAACP and the NRA.

But the language of the bill just passed by the state's House of Representatives, and now being debated by the state Senate, is powerful indeed.

House Joint Resolution No. 22 reads, in part:

> It is the policy of the State of Alaska to oppose any portion of the USA PATRIOT Act that would violate the rights and liberties guaranteed equally under the state and federal constitutions; and in accordance with Alaska state policy, an agency or instrumentality of the State of Alaska, in the absence of reasonable suspicion of criminal activity under Alaska State law, may not (1) initiate, participate in, or assist or cooperate with an inquiry, investigation, surveillance, or detention, (2) record, file, or share intelligence information concerning a person or organization, including library lending and research records, book and video store sales and rental records, medical records, financial records, student records, and other personal data, even if authorized under the USA PATRIOT Act, (3) retain such intelligence information; (and that) an agency or instrumentality of the state may not, (1) use state resources or institutions for the enforcement of federal immigration matters, which are the responsibility of the federal government; (2) collect or maintain information about the political, religious, or social views, associations, or activities of any individual, group, association, organization, corporation, business, or partnership, unless the information directly relates to an investigation of criminal activities and there are reasonable grounds to suspect the subject of the information is or may be involved in criminal conduct; (3) engage in racial profiling; law enforcement agencies may not use race, religion, ethnicity, or national origin as factors in selecting individuals to subject to investigatory activities except when seeking to apprehend a specific suspect whose race, religion, ethnicity, or national origin is part of the description of the suspect.

The bill goes on to say the state legislature implores the United

States Congress "to correct provisions in the USA PATRIOT Act and other measures that infringe on civil liberties, and opposes any pending and future federal legislation to the extent that it infringes on Americans' civil rights and liberties."

If passed by the state legislature's upper house, copies of resolution—a powerful slap at the civil liberties assault by the federal government—will be officially sent to the President Bush, Attorney General Ashcroft, the governor of Alaska, Frank Murkowski, and to the state's three-member congressional delegation.

Ashcroft and his minions appear to be worried about the wildfire civil liberties defense movement that has sprung up against his campaign to gut the Bill of Rights. When Ithaca, N.Y.'s city council recently passed its own version of a Bill of Rights defense resolution, it promptly received a letter from the FBI's Albany regional office claiming that the bill was not needed, since "As you know, FBI investigations are scrutinized by the courts to ensure that proper Constitutional standards are maintained," and that "Unlike foreign intelligence services, FBI investigative techniques must be sanctioned by judges."

Of course, this is a blatant falsehood, since Section 215 of the USA PATRIOT Act expressly allows G-men to rifle through library and video store records without a warrant and without showing "probably cause"—precisely the kind of thing that has prompted all these state and local resolutions.

The strategy behind the Bill of Rights protection movement is to present congressional delegations with evidence of widespread support for civil liberties, so that they will develop the spine needed to overturn the USA PATRIOT Act, or at least let it expire in 2004. So far over 11 million Americans live in jurisdictions which have passed such resolutions, and the campaign is scarcely a year old as yet.

—*CounterPunch.org, May 14, 2003*

An important part of the Bush-Ashcroft assault on civil liberties, much less obvious but more long lasting, has been the appointing of right-wing judges, who besides taking a narrow view of the protections of the Bill of Rights and the traditions of the court, also see themselves as part of the law-enforcement establishment. In the 2002 trial of John Walker Lindh, the young American who found himself fighting with the Taliban when the U.S. Army invaded Afghanistan, and who had the misfortune of being shot and captured by U.S. troops and then facing possible prosecution as a traitor, this willingness of a federal judge to do the bidding of the Justice Department had serious consequences, not just for poor Lindh, who ended up with a 20-year sentence in the federal pen, but for the nation, which lost a chance to expose the abuse of prisoners by American troops before the practice spread to Iraq and became an international scandal of epic proportions. In a sense, one could say that it was Attorney General John Ashcroft and Federal Judge T.S. Ellis who lost the war in Iraq for America by their connivance in silencing Lindh.

There's a lesson or two here. First of all, people need to realize that where judges are concerned, the issue is not whether a judge is pro or anti abortion rights, pro or anti states' rights, or pro or anti capital punishment. The overall integrity of our judiciary, its independence from government interference, and its unflinching respect for all the protections of the Bill of Rights and of court precedent, are crucial to us all. Secondly, the impact of a bad judge or a bad ruling can be profound, and reach way beyond the individual defendant in a case.

John Walker Lindh, Revisited:
A First Glimpse at Bush's Torture Show

Now that we know the truth behind how U.S. forces in Iraq and Afghanistan have been treating captured fighters (and captured innocent bystanders), it's time to revisit the case of John Walker Lindh, the so-called "American Taliban fighter" who is now serving 20 years in federal prison. For had Lindh pursued his case in court, instead of settling and getting slapped with a gag order, he might have exposed the whole prisoner abuse scandal two years ago, and spared the U.S.—and a whole lot of abused or slain POWs—the Abu-Ghraib fiasco.

Lindh, it may be recalled, was among a group of Taliban and Al Qaeda fighters captured and later, for the most part, slaughtered in northern Afghanistan by American soldiers and their Northern Alliance allies.

Initially threatened by U.S. Attorney General John Ashcroft with being tried as a traitor, Lindh was eventually charged with terrorism, consorting with Al Qaeda, and attempting to kill Americans. But he never went to trial. Instead, he pleaded guilty to just two relatively innocuous charges. But for those two charges—the first of which (carrying a grenade), probably innumerable Americans are guilty of, and the second of which (providing services to an enemy of the U.S.), could more properly be brought against a number of major U.S. corporations—Lindh had the book thrown at him by a compliant federal judge in Virginia. The judge, at the government's request, also hit him with a gag order barring him from talking about his experience. As part of his plea bargain agreement, Lindh was even forced to sign a statement saying: "The defendant agrees that this agreement puts to rest his claims of mistreatment by the United states military, and all claims of mistreatment are withdrawn. The defendant acknowledges that he was not intentionally mistreated by the U.S. military."

This outlandish and over-the-top effort to legally muzzle Lindh appears in a harsh new light now that we know the criminal nature of U.S. prisoner-of-war policies.

In the run-up to his trial, it was clear from documents submitted by the defense that Lindh, whatever document he may have been bullied into signing might say, had been viciously treated in captivity. Shot in the leg prior to his capture, and already starving and badly dehydrated, Lindh unconscionably was left with his wound untreated and festering for days despite doctors being readily available. Denied access to a lawyer, and threatened repeatedly with death, he was duct-taped to a stretcher and left for long periods of time in an enclosed, unheated and unlit metal shipping container, removed only during interrogations, at which time he was still left taped to his stretcher. (Hundreds of his Taliban and Al Qaeda comrades actually were deliberately allowed to die in those same containers in one of the more monstrous war crimes perpetrated during this conflict.)

In truth, the government's case against Lindh was always spurious at best. A 20-year-old, white, middle-class convert to Islam from Marin County, California, Lindh had only gone to Afghanistan in August 2001, scarcely a month before the 9/11 attacks and the subsequent U.S. invasion of Afghanistan. At the time of his arrival there, the Taliban government, far from being an enemy of America, was still receiving funding from the U.S. government. Lindh, to the extent that he was ever a fighter with the Taliban (he hadn't had time for a decent "boot camp" training in weapons use), was in fact fighting the Northern Alliance, not America, at the time of the U.S. invasion. His attorneys maintain that he never was an enemy of his own country, and in fact had been trapped with the Taliban in Afghanistan by the surprise U.S. invasion.

What appears to have led Ashcroft and the U.S. government to drop its serious charges against Lindh, and to agree to a settlement on minor charges, was his defense attorneys' plans to go after testimony about his treatment from other Afghani captives being held at Guantanamo who had witnessed it.

Had those witnesses been permitted to testify in his case—as the judge had already said he would probably agree to, given Lindh's constitutional right to mount a vigorous defense—there would have been plenty of embarrassing evidence presented about torture and abuse at the hands of U.S. troops.

This sorry legal history raises a couple of very troubling questions.

First of all, the haste with which the government deep-sixed this case, after first trumpeting it as a highlight in the "war on terror," and the lengths to which the attorney general went to silence Lindh, suggest that the Bush administration well knew what was coming and was determined to keep its criminal treatment of POWs in Afghanistan a secret. Second, the closing off of evidence of torture, to which Lindh himself could have testified, along with any witnesses he might have called—witnesses who might well have included some of his torturers and their superior officers—allowed an official campaign of torture and abuse of POWs to continue and to expand into Iraq, ultimately leading to the Abu Ghraib scandal and the discrediting of the entire U.S. war effort. Last, but certainly not least, Lindh himself, terrified at being railroaded to a potential death sentence or a sentence to life in prison without parole, and already a victim of torture and abuse at the hands of his federal captors, remains almost certainly wrongfully imprisoned—just one more victim of America's criminal violation of the Geneva Conventions and our own constitutional right to a fair trial.

In a fair world, Judge T.S. Ellis, who accommodated the Justice Department by slapping Lindh with a brutally harsh sentence, and by gratuitously silencing him and forcing him to forswear any future claim of torture, would reopen this case in view of what is now known about how prisoners like Lindh were being treated by U.S. forces.

This is not, however, a fair world—or a fair legal system—and as more and more judges like Ellis are appointed to the federal bench, it is becoming even less fair as time goes by.

—CounterPunch.org, June 5, 2004

I suppose if all these assaults on our basic democratic freedoms and constitutional rights were making for a safer America and a safer world, many people would argue that it was a trade-off worth the sacrifice. No doubt that's why the administration has been trying to assure us that in fact they have made us safer, as they did with the much-heralded release in late spring of a State Department report purporting to show that both the incidence of and the number of victims of terrorism were significantly lower in 2003 than in prior years. It wasn't long before a couple of academics, puzzled by the data, discovered that it was actually wrong. It turns out the study had mysteriously omitted the month of December, when there had been several large and bloody terrorist attacks. It had also inexplicably excluded terror attacks against American troops in Iraq, and had arbitrarily eliminated a variety of other terror attacks from the count.

Eventually, the Secretary of State was forced to disavow the report and to order that it be redone, which resulted in a finding that in reality 2003 had been a record year for terrorism. But really, we didn't need those academic researchers, or Secretary of State Colin Powell, to know that the initial report was garbage and propaganda. All anyone had to do was check with the State Department's own internal analysis of the security situation, which is on high alert.

That Terrorism Report:
The Warnings the State Department
Sent Its Own People, But Not You

In mid-June of 2004, Secretary of State Colin Powell admitted that his department's boast that terrorist attacks against America were down in 2003 was a fraud (it only looked at part of the year and in fact attacks were at a record high). Powell claimed that the earlier assertion that terrorism was down had been a mistake.

Some mistake.

In fact, even as it was telling the media that terrorism was in decline, way back on April 29, Powell's State Department was quietly warning Americans abroad, through its consulates and embassies, that things were getting worse, not better.

While average citizens in the U.S. didn't see it, here's the message that the State Department was having its embassy personnel relay to Fulbright scholars and American government employees abroad more than a month earlier:

SUBJECT: PUBLIC ANNOUNCEMENT
WORLDWIDE CAUTION

This Public Announcement is being updated to remind U.S. citizens of the continuing threat of terrorist actions and anti-American violence against U.S. citizens and interests overseas. This supersedes the Worldwide Caution dated March 23, 2004 and expires on October 23, 2004.

The Department of State is deeply concerned about the *heightened threat* [author's emphasis] of terrorist attacks against U.S. citizens and interests abroad. The Department is also concerned about the potential for demonstrations and violent actions against U.S. citizens and interests overseas. U.S. citizens are reminded to maintain a high level of vigilance and to take appropriate steps to *increase* [author's emphasis] their security awareness.

The Department of State remains concerned by indications that al-Qaida continues to prepare to strike U.S. interests abroad. Al-Qaida and its associated organizations have most recently struck in the Middle East and in Europe but other geographic locations could also be venues for attacks. Future al-Qaida attacks could possibly involve non-conventional weapons such as chemical or biological agents as well as conventional weapons of terror. We also cannot rule out that al-Qaida will attempt a catastrophic attack within the U.S.

Terrorist actions may include, but are not limited to, suicide operations, hijackings, bombings or kidnappings. These may involve aviation and other transportation and maritime interests, and may also include conventional weapons, such as explosive devices. Terrorists do not distinguish between official and civilian targets. These may include facilities where U.S. citizens and other foreigners congregate or visit, including residential areas, clubs, restaurants, places of worship, schools, hotels and public areas. U.S. citizens are encouraged to maintain a high level of vigilance and to take appropriate steps to *increase* [author's emphasis] their security awareness.

U.S. Government facilities worldwide remain at a heightened state of alert. These facilities may temporarily close or suspend public services from time to time to assess their security posture. In those instances, U.S. embassies and consulates will make every effort to provide emergency services to U.S. citizens. Americans abroad are urged to monitor the local news and maintain contact with the nearest U.S. embassy or consulate.*

---

*This message was emailed to all Fulbright grantees who were posted overseas in June 2004 by American consular officials, on instructions from the State Department, which operates the program.

Next time the president or vice president—or our equally veracity-challenged secretary of state—claim that the War in Iraq has made America safer, Americans—and especially the credulous American journalists who continue to publish government announcements without first fumigating them—should go to the State Department's website (http://travel.state.gov/wwc1.html) and see what they're telling their consular offices and Americans abroad.

—*CounterPunch.org, June 26, 2004*

Chapter 5

The Inbedded Media

The role of the media in bringing the country to this point of crisis cannot be overstated. For all the shortcomings of the press in the era of yellow journalism, or through Watergate and the Indochina War, there simply is no comparison to today, when a handful of giant conglomerates controls virtually all the images and all the information that Americans get.

The idea that a corporation like Disney, which owns the ABC television network, or Sinclair, which owns many ABC local station affiliates, could be so politically connected to government that they would openly and with no sense of shame block films or broadcasts is simply mind-boggling. Recall that Disney quite publicly blocked the distribution of "Fahrenheit 9/11," Michael Moore's Palme d'Or award-winning documentary on the Bush presidency and his wars on Afghanistan, Iraq and terror, while Sinclair publicly ordered its network of stations not to broadcast a regularly scheduled program of "Nightline" because the corporate managers thought the planned reading of the names of the American dead in Iraq was too "anti-war." Shocking, but no more so than watching *The New York Times*, a paper of incomparable influence and power, allow one of its reporters, Judith Miller, to become a shill for the administration's war marketing campaign, and then, when it became clear that they'd been badly used, not sack her. (Granted, after the *Times* and Miller had channeled pro-war propaganda for the Bush/Cheney warmongers for over two years, the paper finally published a sort of apology in May 2004. But buried as it was on the inside of the paper, it was probably not widely read. Moreover, the article of contrition failed to name Miller and other reporters and editors who had been the propagandists and liars for the administration. Worse, it suggested that the problem had been that the paper—and the administration—had been misled, when in fact the problem was that the administration had been doing the misleading, and that the *Times* had been both gullible and a willing accomplice in a campaign to trick the public into war—a point made by the paper's own ombudsman, Daniel Okrent, in a later article criticizing the paper's war coverage.)

Even more incredible is the way the White House press corps has allowed itself, enmasse, to become nothing more than a prop for presidential photo-ops, with scripted pre-approved questions, no follow-ups, and with legitimate reporters with real questions shunted to the back of the room and left uncalled on.

The once scruffy and unruly media is now a class apart, coifed, manicured, dressed in designer clothes that, in the case of TV reporters at least, are selected by network image consultants—people in short with little care for or understanding of the lives of ordinary viewers. And everywhere, rampant careerism has replaced any notion of dedication to the craft or to the old-fashioned idea of getting information out so people can gain some understanding of and control over the world around them.

It is an environment ripe for manipulation, and the current administration, while displaying an almost bored indifference to the actual business of running a government, has shown an uncanny aptitude and passion for controlling the news.

The war is a case in point.

Instead of following earlier practice, as we saw in World War II, the Korean War or the Vietnam War, in which journalists were basically given free run of the front, subject only to concerns about their personal safety, the safety of those around them, and operational secrecy, in the current conflict, a new technique, initially developed during President Bush I's brief Persian Gulf War—embedding—was refined and used exclusively. All reporters covering this latest Bush war were required to be "embedded" in specific units, where they became one with the troops, and had little or no contact with or understanding of the larger picture. Embedding meant accepting local censorship, and more critically, putting the reporter firmly under the thumb of the local commander.

The result was great graphics and great TV ratings—the reporters and their camera crews were right at the front line of battles on the road to, and inside of Baghdad—but no detached analysis or understanding of the other side, and no messy, disturbing pictures of Americans dying or committing atrocities.

Reporters, American and foreign, who challenged these rules, found themselves being hustled out of the country, or even shot at. More than a few died or were killed under questionable circumstances.

The shocking thing is how few news organizations bothered to question the policy. Indeed, all too many editors and publishers hailed this absorption and co-option of their reporters as a great advance, to the point that during the drive to Baghdad we actually had anchors at the networks exclaiming over the drama of their reporters' live reports, most of which were nothing but PR films for the Pentagon. (Incidentally, I don't discount the role of money in all this. Sending reporters overseas is extremely costly, especially for television, and embedding them where they can get free transportation, food and lodging, and probably free access to communications facilities too, is an irresistible temptation for news managers who are being required by their corporate overseers to regularly produce 15 percent per year earnings growth.)

That this could have happened is shocking in itself, but in fact, the shabby and mindless coverage of the war in Iraq is really simply an extension of what has been happening to American journalism in general, where the concept of embedding reporters—that is, sucking them onto the set to serve as props instead of prods—has already become the norm, particularly in Washington, as this column, written on the eve of the war, explains.

The Failure of American Journalism: War, Protest and the Press

The abject failure of the American journalistic model—long worsening—has become depressingly apparent in the run-up to what appears to be almost certain war with Iraq.

Although there are clear, rational and compelling arguments being made against war both at home and abroad by professional soldiers, seasoned diplomats and millions of ordinary people, the American corporate media, both print and electronic, have become virtual parrots of the Administration line that war is necessary because Saddam Hussein is evil and a clear threat to America.

If the administration's warning that a terror strike was imminent and that Americans should all buy plastic sheeting and duct tape to enable them to protect their homes in the event of a gas or germ attack was akin to someone shouting "Fire!" in a crowded theater, the resulting panic stoked by the media's breathless and uncritical repeating of that self-serving nonsense was like a gang of ushers echoing the cry while goading theatergoers into a stampede for the exits.

Some critics of the media have blamed this on a conspiracy—a conscious desire on the part of the corporate media to support a pro-corporate government agenda. While there certainly is a commonality of interest, particularly as the major media have fallen into the hands of just a few giant corporate holding companies, there is something else at work too. Ordinarily jaded and cynical journalists and their editors seem of late to have entirely lost their grounding in reality. Constrained for years by a tradition that requires them to remain scrupulously "objective" and seemingly devoid of ideology, they have allowed themselves to be manipulated into the role of little more than purveyors of government press releases—and of the dominant ideology.

Standard American journalistic practice calls for reporters to recount faithfully what they are told by official sources, and then to go to the other side for comment. But where war is concerned, the other side is perceived as "the enemy," and is deemed not worthy of comment. Ordinarily, the other easy source of critical comment on government pronouncements and opinions would be the opposition party, but in this instance, with a war in the offing, the Democrats (not much in the way of opposition in any case), have become largely silent, afraid of being labeled unpatriotic. That has left the administration with a free hand to present its case for war in Iraq in the corporate media virtually without comment or criticism.

How different things are in the U.K., where newspapers are expected to have their own political viewpoints, and where journalists are permitted, even expected to have opinions. *The Mirror*, for example, was actually a sponsor of the giant Feb. 15 peace march in London. Imagine *The New York Times* as a sponsor of a political demonstration in New York!

Of course, the feigned disinterest and neutrality of the American media is a fraud. Publications like the *Washington Post* and the *Times* view themselves as part of the ruling Establishment, and rarely if ever challenge the policies of the government except in the margin. In this case, whether to go to war is not a question that is even on the table— only whether or not the U.S. should go it alone if it cannot gain UN support.

As the *Philadelphia Inquirer* put it in a page one news analysis the day after UN inspector Hans Blix undermined President Bush's and Secretary of State Colin Powell's plans to demand a Security Council war resolution by reporting that in fact the inspections were making good progress: "President Bush now faces an unpleasant choice. He must decide whether to launch a final round of diplomacy aimed at repairing the breach with many U.S. allies and thus winning broader backing for war, or to abandon the United Nations, ignore global opinion, and launch an invasion with whatever allies will follow."

There simply was no mention by the author of a third choice: not going to war at all.

In its initial coverage of the demonstrations the evening of Feb. 15, CNN actually focused not on the numbers (the AOL Time Warner network claimed, rather ludicrously and without any attribution, that there had been only 100,000 protesters in New York City), but on alleged violence, with a headline saying, "protesters get rowdy." In fact, despite the presence of an army of police and as many as half a million protesters, many of them angered that the city and the courts had conspired to prevent them from reaching the UN, arrests numbered only two dozen, mostly for the minor charge of "disorderly conduct." Actually, in reading the coverage of the dramatic worldwide protest against war the morning after, one could almost sense, as they wrote of the hundreds of thousands of marchers and demonstrators in New York, Philadelphia, San Francisco and the millions in Europe and elsewhere around the world, some reporters' chafing at the artificial yoke of "objectivity" under which they have labored for months. Finally they could safely and honestly quote some of the obvious arguments against the rush to war—the inevitable wave of terrorism that would follow, the terrible and unavoidable slaughter of innocents in Iraq, the unreality of the Bush Administration's blitzkrieg fantasy, and the lack of any pressing need to unseat Saddam Hussein, whose military machine has withered.

All these are arguments against war the media have known of for months, but as self-constrained as American journalism has become, they can only get into print if someone else besides a journalist says them. And under current practice, even for a reporter to go to some university and seek out an expert to articulate such anti-establishment points of view would be seen as evidence of media bias—or worse, liberal bias. Only when they have been spoken during a legitimate news event, such as a demonstration, can the reporter safely purvey such contrarian thoughts without risk of being labeled biased.

The public is ill served by this choke-collar tradition of so-called "objectivity," but it all works beautifully for those in power. If President Bush or one of his cabinet secretaries says something, it is considered legitimate news, and can be quoted without being challenged. Such statements, though clearly political or even clearly false or lies, are considered to be "facts." In the same way, a police estimate for the number of people at a demonstration, such as the Berlin police estimate of

500,000 protesters in the German capital, can go unchallenged in the *New York Times*, but in the case of an estimate of 400,000 demonstrators in New York, made by organizers, the reporter felt obliged add a caveat. "Crowd estimates are often little more than politically tinged guesses, and the police did not provide one," he warned, but then added, "given the sea of faces extending for more than a mile up First Avenue and the ancillary crowds that were prevented from joining them, the claim did not appear to be wildly improbable." (Actually, on page one, the *Times* article by Robert McFadden said, without giving a source, that there were 200,000 demonstrators in Berlin, only 40 percent of the number reported by Alan Cowell in his story on page 20 of the same edition.)

Like bloodied Christian penitents, the media repeatedly flagellate themselves, citing polls that say the public is losing respect for and confidence in the media. Inevitably, the response to these polls is for editors to yank even harder on the leashes constraining their reporters to the "objective" reporting of stories. Yet this is precisely why the American public has lost confidence in the mainstream corporate media.

As the line between entertainment and news has blurred, Americans, long adept at spotting snake-oil salesmen and deconstructing advertising, have realized that they are getting fed a line by the news media. Their response has been to tune it out, the same way they mute the sound during commercials.

Unfortunately, with so few mass media sources of information available, that response has left the public largely ignorant, and vulnerable to manipulation during times of crisis.

This crisis in American journalism makes alternative politics, like this week's global protests, and alternative media, crucial for the development of any serious opposition the government's plans for war, corporatism, and the assault on civil liberties and democracy.

At the same time, serious committed journalists in the U.S. need to begin a grassroots struggle in the media workplace to challenge the paradigm that has turned them from a Fourth Estate into little more than a slave hut on the Estate of the Establishment.

—CounterPunch.org, Feb. 18, 2003

As I noted earlier, there were those who defied the American government's official constraints on reporters in Iraq. Some American journalists and journalists from other countries took their chances and traveled around the country reporting on war the old-fashioned way. But this approach has meant taking enormous risks, for such brave war correspondents are targets not just of the Iraqi insurgents, but of the Americans, whom the evidence suggests basically have come to view any non-embedded journalists as the enemy.

Killing the Messengers
Deliberate or Accident: It Doesn't Really Matter

When it comes to the killing of three journalists by American troops in two separate incidents in Baghdad over the last 24 hours, there really are only two alternatives, neither one of them very pleasant to contemplate.

Either the U.S. is targeting journalists to punish those who are reporting honestly about the horrors of the war (the bombing of the *Al Jazeera* office) and to send a message to others not to get to close to the conflict (the tank blast at the Palestine Hotel, home base for most of the foreign press corps), or else these were simply the kinds of mindless, accidental yet inevitable atrocities that are going on all over Iraq, and especially Baghdad.

If the explanation is the former—that the U.S. is deliberately targeting journalists—we're talking about murder pure and simple, and someone should be made to pay for the crime. It wouldn't be the first time the Pentagon has targeted journalists or attempted to silence them through threats. Several mainstream American reporters trying to get to Grenada by small boat during the U.S. invasion of that little island (which had been barred to the press by the U.S. military), were threatened with being blown out of the water by a U.S. destroyer. They turned around and stayed clear. Certainly there was a motive in the current case: *Al-Jezeera* has clearly frustrated and angered the U.S. military and the White House. This broadcaster is able to deliver into any Arab or American living room that wants it—free of White House censorship—the scenes of death and destruction that the American media have been submissively censoring out.

But the press in wartime has to expect to antagonize the authorities if it's really doing its job, so while we may be upset at the thought of the U.S. deliberately targeting journalists, we shouldn't be too surprised.

In a way, the second explanation for these two recent attacks is far more awful to contemplate.

Consider. There are basically only a couple of clearly identified places in the Iraqi capital where journalists are known to congregate. One is the *Al Jazeera* office. The other would be the two hotels where journalists have been staying. These locations, like hospitals, are clearly well known to Pentagon war planners and to the pilots and soldiers on the ground who are tossing around high-explosive ordnance. And the official claim is that the Pentagon is trying to avoid injuring civilians.

If they really did hit these two clearly off-limits locations and kill three journalists "by accident" in just one day's fighting, just imagine how many innocents are being slaughtered "by accident" every day of this war in places whose locations don't even register on all those war maps?

We've been asked to believe that while a decade ago, only 10 percent of the allegedly "smart" bombs hit their designated targets, this time around the bombs are "smarter." Are they twice as smart? That would mean they're missing only 80 percent of the time. Three times as smart? That would still leave a 70 percent error rate. Does anybody really believe they're 10 times as smart as a decade ago?

It is significant that when a U.S. pilot accidentally bombed a convoy of Kurdish troops and American Special Forces personnel, reporters were quick to report on the incredible carnage caused by the single bomb—and not a particularly large one at that. Try to find a similar account in the American media of the carnage caused by one of those bombs that fell where it was supposed to fall. I've tried, and haven't been able to find one. Obviously these "precision" weapons don't just cause "collateral damage" when they miss. They make a big circle of destruction around whatever target they hit, too, which virtually guarantees a lot of "collateral damage."

If the American media get off their knees now and start honestly reporting about what is happening at the receiving end of all these bombs and shells, the deaths of these three journalists will at least have served a valuable journalistic function. Americans might finally start to understand what this war is doing to the Iraqi people and the fabric of Iraq.

They might also understand why, after the U.S. occupation of a conquered Iraq begins in earnest, there will be so much resentment and, no doubt, armed resistance.

—*CounterPunch.org, April 8, 2003*

The job of a White House flak has always been to protect the president and to deflect criticism, but with the current administration, which features a president who is demonstrably ignorant and a remarkably poor speaker, the role of the flak has taken on mythic proportions. Add to this that we're talking about a White House administration that took office through fraud and deceit, and that has governed since then through a campaign of lies and deception, and you have a media relations job that has to be like managing one endless Exxon Valdez oil spill. White house flak Ari Fleischer, who came to his job appropriately from the ad industry, not from journalism, handled that task admirably, but eventually, it appears to have become too much for even him.

Ari "the Fabulist" Fleischer Quits the Scene
The Liar's Gone, the Enablers Remain

White House flack and fabulist Ari Fleischer quits his post and says he is leaving because he wants to be with family, because he's been in government service too long and wants to go into the private sector, da-da, da-da—all the usual things people in government positions of power say when they abandon ship. Is there more to this though? We're talking about the public face of the super-secretive Mini-Bush White House. There are no places Fleisher could move to where he'd get the power, influence and public recognition he has obtained over the last two years. So could this be a case of the first rat leaving a doomed ship?

That might sound ridiculous looking at Bush's poll numbers, but maybe Ari knows stuff we don't know. After all, the U.S. economy is pretty close to a sinking ship—the dollar's going relentlessly south, which will eventually mean rising interest rates and a dead economy, or soaring inflation and a return to the era of stagflation, unemployment is edging upward, states are going bust, and now there's talk of the property bubble bursting, which will upset the middle class no end.

Meanwhile, Al Qaeda is successfully sticking a giant thumb into the eye of Bush's anti-terror campaign, reminding everyone why invading Iraq was a pretty stupid idea.

Oh yeah, and Iraq is starting to look more and more like the quagmire that everyone except Bush's circle of Iraqi exile friends and his aggressively ignorant advisers, Rumsfeld, Wolfowitz and Cheney, predicted it would be.

The pundits of the increasingly state-organ-style corporate media have already called the 2004 election for Bush, but this is nonsense. Even if the Republicans manage to subvert some close votes in states where they have the courts in their pockets, it's quite possible that if Democrats manage to put forward a candidate with a modicum of spine and intelligence, who will highlight the domestic and international catastrophes that this unelected, willfully ignorant alcoholic Texas yahoo has wrought, Bush and his gang could end up being swept from power in a wave of voter anger not seen in years. Fleischer, while not a central figure in the new Imperial White House, is a courtesan who is necessarily privy to the thinking of its key players, and may have been hearing worried talk that has led him to decide he should git while the gittin's good.

Fleischer has been a brazen liar for the Bush Administration—so much so that he has been a source of genuine entertainment for what passes for a White House press corps. But he can't have enjoyed the thought that the lies would have to grow in audacity and shamelessness as the economy and foreign policy come crashing down.

A second thought: That wonderful kiss on the head Ari had bestowed by Bush when he said he was leaving. You have to love the imagery there. There's something marvelously feudalistic about it: the monarch bestowing a token of his affection on the obsequious servant who has repeatedly defiled himself defending the honor of his sovereign. Somehow, one can't picture the Imperial Bush, with his new imperial pretensions, hugging or shaking hands with a second tier aide like Fleischer in such a moment.

Finally, there's the matter of that White House Press Corps. Some have speculated as to why Fleischer never resigned earlier. I don't see why that is a puzzle. The man has demonstrated over the years that he has no principles. Like a flack for Exxon/Mobil or Grace Industries, he obviously sees the job of media relations as one big con job, so why would he suddenly feel the need to resign? No, the real question is why no one in the White House Press Corps has had the sense of principle and the courage to say that they would no longer participate in the charade that is being passed off as journalism. They all know that they've been lied to repeatedly, but they are the willing conduits of those lies to the American public. Night after night, one can watch them carrying Fleischer's water, not cracking a smile as they gravely report the latest politically timed raising of the terror alert level, not bursting out laughing as they report on the president's claim that Al Qaeda is no longer a problem.

These people—who call themselves journalists—actually allowed themselves to be scripted into a fake White House press conference, where the president pretended to be selecting reporters to ask questions when they had actually submitted them in advance and he had picked the ones he would answer, and where those few reporters who objected, like Helen Thomas, were unceremoniously dumped in the rear of the pool among the potted palms (with no protest from her shameless "colleagues").

Fleischer will certainly not be missed. He managed to drag the role of Presidential spokesperson further into the slime than it had been since Ron Ziegler's days during the Nixon Administration. The sad thing is that even with the liar Fleischer gone, we're stuck with the same pathetic enablers in the White House Press Corps.

Fleischer's replacement will have no trouble picking up the job of media manipulation from his predecessor. He or she will have able assistance from the people asking the questions.

—*CounterPunch.org, May 22, 2003*

Bad enough that we have paid professional dissemblers on the government payroll to do the same thing that PR organizations do for corporate America: provide a narrative of falsehoods just credible enough that reporters won't have to challenge it, so that the image of competence, concern and integrity can be peddled to the public uncritically. But we also have a mass media that willfully participates in these deceptions. This willingness to play the game, to cover up for the crimes and failures of the government, is even in evidence at the country's top media establishments. Take a look at *The New York Times*, surely the most influential single media establishment in America, if not the world. Having bought into the administration's fraudulent claims that Iraq had weapons of mass destruction (or even, courtesy of its reporter Judith Miller, having deliberately pushed that fraud itself), the self-styled paper of record, instead of exposing the shams and the lies, has tried to explain them away, not only for itself, but also for the president.

WMD Damage Control at *The New York Times*:
Many Presidents Have Lied, But This Time the
Press Went Along for the Ride

As evidence mounts of the Bush administration's gross prevarications regarding evidence of so-called "weapons of mass destruction" in Iraq, and of a never-demonstrated link between Hussein and Al Qaeda, the *New York Times* has taken the lead in the media at damage control.

Instead of trying to deny the lying, which would be a hopeless venture, the *Times* in the lead story of this past Sunday's "Week in Review" section written by David E. Rosenbaum, went with the argument that Bush "exaggerated" and that in any event, many presidents have lied.

Rosenbaum selectively examines some Bush whoppers—his claim on Oct. 7, 2002 that Iraq had "a massive stockpile of biological weapons" and "thousands of tons of chemical agents," and that it was "reconstituting its nuclear weapons program," and his claim on March 17 that "Intelligence gathered by this and other governments leaves no doubt that the Iraq regime continues to possess and conceal some of the most lethal weapons ever devised." Rosenbaum concludes that the president may have "believed what he was saying," and adds for effect that that most reliable of sources, Sen. Hillary Rodham Clinton, says the intelligence briefings she received a week ago "justified Mr. Bush's statements." (He didn't mention that Sen. Clinton has good reason to say this, having voted for giving Bush the authority to go to war last fall.)

For good measure, Rosenbaum also cites Bush's claim, made in his last State of the Union address and on later occasions, that his latest tax cut would benefit "everyone who pays income taxes." Here, Rosenbaum concedes that the claim is factually incorrect—some 8.1 million taxpayers will get no break in the tax cut as designed by the administration and passed by Congress in May. But Rosenbaum goes on to say that since 90 percent of taxpayers will get at least some minimal tax break, the president would have been correct had he said "almost all" people who pay taxes would get a cut.

But Rosenbaum only scratches the surface of Bush's and his subordinates' lies. He doesn't mention that the president, his defense secretary, and his secretary of state lied blatantly in citing evidence of Iraqi purchases of uranium from Niger—evidence that the government knew to have been a gross forgery. He doesn't mention Bush's false claim that an economic study showed that his tax cut would produce a 3 percent growth rate in the U.S. economy, when in fact no such study exists. He didn't mention the lie put forward by the Bush administration that the reason the president had vanished on 9/11 was because of a terrorist threat to Air Force One—a total fabrication. Nor did he mention literally dozens of other documented lies.

It's true that there are lies, and there are evasions and distortions.

The effort to white-wash the latest Environmental Protection Agency report on the environment by censoring comments about global warming was not a lie. It was a distortion and evasion. Likewise many of the administration's claims about Iraq—for example the many claims that the Pentagon and the White House had planned ahead for the post-war situation in Iraq.

It is also true that other presidents have lied, and lied grotesquely.

But in the end, the real point is not whether what the Bush administration has done is a lie, or whether Bush and his cronies have been slick enough to toss in weasel words that can allow them to later claim that what they said was "just an exaggeration."

Thousands of people have died and continue to die because of these distortions, in the case of the war in Iraq. Millions will end up losing vital services because of the lies about the tax cut. This administration's lies about health policy, education policy, about environmental policy, about labor policy, about its judicial appointments, about communications regulatory policy, business regulatory policy, etc., etc., will have profound negative consequences on the lives of tens of millions of real people.

None, or little, of this, has been or will be subject to any real democratic debate.

But don't blame the White House, though. If is, after all, true that there is nothing new, except perhaps in terms of quantity and audacity, about the Bush administration's lies.

What's new is the acquiescence of the media in the lies and distortions by government.

Granted that the American media have never been the noble Fourth Estate of popular mythology, but there was always, in the past, at least a kind of "gotcha" mentality. Even if they shied away from challenging the underpinnings of empire, reporters and editors—and readers—thrived on the excitement of catching politicians in a lie. Now, there seems to be little stomach for, or even interest in doing this kind of thing at the big media conglomerates. Instead, we have the *Times*—

the self-styled national "newspaper of record"— offering an appalling apologia for Bush Administration deception and lying, an apologia made all the more grotesque because the *Times* sets a tone that is widely followed, lemming like, by smaller newspapers across the nation. (The *Philadelphia Inquirer*, in my community, ran an almost identical analysis in its "Sunday Review" section the same day as Rosenbaum's "Week in Review" piece, headlined "Truth is, presidents have often bent facts." At least the *Inquirer* mentioned the citing of forged evidence with regard to the Niger uranium purchase, and a few other blatant lies.)

What's also new is the timidity of the political opposition. Not only are few Democrats openly challenging this administration's lies and distortions; those that do, like Democratic Presidential candidate Dennis Kucinich, are then dismissed by the media as inconsequential "dark horses". Even Vermont Governor Howard Dean, by any standard a leading contender at this point for the Democratic nomination, and a Democrat who has accused the president of lying about the war, is now being savaged by the media, most recently by "Meet the Press," which sandbagged him with questions about inconsequential minutia (such as the number of U.S. troops in Iraq or Afghanistan), questions which the current famously ill-informed and inattentive president would never be able to answer.

The best hope for American democracy is that the public will not be satisfied with the ongoing cover-up of Bush administration lying and distortion.

That may seem a vain hope, but I'm not so sure. As long as the president remains the subject of ridicule on the comedy circuit, it suggests the public is onto what's really going down.

—*CounterPunch.org, June 24, 2003*

For several years, the media situation in the U.S. has been pretty grim, with the Bush administration getting a largely free ride in both its rapine domestic policies and its war-mongering foreign policy. Fortunately, however, the same "pack" policy that makes it so difficult for any major corporate media player to take a stand outside of the mainstream, means that once a serious question does finally get asked, and it gets picked up by a few of those players, the rest feel that they all have to pile on. It appears that by the middle of the summer of 2003, some four months into the American war against Iraq, the continued and growing resistance on the ground, and the sheer ineptness of the occupation authorities, had begun to produce just such a phenomenon. With the American public finally growing dubious about the whole Iraq adventure, suddenly, in a startling turn of events, we started seeing something we had almost forgotten existed—critical questioning by American reporters of official policy.

The Importance of Tipping: Is the Media Finally Turning on Bush?

Tipping.

That's the new watchword.

When does the situation facing American troops in Iraq deteriorate to the point that public sentiment "tips" against further U.S. involvement and against the Bush administration's policy of occupation and "nation building"?

Clearly the signs, for American GI's and for George Bush's reelection hopes, are getting grimmer.

Already 70 American soldiers have died in Iraq since virtual flyboy Bush prematurely declared the war to be "over" in a staged victory rally aboard an aircraft carrier off San Diego harbor.

A search for the terms "guerrilla war" and "Iraq" turns up hundreds of citations, most dating from about the middle of June onward. Some, like an article on June 18 in the *Detroit Free Press*, simply use the term "guerrilla war" in news reports as an unremarkable and most apt characterization of the current military situation in Iraq. Others, like an article on June 23 in the *Christian Science Monitor*, use the term in editorials warning that the situation threatens to become a "quagmire," (another Vietnam-era term that's returning to currency). Still others use the term in articles warning that the current crisis is heading towards a Vietnam-like situation.

Any way you look at it, there is a growing fear among the public and acceptance in the media that the U.S. is not in control of events in Iraq, is not being viewed as a liberator by Iraqi people, and is facing mounting military threats.

The mounting alarm at this shift in coverage seems to be greater at the Pentagon and the White House than concerns about the actual attacks on American troops themselves, though if those attacks continue to increase in frequency and severity, that could change. For now, though, the Bush administration's panic at the spreading popularity of the term "guerrilla war" in the formerly worshipful national media is understandable.

If the American media continue to increasingly portray Iraq as a dangerous hell-hole for American soldiers, and continue to play up the American body count each day, the American public will quickly start to view this Bush military adventure the way they came to view President Johnson's military adventure in Indochina—as a disaster.

This shift in public attitude in Johnson's case took several years to develop. But Johnson had several advantages not available to Bush. First of all, he began as a hugely popular president, having won election in a landslide. Second, most Americans believed that America had been attacked in Vietnam. Few knew or believed until years later that the alleged attack on an American destroyer in the Gulf of Tonkin was a sham. Johnson also had the advantage that he was sending American soldiers into a war that he hadn't started (the Indochina conflict, for America, dated back to the late 1950s, when the Eisenhower administration took over the battle against Ho Chi Minh's anti-colonial revolutionaries from France). In Bush's case, on the other hand, the blame for any military disaster in Iraq belongs unambiguously with him and his advisers. This was a war quite publicly started by Bush, and it is widely understood already that he started it based upon lies made to the American public. It is his war to lose.

Why the sudden shift in the U.S. media, from unabashed war boosterism to increasing skepticism?

The answer is simple: the continued killing of American troops.

For the first time since at least 9/11, the dynamic of the corporate media business is working against Bush's interests. Top management at the media conglomerates may still have a strong political affinity for the Bush administration, with its anti-regulation ideology and its general pro-business, pro-rich policies, but dead soldiers make great news, and the news business lives and dies on ratings and circulation.

Viewers and readers eat up stories about innocent, fresh-faced young soldiers getting killed in the line of duty, particularly by nefarious guerrillas who shoot and run instead of standing and fighting so they can be "lit up" for their crimes. We are hooked on these stories because they get us angry—first of course at those who are doing the killing, but before too long, also at those in power who are putting our "boys" in harm's way.

Add to that the growing awareness that the reasons for sending American troops into Iraq were bogus in the first place, and you quickly shift to a broad opposition to administration policy.

All this could happen—indeed is happening—very rapidly. First the public has to begin questioning the war. Then the media must tip from support for the war to opposition. That appears to be happening already. Then as the tone of coverage shifts, the public will tip further, from skepticism about the war and the Bush administration, to public sentiment in favor of bringing the troops home and for punishing Bush for sending them there in the first place.

Already, Iraq is at a point like Vietnam in the late 1960s, where the government realizes that it can't just declare victory and leave, because it's clear that when U.S. troops leave, a new regime will take power that will be strongly anti-American. The more American troops get slain in Iraq, the less forgiving Americans would be if the U.S. pulled out only to see those lives wasted.

That's where the term "quagmire" comes in. Clearly the U.S. could have quit Vietnam any time, but to do so the administration in power, whether Eisenhower, Kennedy, Johnson or Nixon, would have had to admit to defeat—as Nixon ultimately had to do on August 29, 1975 when Vietnamese troops stormed Saigon and the U.S. Embassy. The same is now increasingly true with Iraq. The longer U.S. forces remain in Iraq, the more American soldiers die at the hands of Iraqi fighters, the harder it will be for Bush and his advisers to call it quits.

Hence the talk of sending more troops to Iraq, in hopes of quelling the insurrection.

A president running for election during a popular war, or a war for the nation's survival, can be hard to beat.

A president running for election during an unpopular war, and a war that the American public doesn't even see as having anything to do with the nation's security, is another thing entirely.

This could turn out to be a very interesting presidential election campaign.

—*CounterPunch.org, July 9, 2003*

The media coverage of the war and of the Bush administration's foibles and misdeeds may have begun to shift over the course of 2003 as the war turned sour, but there is always a problem getting honest coverage of a war, when reporters and editors either unthinkingly or deliberately identify with "our" side. This inability to apply the basic standard of fairness in reporting a story out of Iraq became apparent at the *New*

York *Times* on October 20, 2003, when the paper ran a piece about an incident the day before near Fallujah—a city which would increasingly find itself in the news in later months precisely because of such clashes.

War Dispatch from the NYT: God's On Our Side

It seemed a small miracle that no one was killed or even wounded here," wrote reporter Ian Fisher in a Monday report in *The New York Times* on Sunday's stunning attack by Iraqi guerrillas on a U.S. military convoy in Fallujah, a city west of Baghdad in the part of Iraq American forces call the Sunni Triangle.

Miracle indeed, except that people *were* killed and wounded there. They just weren't Americans.

As a matter of fact the attack on the convoy, which blew up an American truck carrying highly explosive Hellfire anti-tank missiles, resulted in the death of one Iraqi—by some accounts an innocent bystander—and also led to the wounding of several others, probably innocent bystanders too, when American troops at the scene retreated in panic, firing wildly in a 360-degree sweep as they departed the scene.

Fisher conceded in the 19th paragraph of his story that there were "reports, unconfirmed, that at least one Iraqi had been killed in the exchange of fire that erupted after American soldiers returned several hours later," following the initial attack. He made no mention of people being wounded.

According a British newspaper, the *Independent*, six Iraqis were wounded and sent to local hospitals, where one died.

But then, the *Times* is apparently talking about American miracles, not general, all-purpose miracles.

At the *Times*, it seems, it's really our God against their god, and if God is on our side, He only does miracles that affect our side.

A miracle, at least at the *Times*, is when our guys blow away Iraqis—it doesn't matter that much apparently whether they're guerrillas or just ordinary people—and don't get hurt or killed themselves.

This is sports journalism, not international war reporting.

With sports reporting, you expect the local press to hype the home team, to cheer when our side makes a goal or a TD, and to groan and complain when the other side wins. In sports, God is on our side.

But war reporting is supposed to be different.

The trouble is, if readers incautiously read reports written in the style of the *Times*, they'll end up being perplexed by the growing resistance to American troops and to the occupation among Shia people. They'll end up wondering why all those men were dancing and celebrating after the attack on the convoy.

Fisher, in his article, went on to say that the security situation in Iraq is deteriorating, with Shiites as well as Sunni Iraqis joining the remnant Baathists in the guerrilla attacks on Americans.

How to explain this.

Well, one way is to look what God's soldiers are doing as an occupying force.

Attacked, they fire wildly, killing anything that moves. They're not just getting crazy; this is what they are being instructed to do by the generals in charge of the occupation.

They enter mosques and try to disarm local militias.

According to an Associated Press report (which the NY Times ran in abbreviated form the following day, along with an excellent piece by Raymond Bonner on how the war and occupation is proceeding along the Iraq-Syrian border), they may even be executing suspected enemies. Following the Fallujah convoy attack, AP reports that a second American unit returned to the city, where it was attacked also, leading to the death of one soldier. The U.S. unit responded in standard fashion: "Paratroopers raked the area with return fire, then raided a mosque and houses looking for the attackers," AP reports.

Subsequently, the AP reporter Tarek Al-Issawi, who visited a local hospital, writes, "The bodies of the two civilians killed in the Monday attack (an Iraqi and a Syrian truck driver) were taken to Fallujah General Hospital. The Associated Press saw that one of them, Iraqi Nazem Baji, had a gunshot wound in the back of his head and his hands were tied in front of him with plastic bands similar to those used by the U.S. military when they arrest suspects."

It's good bet that this incident won't be viewed locally as a miracle, or even as an act of a vengeful god. It will no doubt be laid to a repressive and increasingly offensive army of occupation.

At least the Times and other American media should attempt to tally all the dead in these incidents, and with civilians dying right and left with almost every attack on Americans, refrain from calling actions in which no Americans die successes or "miracles."

Maybe then we'd all have a better understanding of what's going on in Iraq, and why there's always so much dancing in the street after an attack on our guys.

—*CounterPunch.org, Oct. 21, 2003*

Much that is wrong with the American media can be attributed to the corporate concentration of the industry and the incessant demand for cost cutting at news operations and for ever higher returns. But the journalists who work for these craven outfits must themselves shoulder some of the blame, too. Once a leading player in the movement to organize of the American workforce, and especially in the unionization drive among white-collar workers, all too many journalists in the establishment media have become self-centered careerists, shunning all notions of solidarity and principle in the interest of self-advancement. Their lack of professional solidarity becomes even more pronounced when it comes to an international setting. This was painfully evident when a couple of foreign (Arab) journalists were slaughtered by American troops in Iraq and the international press corps tried to mount a protest.

The Spinelessness of US Journalism: No Solidarity Among the Scribes

There was a moment that spoke volumes last week about the spinelessness of American journalism and its foot soldiers.

It happened as U.S. Secretary of State Colin Powell was beginning a press conference in Baghdad during his brief visit to Iraq.

As he started to speak, all of the Iraqi and other Arab journalists in the hall got up and walked out, along with many reporters and camera crews from European and other countries.

About the only journalists remaining in their seats when the protest ended were the Americans, who on television could be seen shuffling in embarrassment in their seats.

The cause of the protest was the killing, only a few hours before, of two Dubai journalists from *Al Arabiya* by U.S. troops, who "took out" their car as they were driving past a military checkpoint.

As always, the U.S. military command has pronounced the killings to be unfortunate but justified, given occupation soldiers' concerns about attacks by insurgents. Powell, for his part, expressed regret about the incident.

Regrettable indeed, but the truth is that some 26 journalists have been killed in the course of covering this war, including a number who were directly and deliberately targeted by U.S. guns and bombs. That's nearly one journalist for every 10 U.S soldiers killed by hostile fire. If you consider that there are over 100,000 American soldiers in Iraq, and at most only a few hundred journalists, it's clearly a hell of a lot safer being a grunt and a target of Iraqi insurgents than being journalist and a target of American, and Iraqi insurgent, forces. (It's also a hell of a lot more dangerous being a journalist in Iraq than it was to be a journalist in World War II, judging by the statistics.)

You'd think that American journalists would be as outraged as anyone at the killing of one of their own, but it seems not to work that way. For one thing, it's not that many American journalists who've been killed by hostile action on the part of American troops. Mostly it's been foreign reporters.

So in bed are most of the American press corps in Iraq that many of them seem to perceive themselves as part of the team (in many cases, as with *The New York Times'* Judith Miller and the American bomb squad, or Fox TV during the rush to Baghdad, they *have* been part of the team).

Still, it's appalling to see the lack of professional solidarity that was exhibited at that Powell press conference.

This walkout was, after all, not a political statement. It was not about whether the war was justified, or whether the occupation is good or bad. It was a simple act of professional solidarity in protest against rules of engagement that allow American troops to slaughter accredited journalists at will and escape the consequences of their actions. Surely no one—including their editors and publishers, or their readers or viewers—could fault reporters for protesting such rules and the deaths of colleagues that have resulted from them.

But the American reporters stayed glued to their seats, politely letting our veracity-challenged Secretary of State drone on.

It was a shameful display.

Not surprisingly, a few days later, the U.S. Army issued a report exonerating a U.S. Army tank gunner in the killing of a Palestinian cameraman for Reuters, who was shot as he was filming the tank last August 17. The Army, which has never revealed its so-called "rules of engagement," claimed the shooter had thought the man, Mazen Dana, had been aiming a rocket-propelled grenade at the tank. (Forget that RPGs have posed little or no threat to U.S. M-1 tanks, and thus the tank gunner need not have acted in haste, or that Dana was in an area known to be crawling with journalists.)

No doubt, Dana and the two *Al Arabiya* journalists will not be the last of their profession to die in Iraq, or Afghanistan, or Haiti, or elsewhere at the hands of American soldiers.

The least one could hope is that at some point, American journalists would stand with their foreign colleagues and insist on better protection.

—*CounterPunch.org, March 27, 2004*

The cultural imperialism that has infected the Bush administration's entire approach to Iraq from the beginning has its reflection in the American media. This inability to see things clearly because of cultural blinders was clearly in evidence as the confrontation in Fallujah began to build. American reporters who can accept without flinching the mowing down of Iraqi civilians by helicopter and fixed-wing gunships, who can walk disinterestedly past the bodies of clearly executed guerrilla wounded after American troop engagements, simply can't stomach the same kind of treatment when it was meted out to Americans. Yet in retrospect, this kind of moral relativism and wearing of cultural blinders is a disservice not just to the profession, but to the nation, for it has allowed us to let this government walk our nation and our soldiers down a blind alley of hatred, from which retreat will be the only ultimate escape.

The Press and Fallujah: Barbaric Relativism

"Barbarism"—Reuters
"Grisly Deaths"—*The New York Times*
"Grisly assault"—Associated Press
" Savage behavior"—*Washington Post*

Nobody wants to see the kind of ugly spectacle that occurred earlier this week in Fallujah, Iraq, where four U.S. mercenaries were killed and then had their bodies burned, hacked up, dragged through the streets and ultimately hung trophy-like from a bridge over the Euphrates River.

That said, the way this event was covered by the Western press shows a marked tendency to view the war through politically, culturally and journalistically biased eyes.

It may well be appropriate to call the mutilation of corpses barbaric, grisly and savage, or even, as the White House said, "despicable," but then, one has to recall that American troops have long done the same kind of thing. Remember those photos of severed ears and noses hanging from GIs' belts during the Vietnam War, and the bodies of suspected Viet Cong partisans being dragged behind personnel carriers?

More to the point, what is one to call the U.S. occupation force's rules of engagement, which call for American forces to fire off everything they've got in all directions when they come under attack, even if they are in the middle of a residential block?

In fact, it was only a few days before the killing of the four employees of the North Carolina-based mercenary contracting firm Blackwater Security Consulting, that U.S. troops in Fallujah had, in the bland words of a *New York Times* report, "battled insurgents killing a number of civilians."

Civilian deaths in Iraq, including innocent women and children, are the dirty secret of this terrible war and occupation. They number in the tens of thousands by most accounts, though the American occupation authority has blocked Iraqi medical officials from tallying the number, for obvious reasons.

Do we call this random deadly use of force in highly populated areas barbaric, grisly or savage?

No. In fact, the military calls it "justified," on those rare occasions when it actually investigates the killing of innocents. And by and large, that's how the U.S media handles it.

To date, no American soldier has been prosecuted for a war crime in Iraq, or for an improper use of deadly force—though one soldier was disciplined for abusing a prisoner of war.*

Actually, another *New York Times* article that ran the same day as the report on the mutilation of the American mercenaries' bodies gave a hint of about the barbaric nature of the U.S. occupation. Referring to the killing a few days earlier of two Arab journalists, it reported that the U.S. military had "accepted responsibility" for the deaths. The journalists, the military said, had had the misfortune of driving directly behind a vehicle that "appeared" to be running a military checkpoint. As a result they were hit as well when the threatening vehicle was fired on. The Pentagon report added, by way of justification of the deaths, that the journalists were driving in a "beaten zone."

What's a "beaten zone"? An area which is allowed to be saturated with heavy weapons fire.

---

* With the shocking exposure of the systematic torture of Iraqi prisoners of war and other detainees in American custody in Baghdad's notorious Abu Ghraib prison, there have finally begun to be some prosecutions, but these have so far been limited to lower levels in the chain of command, and appear to be aimed at limiting the damage, not at ending the abuse and the violations of International Law.

Barbaric? Grisly? Savage behavior? Despicable? You bet. But nobody in the U.S. media calls it that. Only when the killing and abuse is done at the hands of Iraqi insurgents (actually the White House consistently and improperly calls them terrorists, not insurgents) do such words apply.

And what about the four unfortunate mercenaries? What exactly were they doing in Fallujah, a hotbed of insurrection?

The *Washington Post* quoted government sources as saying the men were contracted by the occupation authority to guard "food convoys" coming into Fallujah.

In fact, these men are part of a private army of thousands of highly paid mercenaries—most of them former U.S. soldiers, though also including many veterans of the South African white military, the Chilean army, and other military units known for their barbarism and savage behavior.

While these people are euphemistically called "private security agents," they are not really anything like the rent-a-cops you find strolling the aisles at your local Kmart. They are a private army, exempt from the rules of war and from government oversight, employed by the U.S. to boost troop strength in Iraq at a time that it is politically impossible for the Bush Administration to do so overtly—and to do things that it would be illegal for uniformed troops to do, such as executions and torture.

The White House may call the killing of the four men a "senseless loss of life," but for the insurgents battling the U.S. occupation, while the deaths may have been brutal, they were hardly senseless. It was, for them, an act of war.

We can expect the government to try to beat the patriotic drum, trying to pump up a jingoistic fervor among the public, but the media should not be joining in this cheap propaganda campaign.

The American public deserves better from its news purveyors.

If journalists are going to call some of the dreadful things that are happening in Iraq barbaric, grisly or savage, they had better start being honest about it, and applying those terms to all the acts that merit such adjectives—no matter who commits them.

—*CounterPunch.org, April 2, 2004*

The failure of the American media to act as a skeptical outsider to the Iraq War and occupation has had a high cost in blood and money. The Bush administration has been uniquely closed, intellectually rigid and willfully ignorant about its own policies and about the environment in which its politics are being implemented, which has led to one disaster after another—the war itself being probably the biggest single disaster the country has been deliberately led into in history. Had the media been even minimally critical during the early stages of this policy, perhaps the whole thing might have been avoided. But even if the war itself was a foregone conclusion, dead set as Bush and his mentor Vice President Dick Cheney were about starting it, an aggressive, inquisitive and critical press could have prevented at least some of the worst blunders that have made the disaster worse. Instead, it was cheerleading all the way—cheering for the cashiering of the entire Baath-linked military and civil service, cheering for the reopening, under U.S. authority, of the hated Abu Ghraib torture center, cheering for the use of American bombers against urban centers like Fallujah and Najaf—until it has become too late.

Imagination Deficit Disorder: Finally, Bush Unites…the Resistance

Back in the mid 18th Century, the East Coast of North America was a pretty rough-and-tumble place. The British, our colonial motherland, had outlawed slavery, but here in the colonies, the inhuman practice thrived everywhere. Similarly, while Britain had developed what was, warts and all, probably the fairest sort of legal system for its day anywhere in the civilized world, things were a lot more vicious and unpredictable in the wilds of North America, where, especially outside of the larger urban centers, justice was a pretty brutal affair in which local prejudice, and might, made right.

No doubt many in England viewed their military actions in the Colonies in messianic terms as bringing the benefits of British civilization to the Americas (it's always been, and remains, a common conceit among colonial and imperial powers). If that meant burning down recalcitrant villages, massacring militias and arresting, imprisoning and hanging hundreds of revolutionaries, so be it. As time went by, the British Crown and the Parliament must have begun hearing concerns expressed by the Redcoat senior command that loyalist troops and the civilian population in the 13 colonies were not measuring up as junior partners in this civilizing endeavor—that local soldiers were inexplicably unwilling to fire on their compatriots in battle, or that they were deserting, God forbid, to the other side, and that the broader public seemed increasingly to view the Crown's troops as the enemy.

Funny thing. Now our army in Iraq is experiencing the same sort of thing, and the top brass here too are acting astonished. In an AP story on Wednesday, Maj. General Martin Dempsey said that during recent hostilities, 40 percent of the new Iraqi "security force" trained by the U.S. to share the burden of battle during the occupation had walked off the job rather than fight, and that one in 10 of the members of that force had "actually worked against" the so-called Coalition of the Willing. That's a 50 percent failure rate.

Martin, who obviously suffers from imagination deficit disorder, expressed surprise and dismay at this record on the part of the newly outfitted Iraqi forces and said, "We have to take a look at the Iraqi security forces and learn why they walked." He went on to say that there seemed to be a puzzling reluctance by Iraqis to take up arms against their countrymen and added, "It's very difficult at times to convince them that Iraqis are killing fellow Iraqis and fellow Muslims, because it's something they shouldn't have to accept," though "over time I think they will probably have to accept it."

Dempsey completely misses the point that what many in the new security forces are no doubt upset about is precisely that it is Americans who are killing Iraqis and Muslims, and that to the extent that Iraqis are killing Iraqis, it's a mess which America has created—all of which no doubt explains why they don't want to join in the carnage, even for a paycheck. Besides, while there certainly are Iraqis killing Iraqis in today's "liberated" Iraq as the general says, I don't think even he would suggest that the number of Iraqis killed by the insurgents even begins to approach the number of civilians killed by US forces over the past year.

The AP story said that the "failure" of Iraqi security forces to "perform" could hurt the United States' "exit strategy" from Iraq, which it says is dependent upon handing "authority" over to the Iraqis.

There are a lot of big assumptions in this one sentence, however, none of which holds up very well on closer inspection.

First of all, is it appropriate to term it a "failure" if Iraqis don't simply follow foreign orders to join in massive American assaults on Iraqi cities like Najaf and Fallujah? Or might that more properly be called the success of Iraqi nationalism? Should Iraqi forces, which are supposedly protecting Iraq, be expected to "perform" for American commanders? And just what is this "exit strategy" referred to here? To the best of my knowledge, the Bush administration has yet to articulate any exit strategy. Oh sure, they've talked about a "handover of sovereignty" or "authority" on June 30, but in the same breath, they always add that the U.S. will continue to maintain over 135,000 troops in Iraq—making it clear that this is something that will not be up to the new as-yet-to-be-named Iraqi government. Some exit. And besides, with all those U.S. troops in Iraq, just what is this "authority" the article refers to that the U.S. will supposedly be handing over to Iraqis? It's certainly not the authority to defend their country, as the U.S. plans to continue with its occupation regardless of the wishes of the new government in Baghdad. And it's not even the authority to make laws, we learned Thursday during congressional hearings. Apparently even that most fundamental responsibility of government will not be granted to this government-to-be, according to administration officials.

Maybe Maj. Gen. Dempsey, and his superiors at Centcom and the Pentagon and in the White House, should stop a moment and try to imagine how they'd have felt, if they'd been police or militia members back in 1760 or 1770, and British troops, dragging some of their neighbors out of their homes and arresting or shooting them, had asked them to join in and help out with the repression. Maybe then they wouldn't be so surprised at the poor "performance" of the new Iraqi security forces.

Nation-building, as Bush was fond of saying back during the 2000 campaign, is a messy business, but it must be admitted that this administration is doing a remarkable job of building a national consciousness in Iraq. It's just not the nation, or the national consciousness, that they had in mind.

—*CounterPunch.org, April 23, 2004*

When it comes to lack of intelligent criticism of foolish government policy, the preparations for the trial of ousted Iraqi dictator Saddam Hussein really takes the proverbial cake, though. Astoundingly, as crucial as it is for U.S credibility in the Arab world for this trial to be perceived as fair under international standards, the Bush administration and its grand vizier in Baghdad, L. Paul Bremer, have chosen perhaps the worst possible person to oversee the whole process. And about this idiocy, there has been not one word of criticism in the U.S. mainstream press.

Chalabi as Prosecutor:
An Appointment to Shock and Awe

The past year of war and occupation has been the occasion for much jaw dropping, but I have to say that as jaded as I have become about one dumb-ass move after another by this incredibly inept administration, I was completely stunned by the idiocy of the Bush administration's latest move: putting a nephew of Ahmed Chalabi in charge of the tribunal that will investigate and try captured Iraqi tyrant Saddam Hussein.

Ahmad Chalabi, recall, is the ethically challenged, sticky-fingered Iraqi exile financier who in the run-up to the American invasion of Iraq was the source of many of the wildly scary—and wholly fabricated—tales of Iraqi weapons of mass destruction. He is the American government's favorite pick to head up a new quisling Iraqi "sovereign" government sometime this summer, and as head of the Interim Governing Council's economic and finance committee, has already overseen the appointment of the country's ministers of Oil, Finance, Trade and the heads of the central bank, trade bank and largest commercial bank. (Chalabi was also convicted in absentia in Jordon of embezzlement in the 1980s, and is still subject to arrest and imprisonment in that country.)

Bad enough that most Iraqis view this fugitive from Jordanian justice with a mixture of distrust and disdain. Now, when the crucial prosecution of Iraq's former dictator—a trial that is certain to galvanize the attention of the whole world—is about to get underway, the U.S. occupation authority has put forward a relative of this tainted character as director general of the tribunal.

Salem Chalabi, who studied law in the U.S. and speaks in an unaccented American English, may be a fine lawyer for all we know, but with his uncle being so directly linked to the Bush administration's war cabinet and the controversial selling of the war to the Senate and the American public, and with Ahmed Chalabi himself such a controversial figure in Iraq, it is beyond dumb—more like idiotic—to have him be the one to direct the trial of Saddam.

If the U.S. wanted to demonstrate the workings of an honest and fair legal system, if it wanted to win the approval of the masses of people in the Arab and Islamic world, it already had an uphill battle ahead of it. The war itself, and especially the subsequent bloody occupation, have soured much of that world on America and its role in Iraq.

At least the prosecution and trial of a man who for years was widely perceived, even in the Arab world, as a monster, offered the chance for the U.S. to demonstrate the one unarguable positive of its invasion of Iraq—the removal of this man from power.

Now that unique opportunity is being squandered because nobody will trust the integrity of the proceedings if the process is headed up by such tainted goods as Salem Chalabi. It's not just that his uncle is Ahmed. Salem himself is linked directly to the Bush administration. His business partner Mark Zell runs a law firm in partnership with U.S. Undersecretary of Defense and long-time neo-conservative Iraqi War hawk Douglas Feith—whose office oversees the graft and scandal-ridden reconstruction program in Iraq.

You have to wonder what they're smoking over on Pennsylvania Avenue and in the Green Zone in Baghdad. If they wanted to rehabilitate Saddam Hussein on the Arab Street, they couldn't have picked a better way to do it than to have a Chalabi run his trial.

Less shocking, but still stunning in its shabbiness, has been the American media's complete lack of awareness of, or interest in this disastrous appointment. President Bush has been accused of being incurious, but the American media, whose job it is to ask questions, is in cases like this even worse. It's willfully ignorant.

CNN, in an interview with Salem Chalabi back in December, when he was already being described as an "architect" of the coming tribunal, didn't once ask him about the propriety or wisdom of his playing a key role in that tribunal. Neither did the *Washington Post*, which also interviewed him for a story at that time. A Google search of the mainstream media turns up no questioning of Salem Chalabi's role as director general.

Even National Public Radio, which one might expect to show some scintilla of intellectual awareness, ran a piece this week interviewing Salem Chalabi about the tribunal without once asking him the Journalism 101 question about his conflict of interest in the case or the propriety of his serving as director general of the tribunal.

Back in December, President Bush seemed to acknowledge the importance of having a fair and public trial of the Iraqi dictator. At a White House press briefing, he said the U.S. would "work with the Iraqis to develop a way to try him that withstands international scrutiny." Uncle Chalabi, around the same time, pledged that the tribunal would "not be a kangaroo court."

Well, the Saddam tribunal seems to be surviving what passes for scrutiny in what passes for a news media in the U.S., but it's a safe bet that any tribunal headed by Salem Chalabi will not withstand international scrutiny outside the U.S.—and particularly in the Islamic world, where it most needs to be respected.

It's a good bet, too, that the trial will be a kangaroo court.*

—*CounterPunch.org, April 29, 2004*

Ahmad Chalabi, of course, who himself, and whose Iraqi National Congress, were in the pay of the CIA for years, was a key conduit for the duplicitous U.S. government campaign of disinformation about Iraqi weapons of mass destruction and alleged Iraqi links to Al Qaeda, and was also a key source for Judith Miller, the *N.Y. Times'* resident propagandist for the Bush administration's Iraq war campaign. When Chalabi's fortunes crashed in April and May of 2004, Miller and the *Times* went down with him. First, editors at the *Times* responded with their cautious and soft-pedaled mea culpa.[10] Then, four days later, the paper's ombudsman, Public Editor Daniel Okrent, unleashed his own critique of the paper's coverage in an essay published in the Sunday *Times* "Week in Review" section. In it, he pointedly named Miller, reporter Patrick Tyler, and the paper's editors, accusing them of having allowed the paper to be used in a "cunning campaign" by those who were promoting war with Iraq.[11] It was a dramatic moment—the more so as the criticism leveled at the *Times* could apply at least as well to the rest of the U.S. corporate media.

So now it was official: We were lied to repeatedly about the causes of the war by the nation's newspaper of record as well as by most of the rest of the corporate media.

---

* Then again, perhaps not. Events have a way of conspiring to cause one Bush administration scheme after another in Iraq to backfire or collapse. In the case of Chalabi, who was paid millions of dollars over the years by the Pentagon to help promote the war, after being passed over for the role of new maximum leader of Iraq, he has begun throwing wrenches into the U.S. occupation, calling the June 30 handover of "sovereignty" a sham and seeking to undermine the U.N. role in selecting an interim government team by suggesting that the international organization had been corrupt in its handling of the food-for-oil program during the Saddam-era embargo of Iraq. With friends like these... (See Associated Press, May 20, 2004, "U.S. Soldiers Raid Chalabi's Home in Iraq," by Sheherezade Faramarzi.)

This Couldn't Have Been Happening! (But It Was): *The Times'* Okrent on the Credulous Judy Miller

The dramatic indictment, by the *New York Times'* own ombudsman, of the newspaper's propagandistic and misleading coverage of the run-up to the Iraq war, and the fighting of that war, and particularly of its uncritical support for the Bush administration's deceptive claims that Saddam Hussein had weapons of mass destruction and was supporting Al Qaeda, offers the hope of a sea change in the American media's supine approach to journalism.

But only the hope of change.

Much will depend first of all on whether the *Times'* own management takes the steps called for by ombudsman Daniel Okrent. He has called on the paper to "launch a new round of examination and investigation," saying what is needed is not more contrition, but rather "a series of aggressively reported stories detailing the misinformation, disinformation and suspect analysis that led virtually the entire world to believe Hussein had W.M.D. at his disposal."

Okrent, unlike the *Times* editors, who in their own semi-mea culpa essay published only four days earlier, had studiously avoided naming names, singles out two *Times* reporters—Judith Miller and Patrick Tyler—as being purveyors of what he called "credulous" and "flawed" articles, though he adds that their editors too, deserve blame for censoring out or downplaying reports that contradicted or undermined Miller's and other propagandistic writers' reports. Hinting that there were even more unsavory things going on at the *Times*, Okrent discloses that some reporters at the paper, thus far unnamed, actively protected their pro-administration sources from "unfriendly reporting by colleagues." He also charges that editors at the paper created a "dysfunctional" system that permitted some reporters in Washington and Baghdad, again unnamed, "to work outside the lines of customary bureau management," while preventing other reporters "with substantial knowledge of the subject at hand" from getting a chance to "express their reservations" about the stories the paper was running. He even discloses that the *Times*, in a major breach of ethics, from January through May 2003 actually had the niece of key Iraq war hawker (and Miller source) Ahmad Chalabi working for the paper at its Kuwait bureau.

Given the extremes to which the *Times* went to expose the failings of its cub reporter Jason Blair, when it was learned that he had been making up stories-a scandal that hurt nobody but Blair himself and the reputation of the paper—it would seem that the paper would have no alternative but to do at least as exhaustive a housecleaning now, when the deceptions and breaches of journalistic standards by its staff have had so much more serious an impact—contributing as they did to the nation's going to war, and to the death of hundreds of Americans and thousands of innocent Iraqis.

But the impact of Okrent's critique of the *Times* goes far beyond the newspaper itself. If the *Times* was guilty of shamelessly promoting a war on behalf of the Bush administration, so was most of the rest of the American media—especially the major television networks, including cable networks CNN and MSNBC, and the *Times'* main competitors, the *Washington Post* and the *Wall Street Journal*.

Okrent says that at times the nation's self-styled newspaper of record "pushed Pentagon assertions" about W.M.D.s and about Iraq's alleged links to Al Qaeda "so aggressively you could almost sense epaulets sprouting on the shoulders of editors."

Indeed, but the same could as easily be said of the anchors and reporters at the major networks, who might as well have been wearing uniforms. The breathless repeating of administration claims about W.M.D.s, about Al Qaeda threats, about other nations' alleged terrorism links, and, after it began, about the magnificent American invasion, all framed with patriotic bunting and backed by rousing musical soundtracks, could have been designed by veterans of the propaganda offices of the former USSR or the People's Republic of China.

So far, no one at any of these other media institutions has uttered a word of remorse or apology for the shoddy and sordid way they all danced to the Bush administration's tune in first stampeding the nation into war and then misinforming the public about the tragic and misguided course of that conflict.

Nor is there likely to be a word said about any of this scandal—which if honestly exposed would lead to the wholesale firing of a regiment of tainted journalists.

Unless, perhaps, the *Times* follows Okrent's advice and really does expose its own failings and its willful complicity in the Bush administration's warmongering. If the *Times* were to disclose how the administration and its paid Iraqi hirelings conducted their campaign of propaganda and deception, the tale would spread far beyond the paper itself, making it clear that the whole media establishment was dancing in a synchronized chorus line. (Just to give one example of this, CNN used the *Times*' Miller as a source in its reports on the U.S. Army's frenzied W.M.D. search last spring.)

Dramatic and surprising as it is for its forthrightness, perhaps the most striking thing about Okrent's critique of his own employer is how it vindicates the alternative media (a point acknowledged only obliquely by Okrent)—and much of the foreign press—which have been reporting accurately on the W.M.D., issue, the non-existent Iraq-Al Qaeda link, and the conduct of the war, all along.

—*CounterPunch.org, June 1, 2004*

Chapter 6

The So-Called Opposition

The 2004 presidential election year is in one sense a watershed moment in history. Four years after the Republicans stole the presidency, Americans are polarized to an extent not seen perhaps since 1964 or 1960, or perhaps even 1936. At least half the nation's voters despise the current president or at least think he has lied about and blundered in Iraq, while ravaging the nation's finances and its Constitution. Even many Republicans are expressing distress about this administration's foreign and domestic policies. Yet astonishingly, the Democratic party, still firmly in the hands of the same Democratic Leadership Council hacks who brought us Clinton and Gore—people who think of golf as a working man's game, distrust ordinary folks and in general act and think more like Republicans—is pissing away this once-in-a-generation opportunity.

After lining up behind John Kerry, the most mainstream, establishment candidate of the group that ran for the nomination in 2002/3, the Democratic Party leadership and its candidate have allowed the presidential campaign to be played out on Bush's side of the field.

The war, of course, is the biggest missed issue. It has clearly been a misadventure from the day the Iraq-obsessed Dick Cheney and his neocon minions decided to have Bush go after Saddam Hussein. The politics of war were based upon deceit, the planning (such as it was), was based on wishful, ahistorical thinking, and an appalling xenophobia towards traditional allies, and the actual conduct of the war and subsequent occupation and counter-insurgency effort were a disaster of historic proportions, even before the evidence of systematic torture of Iraqi detainees became public knowledge. Yet the Democrats, despite having a Vietnam veteran with both a hero's medals and an anti-war record to bolster him, have offered Americans virtually no alternative. Instead of denouncing the war as a colossal $200-billion mistake, and calling for an end to it, Kerry has called for more troops, and more blood and treasure. Like Hubert Humphrey before him, his argument seems to boil down to "I can do it better." Little wonder that like Humphrey in 1968 he has failed to ignite any excitement among the millions of voters who want to see the war ended. Worst of all, as the crisis deepens, Kerry, who voted for the war and who is on record as saying the US can't "cut and run," is unable to turn around and say, "I told you so."

Domestically the situation is not much better. Kerry never had the guts to say that Bush's horrific tax cuts were a disaster. In fact, he attacked his leading primary opponent, Howard Dean, for saying that the Bush tax cut program should be rescinded, saying, in words that echoed his war stance, that he could do it better, by rescinding only the tax cuts for the rich. The problem is that if you want to have a better, fairer society, you have to pay for it, and in the end that means you need taxes. What a progressive politician needs to do is make taxes fair, and explain how the revenues raised will be used to make the country a better place for all. Of course, doing that would mean serious tax reform— much higher taxes on the wealthy, a restoration of the estate tax, a real corporate profits tax and an end to tax havens and loopholes, and an end to the cap on Social Security income subject to taxation. Again, Kerry, as a DLC candidate beholden to corporate interests, cannot do this, which leaves him in the position of having to admit that he "won't have the money" to do many of the things he claims he'd like to do.

Now there's an inspiring campaign slogan!

In the same way, Kerry has blown that other big democratic issue—jobs. The Bush administration virtually handed this issue to the Democrats on a platter, losing millions of jobs over the last few years to tax-subsidized off-shoring of white-collar jobs and tax-subsidized plant closings and relocations overseas. But Kerry, again beholden to the same industries that support these anti-labor policies, has been unable to go beyond saying he would require companies to give several months' notice of plans to shift jobs overseas. Again, it's hard to see people racing to the polls over this one.

Each time a domestic issue comes up, Kerry seems to have some limp proposal to slightly soften the current Bush policy, while leaving the basic problem unsolved.

Since it's going to take a heavy turnout of Democratic voters to defeat an incumbent president—even a uniquely unpopular one—this DLC-style strategy seems doomed.

It's as if there was no opposition party to turn to.

Clinton, Bush and Impeachment:
It Was the Lying, Right?

Everyone agreed that it was not the sex. It was the lying, right? If having extramarital sex in the White House were an impeachable offense, the impeachment of presidents would long ago have become a routine affair. We'd have seen Roosevelt, Ike, Kennedy, Johnson, Nixon and Bush the Elder in the dock for sure, and maybe Ron, too (though he at least could credibly have said, "I don't remember" without facing a perjury count).

But everyone agreed it wasn't the sex that got President Clinton in trouble. It was the lying. The audacious bending of the meaning of the word "is" and the word "sex."

But has lying ever been practiced so blatantly as it is being practiced today in the White House?

At least President Clinton's lies were about his personal behavior. This administration has done its share of that kind of lying, to be sure. For example about the President's cowardly conduct during the 9/11 attacks, or about Vice President Cheney's dealings with Enron executives as the company was tanking. Or about President Bush's year as an AWOL guardsman during the Vietnam War.

But this administration's lying has gone far beyond that, and has led to the deaths of thousands, including well over a hundred Americans (and counting).* This is prevarication on a scale that rivals the Johnson Administration's lie about the purported attack on an American destroyer in the Gulf of Tonkin, or the Nixon Administration's lie about its secret war in Cambodia.

Like Johnson's big lie, which led to the deaths of over 50,000 Americans and of millions of Southeast Asians, the Bush Administration's lies about Iraq—that it had biological and chemical weapons ready to use and that it was well on the way to developing nuclear weapons or that it was directly supporting Al Qaeda—were deliberately designed to trick Congress and the American public into supporting a war that otherwise would not have happened—in the first instance against Vietnam and in the second against Iraq.

Both of these deceptions were murderous lies.

Remember: Nixon's lie about U.S. aggression against the neutral nation of Cambodia—another murderous lie—was one of the articles of impeachment that were voted against him in the House of Representatives. Johnson never had to face the music for his monstrous lie, but it, and its consequences, did force him to decide against seeking another term of office. Perhaps he realized that had he not decided not to seek a second elected term of office, he too might have ended up facing an impeachment resolution.

---

* Over 800 by the end of May 2004 and rising fast.

Now it's Bush's turn.

But where are the voices calling for his impeachment? (Not in Congress, though out in the hustings, they appear to be lining up behind Ralph Nader.)

Where is the public outcry demanding that he be called to account for his shameless and bloody deception of the American public and the Congress?

It is likely that with American troops still patrolling the streets of Baghdad, and still getting attacked and killed there, and with most Americans still reveling in the thrill of the military's quick victory over Saddam Hussein's army, nobody's ready to call Bush and his cronies on their crimes of falsehood.

But this buoyant nationalistic mood is liable to shift dramatically as the Iraq situation continues to deteriorate, and as the American body count continues to rise. Particularly if, as is likely, the economy stays in the doldrums.

At some point it will start to become politically acceptable to start asking, "If everybody's mad at us, why are we over there?" Once that happens, the next question will be "How did we get into this mess in the first place?"

That's when Bush's Big Lie will start to loom large in the public's assessment of this administration.

As for impeachment, as long as Congress remains in the hands of the Republican Party, it's not likely. That makes the 2004 election doubly important. Even if Bush manages to eke out a narrow victory again in 2004, it is critically important that Democrats regain control of at least one house of Congress.

It may seem hard to imagine today, but if the voters manage that, we may yet see another impeachment drama.

—*CounterPunch.org, May 31, 2003*

This next piece, like the preceding one, represents a bit of wishful thinking on my part. It is, I suppose, still possible that voters will see the madness of the Republican program, and that they will at least return one house of Congress to Democratic control, even if they return Bush to the White House, but by late spring, the odds seemed already to be against it. Back in the fall of 2003, however, it was possible to be at least mildly optimistic.

The Democrats in 2004:
Perfect Storm or Same Old Doldrums?

A number of factors appear to be coming together—a perfect political storm if you will—to suggest that the 2004 elections could be a watershed in American politics instead of the Democratic Waterloo many were anticipating only six months ago.

First of all, the growing cynicism about and disinterest in politics on the part of the majority of American citizens appears to be convincing political strategists in both parties that the Clintonian strategy of seeking out and winning over the undecided voter is a waste of time and money. Since so few of these swing or so-called "independent" voters will vote anyway, since they are so easily swayed back and forth in their choices, and since winning them involves a huge risk of alienating otherwise assured partisan voters, it is and has always been a foolish strategy—as Al Gore found out.

This raises the possibility of a more ideologically driven campaign, with both parties appealing to what is left of their principles in an effort to get their more ardent supporters active in the campaign and to the voting both on election day.

Bad news that, for the Democratic Leadership Council and for Republicans in Democratic clothing like Joe Lieberman.

I'm not deluding myself that the Democratic Party will suddenly become the party of FDR in '36, but it and Democratic candidates for national office clearly will have to give those remaining 13 million trade union members, along with the nation's black and Hispanic voters, its low-wage hamburger flippers, and its idealistic students, a reason to campaign and to vote.

Those fabled soccer moms of the 2000 campaign will not be courted so ardently this time around. In this campaign, they may simply have to decide for themselves whether abortion rights, adequate school funding and clean air trump feel good images of family men bussing their wives in public or talking about the need for morality in government.

Second, the Bush/Cheney/Rumsfeld all-war-all-the-time strategy of maintaining Americans in a state of jingoistic fervor, while keeping everyone on edge with color-coded terror alerts, appears to have backfired. Yellow and orange Homeland Security alerts don't have everyone jumping for the duct tape and plastic any more. And meanwhile, things are falling apart rapidly in both Afghanistan and Iraq. A few months ago, if Iraqi guerrillas had managed to pull off a Lebanon-style mass bombing of American troops, a pumped-up American public probably would have demanded a massive infusion of more heavily armed troops to crush the bastards. Now, after months of quagmire-like occupation, with Iraq no better off than it was at the end of the American assault on Baghdad, with American GI's getting picked off at a rate of about one per day, such a military disaster would probably, Tet-like, lead to popular demands for the U.S. to simply pull out of Iraq, leaving the country to its own devices.

The Bush administration is desperate to avoid going into the 2004 election with a messy Iraq occupation still on its hands, but there is probably no way out at this point. The attacks on the U.N. compound and the latest horrific mosque bombing have pretty much obliterated any chance that other countries—already angry at U.S. unilateralism—will step in to help with the occupation (does anybody seriously believe that it was the U.S. that decided, after that latter blast, to delay the planned takeover of occupation duties in Najaf by Polish troops?). At the same time, it has become politically impossible at this point for the Pentagon to send in more U.S. troops—something it might have gotten away with two months ago but which now would be portrayed as a replay of Vietnam.*

Neither can Bush adopt the Nixonian approach of declaring victory and pulling out. The Nixon "secret plan" for ending the war in Vietnam, recall, was to hand the war over to the South Vietnamese government and army, providing it with sufficient firepower to allow it to hold off the inevitable Communist victory long enough to either get him through his term or to allow him to lay the blame for the "loss" of South Vietnam on Saigon.

But Iraq has no government or army to hand things over to, and the likelihood that its feuding tribes and religious sects could be cobbled together into something that could pass for a government at least through next November, or that the semblance of a puppet army could be created that wouldn't simply fuel further chaos, civil strife and attacks on U.S. troops, is next to nil.

My guess is that Karl Rove is probably kicking himself for that hubristic staging of a Bush carrier landing. If anyone ends up using it in campaign commercials, it will probably be the eventual Democratic presidential candidate. My suggestion is for a "Mr. Bill"-style commer-

---

*Hence the deceptive approach of "stop-loss" orders forcing existing troops in Iraq to stay there beyond their regular tours of duty.

cial featuring the KB Toys Bush flight-suited action figure, mocking his declaration that "Major conflict" in Iraq is over. This would capitalize on the new penchant among pundits to suggest that we need to have grownups in charge in Washington, instead of the testosterone-addled adolescents who are running things these days.

The economy too, is likely to be in sorry shape during this campaign. Anyone who thinks that corporate America is going to start investing, with the prospect of those huge budget deficits on out to the horizon, with over 6 percent of Americans unemployed, and with everyone extended to the limits on their credit, is simply delusional. One in five Americans has been laid off at some point in the last two years, which means that just about everyone knows or has relatives who have been laid off, and that everyone is worried about their own job security. That's hardly fertile ground for an economic boom.

The best that Republicans can hope for is perhaps a stock market rebound, but that won't help that Democratic base or lowly wage-earners to which it appears the party will now be turning. Besides, with interest rates now moving up, even a market rebound seems unlikely.

Of course, the Democratic Party and its presidential candidates have shown an uncanny ability to do the wrong thing in recent years. It's still possible that Democratic candidates, whose lust for corporate affection resembles Clinton's insatiable and self-destructive appetite for young women, could adopt the losing strategy of trying to appeal yet again to Republican voters. Candidate Howard Dean, for example, whose basic position on most economic issues is close to Lieberman's, could end up campaigning after the primaries like a centrist and losing those crucial union and minority voters.

If whoever wins that nomination does decide to appeal to the party's traditional base this year, however, and goes after Bush and Republican congressional candidates on the key issues of the war, the economy and the massive tax breaks for the rich and corporate America—okay, an iffy proposition, I admit—November 2004 could bring dramatic changes.

—*CounterPunch.org, Sept. 2, 2003*

Facing the Music: Courage and the Democrats

On the eve of the U.S. invasion of Iraq, the White House and Pentagon made much of their new war strategy of "Shock and Awe," saying that it was intended to focus tremendous firepower on a select few targets of the Baathist power structure and military leadership, shocking and awing the country, while doing little damage to the larger society and population. As described, the strategy was to be a sort of mini "neutron bomb" that would selectively destroy the key ruling elite while leaving Iraq's people, society and infrastructure largely intact.

In fact, the reverse has happened.

The bombs and assaults of the so-called "Shock and Awe" campaign did little damage to the Iraqi power structure, which largely melted away into hiding, and the army simply evaporated, with most soldiers just doffing their khaki's and walking away from battle in their civvies. What clearly was effectively destroyed by the U.S. military campaign, and its inept aftermath, was most of the country's essential infrastructure of power, communications, water and sewers, its economy, its schools, and its healthcare system. If "Shock and Awe" was envisioned as a kind of "neutron bomb," the reality has been more of a classic nuke.

The astonishing thing is how little the American public seems to care about this incredible and unprecedented disaster.

When former Philadelphia Mayor Wilson Goode and his police decided to flush out a cult group of back-to-nature communalists in West Philadelphia, known as MOVE, they opted for a satchel bomb dropped by helicopter onto the roof of the MOVE house. The plan, supposedly, was to slowly burn down the building and drive the holed-up MOVE people out into the waiting arms of police. The reality was an out-of-control conflagration that killed 11 people, including five children, in the house, and burned down several residential blocks and 60 houses. When that happened, whatever Philadelphians thought of the controversial group MOVE, it spelled the end not only of Goode's political career, but also of the free reign Philadelphia police had enjoyed since the days of Mayor Frank Rizzo.

Similarly, on a national scale, when President Lyndon Johnson lied to the American public about a fraudulent attack by North Vietnamese speed boats on an American destroyer in the Gulf of Tonkin, and then sent half a million troops to Vietnam claiming that he would bring an end to that conflict, only to have it turn into a bloody disaster, he was driven from the White House.

Idiotic or dishonest behavior, resulting in public policy disasters, has led to public dismay and punishment at the ballot box in the past. Indeed, it has done exactly that in California, where Gov. Gray Davis' inept handling of the state's Enron-induced energy crisis, and his inability to contain the state's ballooning budget deficit, has led to a recall campaign that could bounce him from office next month.

Oddly, however, we have an unelected president in Washington who has, on multiple fronts, made the ultimate hash of domestic and foreign policy, and yet he is still considered likely to win re-election next year.

Consider:

- Bush led this nation into a bloody and costly war of aggression based upon blatant lies, self-deception and ignorance, a war that America cannot win, and that the country now cannot easily walk away from. This war has killed thousands of innocent Iraqi civilians and hundreds of GIs, will cost hundreds of billions of dollars, is tying up the entire U.S. military, and has, like Vietnam before it, demonstrated not the might but the impotence of American military power.

- He has put the government and the economy on a path to bankruptcy so serious that even the International Monetary Fund, normally a docile handmaiden of U.S. hegemony, has criticized it as irresponsible and unsustainable.

- He has abrogated a host of treaties which, painstakingly negotiated over decades, had been leading, albeit stumblingly, to a safer, more humane world.

- He has launched an unprecedented assault on the environment, undermining global efforts to confront the threat of global warming, opening up remaining U.S. old-growth forests to commercial exploitation, and gutting clean air and clean water regulations.

All this and still, if polls are to be believed, the general public response remains largely a collective yawn.

Part of the problem is the media, which have grown far more concentrated, and far less combative over the last decade or so. Aaron Brown, for example, on CNN, can do a story on Iraq, and then casually segue into a piece on the World Trade Center Towers by musing, "Everything seems to be linked to 9/11 these days," thus buying into the White House disinformation campaign that the war against Iraq is part of the administration's War on Terror, despite no evidence linking Iraq with Al Qaeda or any international terrorist activities. Likewise, *The New York Times* can report on the Bush administration's desperate efforts to enlist the U.N. in the Iraq occupation without clearly explaining that that same administration had earlier not only ignored the U.N.'s rejection of a war resolution, but had openly and blatantly lied to Security Council members about Iraq's war capabilities and alleged links to terrorism—in fact even spied on them.

Part of the problem too is cowardice on the part of the ostensible political opposition party. Leading Democratic candidates—meaning those candidates whom the above-mentioned complicit corporate media have in their wisdom designated as leading candidates worthy of routine coverage—have refused to seriously challenge the policies of the Bush administration. Howard Dean, the ostensible front runner, while opposing the war and the government's enormous tax cuts, has said he supports the continued occupation and even the "preventative war" strategy that was used to justify the conflict in the first place. Sen. John Kerry, billed as Dean's main opponent, actually voted for the president's authority to go to war, and now pretends he was deceived, though plenty of his colleagues, including Sen. Robert Byrd and presidential candidate Rep. Dennis Kucinich, were well aware of the lies as they were being spoken. Neither Dean nor Kerry is offering much beyond warmed-over Republican economics in their domestic policies. Indeed, as columnist Matthew Miller observes, so tame are today's Democrats that they would probably consider Richard Nixon's 1970s environmental, health and welfare proposals too radical.

In fact, some of the Democratic candidates, notably Kucinich, but also Carol Moseley-Braun and Al Sharpton, are taking real aim at the Bush administration's follies, foibles and falsehoods, and in Kucinich's case, are proposing a set of real, progressive alternatives. The corporate media, however, ignore them, casting them as minor candidates, though by all accounts Kucinich is drawing large, enthusiastic crowds on the stump in Iowa and New Hampshire, and though, at joint appearances of all the candidates, it is often Sharpton who wins some of the biggest rounds of applause.

Still, President Bush for the most part continues to get a free ride, from both the media and the public.

Things may yet turn around. As the situation in Iraq continues to deteriorate, and as the growing U.S. deficit continues to drive interest rates higher and the economy and stock market south, the public is bound, at some point, to start thinking for itself instead of listening to the coiffed and complicit talking heads of network "news" programs.

At that point, Bush will have to face the same music as President Johnson and Philadelphia Mayor Wilson Goode.

The question is, will that moment come in time for the November '04 elections?

A dose of political courage among the "major" Democratic candidates for national office could speed things along.

—*CounterPunch.org, Sept. 5, 2003*

General Hysteria: The Clark Bandwagon

Judging from the hoopla and hype in the media, from CNN to the *NY Times*, the decision by retired four-star general Wesley Clark to throw his hat into the ring as a Democratic Party presidential contender is something akin to the Second Coming. He's a genuine hero, we're told, and Americans, particularly in key states like Texas and the Southeast, will go for his military background.

What is this passion for generals and other guys in uniforms as leaders, anyhow? There was the same kind of fawning adoration being expressed about John McCain during the Republican primaries last time around. (In fact, it was in a pathetic effort to capture some of that adoration that George Bush, the National Guard AWOL and scofflaw, donned his now infamous flight suit and did an orchestrated and carefully staged landing on an aircraft carrier flight deck.)

What, it's fair to ask though, does Sen. John McCain's Vietnam-era bomber flying and POW experience, or Sen. John Kerry's Vietnam-era river patrol boat captaining experience, offer in the way of presidential leadership skills? At least Clark, as a former Supreme NATO commander, and former head of the U.S. Army's Southern Command (Latin America), can claim some executive experience.

But running a military operation, whether a small riverboat or an army division, is nothing like running a country, at least in what still passes for a democracy. Military officers run things by ordering people to do stuff. Presidents must lead by convincing both the public and the Congress to do what they want done.

Is it courage people are looking for? Well, presumably both Kerry and Clark have shown courage under fire, as attested by their Silver Star medals from the Vietnam War, but that is not the same as political courage. Political courage is not about putting one's life on the line. It's about being willing to stand for things that might lead to one's losing an election, because it's the right thing to do. Has either Kerry or

Clark demonstrated that kind of courage? If anything, it was Kerry's decision to come out against the war in Indochina, after he returned from it, which showed some political courage, but sadly, it's his legacy as a fighter, not an anti-war activist, that candidate Kerry is touting on the campaign trail.

Candidate Clark's initial forays into the public forum have not been encouraging in the political courage area. In a CNN interview, he backed off of his earlier embrace of the term "liberal," saying instead that he preferred to eschew labels. On the matter of the war, he now equivocates and says in a *New York Times* piece today that he probably would have voted with the congressional pack and authorized war (which is no doubt true). This is courage?

Americans in the past have turned to generals and military leaders of other rank many times to lead the country, beginning with George Washington. There were also, among others, Andrew Jackson, Ulysses Grant, Theodore Roosevelt, and of course more recently, Dwight Eisenhower. Their records as presidents have been probably no better or worse than civilian presidents. While opinions about Grant as a Civil War general are mixed, most historians agree his post-war presidency was a disaster. Teddy Roosevelt, on the other hand, is rated a success. Eisenhower, who is often credited with having had the prescience to warn of a military-industrial complex, actually oversaw the institutionalization of a permanent war economy, set the country on its grim course in Indochina, deepened the Cold War, and allowed America's malignant race crisis to fester during his two terms of office.

In retrospect, America's experience with soldier-presidents in the White House has been at best a mixed bag.

Michael Moore says he looks forward to a Clark candidacy. He cites Clark's observation that wars should only be "a last resort," and his defense of liberalism and political dissidence, as well as the ex-general's support for abortion rights, affirmative action and his opposition to the USA PATRIOT Act. Moore says we're at war in America, and need to oust President Bush from office, and he suggests that maybe a general is what the Democrats need to accomplish that.

It might be that Clark will turn out to be one of the more liberal of the Democratic candidates (though he's unlikely to take a stand against NAFTA, the way Rep. Dennis Kucinich has done). More likely, he'll turn out to be a kind of Clinton-style centrist—no surprise since it now appears that it was Clinton who really pushed Clark into running, not, as originally claimed, an internet draft movement.

It's safe to say that Clark's entry into the Democratic primary race will enliven the contest. But leftists, progressives and liberals should be on their guard, and avoid allowing themselves to be sucked in by a Clark bandwagon.

A Democratic presidential nominee with a four-star dress uniform hanging in his closet might be nice to have for the 2004 presidential race against military poseur George Bush, but the man wearing it still has a lot of explaining to do before he should get our support.

—*CounterPunch.org, Sept. 19, 2003*

The general vacuity and political cowardice of the Democrats has produced a dismal situation, in which otherwise potentially progressive voters, with nowhere to turn, end up either staying home in disgust or falling for the appeal of charlatans. California's recall demonstrated this clearly. With the mainstream state Democratic Party putting up Grey Davis or a replacement who was indistinguishable from him, many people fell for the fake populist Schwarzenegger, or just skipped the whole thing. There's a lesson here, but is anyone paying attention?

A Black Day for Democracy: Schwarzenegger and the Failure of the Dems

The election of Arnold Schwarzenegger as governor of America's largest state represents a kind of milepost in the decline of American democracy. This is not "Reagan II, the Movie," as some have suggested—a second actor being elected governor of the tinsel state. Reagan, for all the criticism that he was "just an actor," in fact had paid his political dues, leading the actors union and getting involved in a variety of campaigns—for example against Medicare—before jumping into electoral politics to run for governor. While he certainly relied on his actor's charm to manufacture a marketable persona, he had a conservative political agenda and was fairly candid about it.

Schwarzenegger, in contrast, has no political background. He is a total artifice, a creation of a group of Republican backers who care little or nothing about his personal beliefs or ideology, and see him as a vehicle for restoring Republican control in a state that has been becoming increasingly Democratic.

What is incredible, and terribly demoralizing, about this election is that a majority of voters in a state holding a fifth of the U.S. population bought the product. In a moment of nihilistic fury at the corruption and cronyism of the Democratic Party apparatus and its titular head, Gov. Gray Davis, even a large number of Democrats cast their votes along with the state's Republicans for a man who stands for nothing but himself, who is a long-time misogynist with a history of assaulting women, and who is in thrall to business interests (who can be expected now to gut the state's once model regulatory apparatus).

Make no mistake: the Democratic Party richly deserved this debacle. California Democratic politicians have long taken their traditional liberal, labor and minority base for granted. The ultimate Clintonians, California's Democratic leadership bought into the neo-liberal idea of deregulation, bringing on the state's electricity crisis; they have endorsed right-wing get-tough approaches to crime that have made the state a leader in prison construction, and in the grotesque mass incarceration of minorities, and most seriously they have surrendered to the three-decades long Republican-led drive to limit property taxes (a grossly favor-the-rich campaign), refusing to offer progressive alternatives that would tax corporations and the rich to pay for schools, roads and other essential local services. Little wonder then that in a crisis, that progressive Democratic base not only failed to turn out to defend an embattled Democratic politician, but in many cases actually voted for his nemesis.

The sad thing is that they didn't have to do it.

There was an alternative, and I don't mean Lt. Governor Cruz Bustamante, who despite his Hispanic name and working class background was just another cog in the Clintonian pro-corporate Democratic machine.

The alternative was Peter Camejo, the Green Party candidate—a genuine progressive and, like Bustamante, a Latino.

Why the huge wave of Democratic support for Schwarzenegger?

My guess is that these normally Democratic voters weren't really thinking. They were understandably angry at Gray Davis and the Democratic Party. That would explain the yes vote on the recall, and the failure to vote for Bustamante, who is really just a better fed and less hirsute Davis. But if they had been thinking, they wouldn't have voted for Schwarzenegger, who will in the end do nothing to help the state's school system, which is beginning to rival Mississippi's, especially in urban districts, in terms of poor outcomes, and who is likely to continue with deregulation schemes while gutting environmental protections and undermining organized labor. Now Arnold, who has admitted to admiring, if not the actions of, then at least the style of countryman

Adolf Hitler, has managed to copy his mustachioed mentor, in portraying himself as a muscular leader (the Austrian word for that is *Fuehrer*). And millions of Californians—many of them registered Democrats according to exit polls— apparently liked that.

Well, an awful lot of Germans also liked that one back in the election of 1932.

Of course, that's not to say Arnold is Adolf. He has said he despises everything Hitler did and stood for, and we have no reason not to believe him. California is not about to become a fascist outpost on the North American continent because of his election. (If fascism is to come to America, it will arrive in Washington, not California, and more likely in creeping form via actions of the Pentagon and the Justice and Homeland Security Departments than overtly via election.)

What is dismaying about this recall election is how many Californians were willing to vote for that empty muscle shirt with the carefully dyed and coifed hairstyle above, and the carefully scripted and equally empty slogans. (Equally dismaying is the poor showing by the Greens' Camejo. If there were ever a time for dissatisfied progressives to turn to a third party for a protest vote, this was it. For Camejo, who was articulate, campaigned aggressively, and who was able to get unprecedented state-wide attention in a heavily viewed televised five-way candidates' debate, to have still garnered less than 3 percent of the vote, means that hard-line third party advocates need to seriously reassess their strategy of shunning, and running against, the Democratic Party. For whatever reason, that strategy ain't working.)

Gen. Wesley Clark, the "muscle man" in the Democratic presidential primary campaign, has meanwhile offered an Arnold-like example of vacuity in announcing his candidacy with a speech that called for moving the country "forward, not backward," a line that somehow managed to evoke wild cheering from his audience.

Nature may abhor a vacuum, but apparently California voters, and American voters in general, love it. Schwarzenegger's big win in California—based as it was on such deliberate emptiness—is likely to reinforce this tendency in a national Democratic Party that for years, and especially since the election of William Jefferson Clinton, has consciously and carefully stood for nothing.

If the California electorate is in any way indicative of the state of the national electorate, the outlook for 2004, and for American democracy, is grim.

—*CounterPunch.org*, Oct. 9, 2003

Then again, maybe we shouldn't get all worked up about it, if this is all just a part of God's plan. That, at least, is what a surprisingly large number of Americans reportedly think these days. Some of these teleologists, incredibly, are actually in positions where they are making life-and-death decisions. If we're to believe him, one of them is even the commander-in-chief. Welcome to our faith-based military and foreign policy, where you don't have to think much about your decisions, and certainly don't have to apologize if they don't work out they way you said they would, since it's really all His doing.

Take a Ride in God's Humvee: A General Theory of Theology

God. You just gotta love Him, you know?

I mean, what if U.S. Army Lt. Gen. William Boykin is right and God did keep those chads hanging, and did put George Bush—and all those other presidents numbered 1 to 42—in the White House?

Wow!

Think about it. That means He put Calvin Coolidge in the White House. And Herbert Hoover. He must have been the one who came up with the idea of having all those dead people in Chicago vote for John Kennedy. And he sure loved Franklin Roosevelt and all that liberal New Deal stuff. Why, he put Bill Clinton in, too. Twice!

Then again, He got rid of a bunch of those presidents too—the ones who didn't get to fill out their two terms, for example—like Jack Kennedy. Bang. That would mean He was behind the plumbers and the Watergate break-in; a very neat way, you must admit, to ease Tricky Dick out of the big house and make way for Gerald Ford. I guess it means He was behind Bill Clinton's blowjob too, though He also must have decided in His infinite wisdom not to push that one to the limit. For some reason He wanted Bill to finish out his allotted time.

Turning to the War in Iraq, if the good and godly general is on the money, God helped us "win" the battle against those idol-worshipping Iraqis—you know, to get us to the point where His man in the White House and the flight suit said "major combat" was over—but then He left things kind of hanging. Why? Well, we know the Lord works in mysterious ways, but it's safe to say there's got to be some reason why He left the post-invasion situation so muddled. Maybe it is so that Boykin and fellow evangelicals in and out of uniform can have some time to wander the desert converting all those confused and lost souls in Babylon.

He must, one assumes, be the One who is helping the ousted Saddam Hussein hide from the thousands of American soldiers who are nightly scouring the back alleys of Tikrit trying to find "Elvis." Don't ask why. He has His reasons.

He has to have been behind the hiding of Osama Bin Laden too, and you've got to admit, that's a mighty fine job He's doing there. Nobody's seen hide nor hair of that lanky, bearded angel of death since 9/11/2001, except on video. And it must be our God who's protecting Bin Laden, too, because we certainly wouldn't want to suggest that Allah was behind it, and doing a better job then our Guy, would we?

But here the theology gets a bit complicated. What if Satan's at work out there too? Maybe he's the one who's been organizing these difficulties and making it hard for God. Maybe old Lucifer managed to pull off that attack on the WTC, and maybe he's the guy who's been keeping Saddam and Osama a step ahead of God's Humvees.

Funny though. I always thought God had the big guns, and that Lucifer was just a gnat in comparison. Shouldn't the Big Guy be able to know what the devil's up to and spot two ugly little human vermin, delivering them to His American soldiers?

Not being a believer myself, I've always wondered how these religious types like Gen. Boykin manage to be so all-fired certain that God's on their side. I mean, if God organized this Iraq War, He's sure made a hash of it, hasn't He? His army has shown a nasty tendency to blow away innocent children, many of them too young to have even started reading that idolatrous Koran the general's so down on.

I guess we just have to assume that it's all part of His plan, including the messy stuff. Like that budget deficit His latest president has created here in God's country.

Or maybe, like Osama and Saddam, that deficit isn't the Lord's fault either. Maybe Satan hasn't just been whispering in their ears. Maybe he's been whispering in George Jr.'s ear too.

When you start trying to figure it all out, you realize that this theology stuff is just too complicated. Maybe we'd better just leave it to the generals.

—*CounterPunch.org, Oct. 23, 2003*

Speaking of God and those who invoke Him, how about that sanctimonious born-again president of ours? Last time I heard, lying was one of those sins you were not supposed to do. Yet this is a president who has been making quite a practice of lying—big lies to get Congress to approve everything from war to Medicare bills, and, almost more astounding, little lies to duck having to take responsibilities for his own bad decisions. It's a good thing the president is a Christian, and not a Catholic. If he were the latter, he'd be spending so much time in confession booths there's be little time of him to squeeze in his daily exercise routine, not to mention governing.

Big Lies and Little Lies: The Meaning of "Mission Accomplished"

Remember when George Bush the candidate said he would restore integrity to the White House?

The reference, of course, was to the Clinton White House, which had gained a certain notoriety because of Bill Clinton's famous finger-wagging episode, when he told the American public that "I did not have sex with that woman," and for his later performance under grilling by Ken Starr, when he said his answer to a question depended on "what the definition of `is' is."

Bush, the Andover Prep grad who adopted a Texan drawl and the mien of a straight-shootin' cowboy for the campaign, managed to convince a scandal-weary public that he wouldn't stoop to such things. He'd tell it straight.

Of course, we've had some pretty big whoppers out of this White House, and this president since then. There was the Niger yellow cake tale, the supposed bio and chemical weapons in Iraq, and the lie that the president was flying around the country in Air Force One after the 9/11 attacks because of a supposed threat to attack Air Force One, for example. There was the lie that he'd fund Americorps. There was the lie that he would be the Education President. But the real classic, the lie that puts him right down there with Cheatin' Bill, came at Bush's last press conference.

That's when he denied, in response to a reporter's question, that the White House had been responsible for a big red, white and blue banner saying "Mission Accomplished," placed prominently across the front of the superstructure of the carrier Abraham Lincoln on the occasion of Bush's staged jet landing on the ship on May 1. It wasn't the White House advance team that planned that backdrop, Bush told reporters and the viewing public with a straight face. It was those Navy lads on the ship. And by the way, that phrase didn't refer to the War in Iraq, he continued. It referred to the ship's mission. Which was indeed over.

Uh-huh.

The White House was quickly forced to admit that in fact, not only was the banner and the slogan the White House's idea; the White House had produced and delivered said banner to the ship in time to have it mounted for the president's landing stunt.

Of course the president knew this when he lied to the press about its pedigree.

But he was in a jam. George Bush is just not the kind of guy who likes to admit when he's goofed.

As the guerrilla war heats up in Iraq, and the numbers of American dead mount, the "mission accomplished" line, like the "Bring 'em on" line, is returning to haunt him. But this time, instead of just showing him to be out of touch, we see the real character of the man. Caught in an embarrassing situation, he'd prefer to lie his way out than face up to his responsibility.

If he'd gone to law school instead of business school, Bush might have said it all depends upon what your definition of "mission" is. As it is, though, he's stuck looking very much like the little boy with cookie crumbs on his lips who denies that he broke the cookie jar.

This incident could prove to be Bush's undoing.

Americans are a cynical lot when it comes to politics. We know that the political class is basically a bunch of thieves and extortionists, but we expect their crimes and deceits to be of epic proportions. If a presidential candidate takes a million dollars from the pharmaceutical industry and then has the FDA grant extended patents to them, or takes millions from Boeing and then grants the aircraft maker a six-billion-dollar sweetheart lease on planes for the Pentagon it could have bought outright for much less, nobody gets worked up. That's the way Washington works, we figure.

But tell a little lie, whether it's about some nookie on the side or some questionable campaign trick, and people feel angry and insulted.

That's what Bush has done now. In trying to blame his ineptness and false optimism concerning the Iraq War by laying it on the guys in the sailor suits, this son of privilege has insulted our intelligence. Worse yet, he got caught. Even rank-and-file Republicans are miffed.

As voters, we're willing to forget many things. We'll forget about the stealing of an election, about scandals like the doctoring of a report on global warming, even about the deliberate outing of a CIA agent.

But we won't forget being taken for yokels with a cheap lie.

If the gang of Democrats running for president are smart, they'll start using the phrase "Mission Accomplished" as often as possible as a laugh line in their speeches. If they do that, by the time the campaign for president is in full swing next fall, the Democratic presidential candidate will be able to run "Small Soldiers" ads featuring action figure George Bush strutting around in front of a "Mission Accomplished" banner.

—*CounterPunch.org, Oct. 30, 2003*

One thing that has repeatedly caught me by surprise is how much support George Bush continues to command despite his severe and obvious shortcomings—his lack of intellectual rigor or curiosity, his lack of truthfulness, his inability to admit a mistake or to correct one. Somehow you imagine that for someone to get to the point that she or he becomes a governor, or especially a president, they must have exhibited some sort of character—the kind of traits that would draw people to them as leaders. And yet here's a guy who seems to exhibit no such qualities holding the top job in the land. Indeed the best people have been able to say of the guy is that he's fun to be around, which was probably true of Bozo the Clown and Peewee Herman—nobody's idea of White House material. Yet every time I think Bush has finally done something so reckless or stupid or dishonest that the public will drop him, I find his poll numbers still riding high. What's the deal here?

Bush's Brand of Leadership: Putting Himself First

One of the more amazing things to contemplate in this bizarre polity called the United States is that George Bush, probably the least engaged, most willfully ignorant, and most bungling and disastrously inept president the country has ever had, is still viewed by many Americans as a "strong leader."

Yet how's this for leadership?

In the midst of a conflict that has so far killed hundreds of Americans and maimed several thousand, more than half of them since May 1, 2003 when he prematurely declared "major conflict over" and "mission accomplished," Bush has had to order his man in Iraq, L. Paul Bremer, to rush back to Washington, D.C., canceling a meeting Bremer had scheduled with the prime minister of Poland, to participate in yet another panicky executive session on how to fix the mess in Iraq.

At the same time, Bush's CIA has had to leak to the press its latest secret report on the deteriorating situation in the war in Iraq because the Agency was reportedly worried that its highly critical report wouldn't reach the attention of the president if they went through normal channels. (The ploy may not have worked, though. Given this remarkably incurious president's admission that he doesn't read the papers, and gets his news entirely through his staff, he may not even know about the CIA leak.)

Similarly, Lt. Gen. Ricardo Sanchez, head of ground operations in Iraq, recently began blatantly and pointedly referring to the worsening conflict in Iraq as a "war," reportedly to counter the false and fraudulent optimism being expressed about the Iraq crisis by key Bush advisers like Secretary of Defense Donald "We-have-a-Plan" Rumsfeld, National Security Adviser Condoleeza Rice and Vice President-in-hiding Dick Cheney. Sanchez, who is confronting a mounting guerrilla insurgency that is now hitting his troops with increasingly deadly attacks at a rate of 35 times a day, is reportedly afraid that the president may not know how bad things are getting.

Leadership?

Everyone outside of the White House knows that the war on the cheap that Bush began with the unprovoked invasion of Iraq in March 2003 is failing and that the American and "coalition" troops in Iraq are far too few to control the increasingly restive occupied population. Yet faced with the reality that Americans don't want more troops sent into this mess, Bush has put his re-election before the safety of those troops already over there. Astonishingly, he is actually planning to *reduce* the number of troops in Iraq, making up for their diminished ranks by increasing the use of bombs and heavy artillery.

As the CIA, in its leaked report, makes clear, this is clearly a recipe for higher casualties among the remaining troops, both from "friendly" fire and from guerrillas, who will face fewer U.S. soldiers. As the CIA also says, it's a recipe for higher casualties among Iraqi civilians, who will inevitably be hit by the indiscriminate bombs and artillery, and who will just as inevitably join the guerrillas in increasing numbers. It's also a recipe for a quagmire.

By putting his re-election ahead of solving the Iraq mess he has created, Bush, if returned to the White House in November 2004, will face the choice of dramatically escalating the U.S. war in Iraq with far more troops and almost certainly a national draft, or of withdrawing, leaving Iraq to collapse into the same kind of civil strife and chaos that has overtaken Afghanistan—his other war disaster. (One report coming out of the Bremer meeting suggested that the White House, despite the obvious failure of its efforts in Afghanistan, is considering going with the Afghan model for Iraq, appointing a U.S.-backed leader to run the country, instead of trying to develop a constitutional government.)

If this is strong leadership, you have to wonder what a weak leader would do.

Domestically, meanwhile, this "strong leader" has basically handed the country over to the nation's CEOs and major investors, turning the US economy into a get-rich-quick Ponzi scheme. Those with enormous wealth will be able to reap tremendous profits in the short run and hang on to them because of massively skewed tax cuts and loopholes for upper bracket taxpayers and investors, and then cash out before the economy collapses under the weight of the almost unimaginably huge deficits caused by those tax cuts.

Now, one might imagine that President Bush is simply doing what comes naturally in shifting all this wealth to the ruling elite, but cynical as I generally am, it's actually hard to imagine that this scion of a multi-generational blue-blood clan of Republican political leaders really wants to go down in history as a nation-wrecker. Maybe Bush Jr. has been such a weak, ignorant and manipulated leader that he has allowed himself to be lured into this disastrous economic policy.

It should not be terribly surprising that such a weak and inept president has been able to be portrayed as a strong, incisive leader. Since the 9/11 attacks, the corporate media has been, at least until recently, little more than a White House propaganda machine. This might have continued on through next November, but the war in Iraq has refused to play along. As America's fortunes there go demonstrably south, the compliant media has been compelled, slowly and painfully, to begin honestly portraying how badly things are going. This has led to the first doubts among the electorate about the president's real leadership qualities.

It remains to be seen whether this new skepticism will spill over into domestic policy. If it does, it won't be thanks to the bleating of the journalistic sheep grazing in the mass media, but in spite of them.

—*CounterPunch.org, Nov. 14, 2003*

For all his shortcomings, for a short while there Howard Dean had them sweating in Republican and Democratic DLC headquarters. His unflinching attack on the War in Iraq, and his uncomplicated call for a rescinding of Bush's and the Republican's colossal tax cuts really seemed in late 2003 and early 2004 to have struck a chord with the voters. Then something happened. I believe you can trace the collapse of the Dean campaign to a biblical moment.

Al Gore's Judas Kiss: Dean Joins the Party

Pity Howard Dean.

Just when it looked like he was getting somewhere, with the polls showing him moving decisively ahead in New Hampshire and Iowa, and even starting to climb out of the cellar in South Carolina, in steps Al Gore with his endorsement.

The Judas-like electoral kiss of death.

What on earth does Howard Dean, the self-styled opponent of the Democratic Party powerbrokers, want with this sell-out has been?

The New York Times opines that Gore would somehow bring blacks into Dean's camp.

Excuse me, but wasn't Gore the guy who, when running for the Democratic nomination, chose to trash black voters in the New York primary in 1988, with the help of Mayor Ed Koch? This guy, who couldn't stand up and demand a Florida recount based upon the blatant disenfranchisement last election of hundreds of thousands of black voters, is the African-American's friend?

Others suggested that as a southerner (while he was raised mostly in Washington, D.C. by his senator father, he was born in Tennessee and resides there sometimes) he would help Yankee Dean there, forgetting that Gore in fact lost every single state in the Old South, unless you count the stolen state of Florida (though Florida, with its right-wing Cubans and its relatively liberal population of northern retirees, hardly fits the Old South demographic).

Still others suggest that Gore's endorsement will suck union votes away from Dick Gephardt? But whoa! Isn't this the same Al Gore who so ardently backed and continues to back President Clinton's crooked NAFTA job destruction treaty?

So far, nobody's been so silly as to suggest that Gore—whose spouse Tipper has made a career of trying to promote censorship of rock and roll—will help lure young people back into the Democratic fold. He had no success in that area in 2000, and is unlikely to be much help this time either. And we won't even talk about environmentalists, since

Gore sold out on that issue so long ago it's an old story.

So what does this ardent militarist bring to the anti-Iraq War Dean campaign?

Arguably what Gore brings to the table is the one thing that Dean doesn't need: a link to the Democratic Leadership Council—that group of Republicans in Democratic clothing who brought us the Clinton presidency, welfare "reform," the Effective Death Penalty Act, NAFTA, deregulation of the power industry, the concept of pre-emptive strikes (remember the illegal bombings of Sudan and Afghanistan?), etc., etc.

The proof of what is really going on is the widespread observation among the punditry that the Gore endorsement primarily hurts the candidacy of Joe Lieberman, Gore's 2000 running mate. Why this consensus? Because the lackluster Lieberman was for a time the favored candidate of the DLC. By endorsing Dean, Gore is taking that mantle off of Lieberman, who has all the fire and charisma of a dish rag, and draping it on Dean. Dean has plenty of problems—a record, as Vermont's governor, of backing cuts in Medicare, and supporting the death penalty for example—but up to now he has shown one characteristic that made him stand out from the rest of the so-called Democratic "front-runners"—John Kerry, Wesley Clark, Dick Gephardt and Joe Lieberman, Put simply, he has not been the candidate of big corporate interests. There was even the hope that, by sticking with a populist campaign and relying on his burgeoning network of small contributors, Dean could battle his way to the nomination and then on to the White House without becoming beholden to those interests.

Gore's endorsement betrays, and probably ultimately dashes those hopes.

A corporate whore of the first order, Gore's 2000 presidential campaign took money from pretty much all of the same powerful groups that bankrolled the Bush campaign—oil companies, pharmaceutical companies, physicians, hospital companies, the insurance industry, the communications and power industries. Indeed, the difference between the two campaign contributor lists of Bush and Gore was really a matter of emphasis, not substance. Bush got the big oil bucks, Gore got the big medical bucks. They both got big defense industry bucks. More generally, they both got big contributions from big business, which is the main point. Dean can still refuse this Judas kiss and the purse of silver coins that will follow, but he hasn't done so yet (and indeed as Josh

Frank noted in this space yesterday, he has already started collecting some of those tarnished coins, from the likes of corporate outsourcing providers IBM and Hewlett-Packard and recently-SEC-sanctioned Wall Street investment banks Goldman Sachs and Morgan Stanley). Indeed, the Gore endorsement, more than anything else, has to be seen as a coded message to the big corporate interests, which have no doubt been watching the Dean bandwagon in some dismay, that it's okay to back the former governor of Vermont; that despite his occasionally anti-corporate rhetoric, he's "one of us."

One has to wonder why else the Dean campaign would have turned to Al Gore. If the Dean campaign to date has stood for the "real" Democratic party (a highly questionable assertion in the first place, since Dennis Kucinich already had that spot pretty well occupied), Al Gore, throughout his political career, has willingly stood among the usurpers, the fake Democrats, the posers who toss off a few populist lines during campaigns and then do the bidding of corporate interests while in office.

It will be interesting to see how Dean's enthusiastic minions, the youthful activists and 30-somethings who see in their candidate someone who is outside the corruption of the Democratic Party apparatus, react to seeing him slowly sucked into its greasy clutches.

—*CounterPunch.org, Dec. 10, 2003*

Histrionics About Howard:
Dean and His Democratic Detractors

As one who has been extremely cynical and suspicious about the candidacy of Howard Dean for the Democratic Party's presidential nomination, I have to confess that the more I hear the other candidates criticize him, and the more I hear him respond to their vapid and treacherous charges, the better he looks.

Take the recent criticism of Dean's comment concerning Osama Bin Laden. At the nationally televised debate last weekend sponsored by the *Des Moines Register* newspaper, John Kerry, supposedly one of the more liberal of the Democratic presidential wannabes, tried to make Dean look like a limp-wristed liberal criminal coddler by recalling Dean's recent observation that Bin Laden, if captured, would have the presumption of innocence.

Well, wouldn't he? Or was Kerry suggesting that such legal niceties as a fair trial could be dispensed with in this particular instance in favor of a good old-fashioned public lynching?

Dean, who could have given the yahoos in the television audience the red meat some are looking for by joining the call for Osama's head, instead said simply that as president he would be bound to protect the rule of law, and that while he assumed Bin Laden would be convicted and sentenced to death for his alleged crime of masterminding the attack on the World Trade Center towers, he would also have to be tried in accordance with the law, which includes giving him the presumption of innocence.

That solid defense of the Constitutional right to a fair trial stands at once in stark contrast with the position of the current occupant of the White House, who has locked several American citizens up indefinitely without charges, without trial, and without access to a lawyer or even contact with family members. It stands in equally stark contrast to Kerry and the other candidates, none of whom jumped to Dean's defense.

Dean got the same kind of unprincipled criticism from Kerry and Lieberman a few weeks ago when he made the rather obvious observation that the much ballyhooed capture of Saddam Hussein had done nothing to make the U.S. safer or more secure—a point that was underlined readily by the continued slaughter of U.S. soldiers in Iraq and by the elevation of the Homeland Security Department's risk index, as well as by a series of high-level threats to U.S. bound airliners, necessitating, in some cases, F-16 escorts to some flights (presumably to shoot them down if they showed signs of veering towards buildings) and cancellations of others.

Dean's earlier comment about wanting to be the candidate of the guys who drive pickups decked out with confederate flags prompted a similar attack from his rivals. For saying that he does not want to write off the South in the election, and wants to challenge the Republicans' so-called "Southern Strategy" of using racial code words to pry Southern working class whites away from their traditional support of the Democratic New Deal coalition, Dean was attacked by candidates Lieberman, Kerry, John Edwards and even by Al Sharpton, all of whom accused him both of racial insensitivity to the supposed hurt feelings of blacks and of paternalism towards whites.

Excuse me, but just how does it hurt black feelings to say that working class people—black and white—are being screwed by a Republican strategy of tricking whites into voting against their own class interest by appealing to their racial fears? And how is it paternalistic to point out to the guys who put Confederate flags on their pickup trucks—and there certainly are a lot of them in the Southland, most of them really decent folks at heart, who do exactly that—that they have been duped and used by the Republican Party? It's a fact, and it's high time that someone among the Democrats had the *huevos* to point it out. Dean has been taken to task by his Democratic rivals too, for calling for a repeal of the entire Bush tax cut package, with Kerry in the lead saying that he would preserve the portion of the tax cuts that went to the middle class.

Has anyone looked at those alleged middle-class tax cuts Kerry and Lieberman want to save? They are so small as to be insulting. Few would miss them if they were gone, and they weren't across-the-board in any case. Dean is right. It would be far better to wipe them out and start from scratch. Far fairer, and far better for the economy, would be a one-time cut in the Social Security FICA tax, which would go disproportionately to those at the lower end of the economic scale, and which would be spent immediately back into the economy.

While Dean hasn't had the guts to join Congressman Dennis Kucinich in calling for a slashing of the military budget—the only way the U.S. government will ever truly be able to fund all the real needs of the American public—or for making the tax code more progressive, it was still bracing to hear him tell Kerry, and by inference most of the other candidates at a debate hosted Tuesday by National Public Radio, that Kerry's call for keeping much of the Bush tax cut in place while proposing a host of new funding initiatives was "hogwash," as indeed most of the human services spending promises made by Democratic presidential candidates in the past several decades have been. Further, Dean gets points for explaining that any benefits middle class families may have thought they were receiving from the Bush tax cuts have long since been gobbled up by higher property taxes and state sales and income taxes necessitated by Bush cuts in federal aid for schools, police, roads, etc. Not to mention the higher energy prices and interest rates that have been the result of Bush administration policies. Senator Lieberman blasted Dean saying that no Democrat has been elected president who ran on a call for higher taxes, but this criticism coming from a guy who, with Al Gore, blew the 2000 election while shamelessly promising program after program to every wedge group a pollster could identify didn't carry much weight.

Dean is far from perfect, and he shows a worrying tendency to back away from some good statements and positions when confronted (especially when compared to candidate Dennis Kucinich, who has stood solidly by all his positions and who is helping to keep Dean honest with regard to his opposition to the Iraq War). But not always. It was refreshing to see him stand firm for the Constitutional right to a presumption of innocence and the right to a fair trial. It has been refreshing to hear him call the Republicans' Southern Strategy for what it is—a racist gambit that has hoodwinked a generation of white stars-and-bars waving Southerners (as well as a large cohort of northern white suburbanites, who keep their own Confederate flags neatly hidden away in their racially frightened hearts).

Dean may not be a progressive candidate. His position on the death penalty is indefensible; his record as governor could hardly be called liberal, and his position on globalization and trade agreements, not to mention the military, is pretty wishy-washy.

But I have to confess, listening to the treacherous and petty Republican-style attacks of his weasely rivals for the nomination, and watching him stand his ground for (the most part), with humor and dignity, is exhilarating, after years of the likes of Carter, Mondale, Dukakis, Clinton and Gore.

If nothing else, a Bush-Dean match-up would, for the first time in a generation, offer us the spectacle of a genuine political street fight, with real punches thrown and real blood on the pavement.

—*CounterPunch.org, Jan. 7, 2004*

Kerry meanwhile, continues to disappoint. The man simply cannot seem to take a stand on principle. Take the case of Taiwan, which should be pretty straightforward. Here, after all, is a clear example of a nation of people who have, in the face of threats and intimidation, courageously chosen a democratic path. They obviously need and deserve our support in the face of threats of invasion from China, which claims the island as an integral part of its territory. Part of Kerry's claim to leadership is that he has served for years on the Senate Foreign Relations Committee, and yet, his comments on Taiwan relations show him to be either curiously ignorant about the situation there, or what's more likely, more interested in collecting campaign contributions from the companies that want ever better relations with China.

Selling Out Democracy: Kerry's China Connection

The world's struggling democracies and democratic activists should not be terribly sanguine about the prospects of a John Kerry presidency.

Not if Kerry is serious—and the man aptly described as resembling a dead Abraham Lincoln is nothing if not serious—in his thinking about Taiwan.

In a January debate among the Democratic presidential hopefuls, Kerry said that Taiwan should adhere to a "one-country, two systems" approach in its relations with the People's Republic of China.

Now this long-time member of the Senate Foreign Relations Committee surely knows that "one-country, two systems" is one of those clumsy shorthand linguistic formulations popular with the Chinese Communist Party, developed in this case during negotiations with the British during the process of the handover of their colony of Hong Kong to Chinese sovereignty. The slogan was described by China at the time to mean that Hong Kong would become a part of China, but would be allowed to keep its traditional freedoms of speech, press, religion, etc., and control over its own economy and courts.

There were promises that after 2007, the public would for the first time even get to elect their own governor, and that later, after 2011, they could elect their legislature, a majority of which under the British were appointed by business interests or the colonial authority. The important point in all this, however, was that China had sovereignty over Hong Kong. Hong Kong law would be subordinate to Chinese law, and Hong Kong government actions would be subject to Chinese veto. In fact, since the 1997 handover China has put considerable pressure on those freedoms it permitted, is now backing off of its promise to permit election of the governor, is saying election of the full legislative counsel may be put off for three decades, and is even accusing democratic activists of being "unpatriotic."

Taiwan, as would-be president Kerry surely knows, is an entirely different situation. It is in no way subordinated or subject to Chinese rule or law. The island has been completely independent of and separate from China since 1949, when Mao Zedong's victorious People's Liberation Army drove the corrupt Nationalist Army of Chiang Kai-shek to retreat there, where he established a ruthless dictatorship over the local Taiwanese population and claimed his government was the legitimate heir to the Republican China founded in 1911 with the overthrow of the Manchu dynasty. Over the years, while the People's Republic remained a stifling Communist one-party dictatorship, Taiwan has evolved into a rough-and-tumble democracy. The majority Taiwanese through the pro-independence Democratic Progressive Party, currently control the presidency, but also play a major role in the old Kuomintang, or Nationalist Party of Chiang Kai-shek, which advocates a more conservative domestic economic policy and a conciliatory approach towards China.

The reality is that virtually no one in Taiwan, regardless of party, wants anything to do with the massively discredited "one-country, two systems" charade which China foisted on the people of Hong Kong. While there is bitter debate over whether to boldly confront China by eventually declaring full independence, or to maintain the long-standing ambiguous stance of pretending that there is only one China but that eventually the Communists will fall and Taiwan will rejoin a reborn pan-China "Republic," Kerry's notion that the Taiwanese people must or ought to accept Chinese sovereignty on the Hong Kong "one country, two-systems" model is either ludicrous or a treacherous betrayal of a people.

Some in the Kerry camp have tried to suggest that the candidate simply misspoke, and meant to say he supported the "one China" policy established during the Nixon administration, when the U.S. stopped recognizing Taiwan as being the real China, and acknowledged Beijing as the government of China. In that formulation, the de facto independence of Taiwan is acknowledged by the U.S., which has embassy officers there (in all but name), sells it defensive weaponry, and, on occasion, even provides it with military back-up when China threatens (as it has been doing lately in the run-up to the presidential election in Taiwan later this month). The problem is, Kerry is not particularly given to blurting out gaffes, and besides, his background on the Foreign Relations Committee has surely made him quite familiar with the nuances of the China/Taiwan relationship. He can't claim ignorance.

Besides, Kerry has something of a history of selling out the Taiwanese.

As early as April 25, 2001, before he was a candidate for president, Kerry, in a speech on the Senate floor, actually berated Pres. Bush for asserting that U.S. policy was to defend Taiwan against attack by China. While Bush's statement was indeed a more direct promise of support than any president had made in recent years, Kerry's rebuke was a more glaring backing away from support of Taiwan than any president or major policy maker in memory.

It's worrisome too that Kerry was another recipient of funds from Johnny Chung, a Taiwanese-American businessman and his associate, Liu Chaoying, a Hong Kong businessman, whose political activities became a scandal during the 1996 Clinton campaign. It turned out that Liu, whom Kerry helped in his effort to get a Chinese-based company listed on the New York Stock Exchange, was actually an officer in the Chinese People's Liberation Army, which was also an owner of the company in question.

While it's a stretch to imagine that Kerry is or was acting in the interests of the PLA (particularly given that its ownership of business interests, while wide-ranging, is also carefully concealed through front companies), his willingness to accept money from such China-linked businesses, whether foreign or American, suggests where the real problem lies.

China these days is a multinational corporate wet dream—easy money to be made and lots of it—and politicians on both sides of the aisle in America are being buttered up with legal campaign funds designed to induce them to adopt foreign policies that favor China business, and that might make China's rulers favorably disposed towards the U.S. One way to keep Beijing happy: put the screws to Taiwan.

If this is the kind of pro-corporate foreign policy we can expect from a Kerry presidency, the future looks grim not just for the democratic citizenry of Taiwan, but for struggling democracy advocates in other parts of the world (Vietnam, Indonesia, Burma, Nigeria and of course Iraq come immediately to mind) where the amount of money to be made likely trumps other more progressive concerns.

—*CounterPunch.org, Feb. 24, 2004*

Before Kerry became corporate America's Democratic standard-bearer, he faced some competition from another candidate, retired Gen. Wesley Clark. That the Democratic Leadership Conference crowd would turn to such a candidate is no surprise. But the general also got some support from an unanticipated quarter, when filmmaker and corporate gadfly Michael Moore promoted his candidacy, while trashing Dennis Kucinich. Now I love Michael's films as much as the next progressive viewer, and his latest film, "Fahrenheit 9-11," is a devastating exposé of the Bush crew. So I really was stunned that he'd do this.

Dude! Where's Your Politics?
Michael Moore Smears Kucinich

Film producer and journalist Michael Moore, who has decided to endorse and actively campaign for retired Gen. Wesley Clark for the Democratic presidential nomination, has crossed the line in attacking at least one of Clark's rivals.

Moore, in emails to supporters, and on his website (www.michael-moore.com), asks forbearance on the part of those who have been pointing out Clark's negatives, notably his role in the bombing of civilian targets in Serbia during the NATO Kosovo campaign, his dangerous order (disobeyed fortunately by a British commander) to have NATO troops confront Russian troops at the Pristina airbase where they had landed a contingent without NATO permission, and his record of supporting Republicans in the past.

Moore backs up this questionable plea for grace by claiming that Dennis Kucinich—the most consistent and outspoken opponent of the Iraq war of all the Democratic candidates, and the only member of Congress running for the presidency who had the guts to vote against the November war resolution which Bush used as his "Tonkin Gulf" authorization to invade Iraq—is himself a waffler on the issue of the war.

How so?

As Moore explains, "Dennis Kucinich refused to vote against the war resolution in Congress on March 21 (two days after the war started) which stated `unequivocal support' for Bush and the war (only 11 Democrats voted against this—Dennis abstained)."

After this nasty charge, he goes on to play coy, saying, "What's the point of this ridiculous tit-for-tat sniping? I applaud Dennis for all his other stands against the war."

But putting aside for the moment whether it makes sense—in the interest of ousting Bush—not to look too hard into the pasts of the various candidates for the Democratic nomination, as Moore is urging us to refrain from doing, let's look at the truth of this particular libel against Kucinich.

What exactly was that resolution in March '03 that Kucinich abstained on (he voted "present" rather than yes or no)? It called on the members of Congress to "express support and appreciation of the nation for the president and the members of the armed forces who are involved in Operation Iraqi Freedom."

This was not a further authorization for war—something which Kucinich, who had voted against the original war authorization, would certainly have opposed. Rather, as the politically savvy Moore clearly knows, it was a meaningless "feel good" resolution, and a blatant Republican effort to "sandbag" Bush critics in Congress by offering up a "support the troops" resolution that they would find it politically hard not to vote for. The trick was, the resolution didn't just say Congress members supported the troops and their families; it also said they supported the president.

As Kucinich spokesperson David Swanson explains, "Dennis supports the troops, but he doesn't support the president, so he couldn't support the resolution. But he didn't want to vote against support for the troops, so he voted `present.'"

A purist might argue that Kucinich should have simply called the resolution for what it was—a dirty trick designed to silence war critics—and voted against it, which, as Moore correctly notes, a handful of Democrats did in fact do. But given the simplistic way the corporate media reports such matters, and the way Republican opponents could be counted upon to use it in a campaign, it is also understandable why Kucinich chose to simply abstain. (Just look how Moore and Clark are using it now!)

Moore is in fact shamelessly playing the Republicans' game by trying to paint this decision by Kucinich as a waffle on the war. He and Gen. Clark shouldn't be stooping to this kind of misrepresentation in order to win the nomination. In any event, such an effort, if it is designed to win over Kucinich supporters to the general's cause, is going to backfire.

As for the notion that people shouldn't examine the past positions of the candidates for the Democratic nomination, this is a recipe for disaster. Candidates' pasts don't only reveal their political views; they reveal their ability to stand up under pressure, their political connections and liabilities, and their basic character. We ignore such records at our risk.

President Nixon, in 1968, tried to remake himself as a peace candidate, running against Hubert Humphrey. 25,000 more dead Americans and a million dead Indochinese later, we saw just what a man of peace he was. But of course, his past years as a cold warrior should have made it clear to anyone paying attention that his "peace" image was a sham. The same can be said of President Clinton, who ran in 1992 as a champion of minorities, gays and labor, but who then abolished welfare, enlarged the prison-slave system, and passed the NAFTA job destruction treaty. Anyone who examined Clinton's history as governor of Arkansas would have been able to see this was no man of the people.

Furthermore, we need to know the past actions of the candidates, because if there is anything embarrassing in their records, and they win the nomination, we can be certain that Bush's campaign will dig it up and use it to the hilt in the general election.

No, Moore is wrong to suggest that we voters stop looking into the candidates' pasts, though it's obvious in Gen. Clark's case why he'd be saying that.

Even worse is misrepresenting those pasts, as Moore is doing in Kucinich's case.

—*CounterPunch.org, Jan. 16, 2004*

Well, by April, 2004, both Gen. Clark and Rep. Kucinich were history, though Kucinich continued to campaign with his characteristic upbeat bravado as a way of keeping John Kerry honest—a major challenge for Kerry given his campaign's misbegotten decision to play to the middle, and given Kerry's unwillingness to take a stand for ending the Iraq War. Meanwhile, a new threat is looming—the Iraqification of the American politics. The danger is that the Bush administration, intent upon rigging the establishment of a new government in Baghdad so as to ensure the selection of a pro-U.S. regime, will bring that strategy home to the U.S. this November. Given the Bush campaign's experience in twisting the results in 2000, it seems likely that they'll try the same thing in 2004. Already, many of the key elements are in place—political cronies on the bench, aggressive voter registration roll purges in the works, electronic voting machines subject to tampering, and a record campaign war chest for anti-Kerry propaganda and dirty tricks.

Beware the Iraq Election Blowback: Rigged Votes and Puppet Governments

With Iowa just having dramatically demonstrated to us the unpredictability of the democratic process, you start to understand what's motivating all those Shiite demonstrators in Iraq.

They see how Bush and his viceroy, L. Paul Bremer, and their handpicked quisling officials in the provisional authority, are trying to rig the summer "sovereignty" exercise by running elections through open ballot caucuses, and are demanding instead an election by universal suffrage.

Of course, if there were a real open one-person, one-vote election in Iraq, odds are that the outcome would be a government that would promptly demand that the U.S. pull out, immediately, lock, stock and barrel.

That's why Bremer is running back and forth between his Baghdad palace and Washington, and inviting in the U.N., trying to come up with some kind of a scheme in which the government could be somehow elected, but would have to agree in advance not to order the U.S. to leave.

Some kinda "sovereignty!"

I checked my dictionary, and the definition of the term sovereignty was "supreme and unrestricted power." That's pretty unambiguous wording.

Clearly if you have a government, but it can't tell an occupying army to scram, you don't have a sovereign government.

Although the corporate media are still content to repeat uncritically the White House's use of the term sovereignty, the dictionary definition of the word is rather hard to get around, and it makes a joke of the so called "handover of sovereignty" being planned by Washington for Iraq for this June 30. In fact, contemplating Iraq's future administration, the term "puppet government" comes most readily to mind. My dictionary defines that as "a state that appears independent but is controlled by another."

At least in Hong Kong, when they talked about the handover of sovereignty in 1997, the British and the Chinese didn't play games. Everyone knew were talking about handing the sovereignty over Hong Kong from the British to the Chinese, not a handover of sovereignty to the people of Hong Kong.

In the current instance, what we're talking about is the handover of sovereignty in Iraq from the U.S. to...the U.S.

No wonder tens of thousands of angry people are marching in the streets of Baghdad and other Iraqi cities demanding a real election.

What they need to remember, though, is that we have a president here in the Land of the Free and the Brave who has every reason to fear such a process, not just in Iraq, but at home in America.

Bush knows he himself would not be president today if the U.S. presidential election in 2000 had been conducted by universal suffrage rules. He lost the popular election by almost half a million votes.

No wonder he favors a rigged system in Iraq—it worked for him.

Meanwhile, beware the blowback of American imperialist election fraud overseas.

The same folks who are busy trying to limit, restrict and manipulate the operation of democracy in Iraq, such as it is, are also busy here at home trying to do the same thing.

While the Democrats busily play the semifinal game of democracy in the primaries, the Bush election juggernaut is hard at work rigging the final match that will be played in November.

Hence the gerrymandering of congressional districts in key states like Pennsylvania and Texas, which will virtually ensure that the next congress will be Republican, whoever is president. Hence the effort to pack as many conservatives onto federal and state benches as possible before then. And hence the push to get all states to buy into electronic voting, which will mean using computers made by companies owned and run by Republican campaign backers, which are demonstrably easy to hack and cheat with, and which leave no paper trial.

Americans, and the Democratic presidential candidate, whomever he may be come July, should watch Iraq carefully this spring and early summer. It may indeed turn out to be a dry run for the November election here in the U.S. Watch for massive fraud, courtesy of the likes of Diebold Corp's voting machines, and the mysterious disenfranchisement of a majority of the Shiite electorate.

What, by the way, do you call a democracy where the people no longer have sovereignty?

My dictionary suggests the term dictatorship: "a system of government where the ruler is not bound by a constitution or laws."

—*CounterPunch.org, Jan. 21, 2004*

Unfortunately, it may not even be necessary for the Bush campaign to resort to underhanded means to win re-election. The Kerry campaign's apparent decision to basically re-run Al Gore's uninspiring and ultimately doomed centrist campaign of four years earlier seems destined to hand a victory to Bush anyway. At this point the best hope for Kerry is that the war in Iraq will continue to worsen, sinking Bush first. The race may end up being all about which campaign self-destructs first.

Presidential Occupations:
Bush and Kerry Share a Problem

These days, presidential candidates George Bush and John Kerry have a lot in common, and I don't mean the fact that both are rich New England preppies and Yale Skull & Bones Club alums. I'm talking about how both are walking a knife's edge, trying to avoid political disaster.

First look at Bush. Confronted with the very real risk of losing the war in Iraq before the November election, he has in desperation turned for help to a bunch of Saddam Hussein's own top military brass. The U.S. did the same thing with key Nazi's from Germany's secret police and its military scientists, but this was done secretly, only coming to light years later. Bush has had to hire his Baathist villains in public, and now has to hope that the project won't so poison public attitudes in Iraq towards the occupation that the whole country turns on us and boots us out.

As for Kerry, he and his Clinton/Gore campaign advisers have decided (surprise, surprise!) that the key to victory in November is for him to convince disenchanted Republicans and the uncommitted that he's no liberal, while still letting the liberal Democratic base feel he is one of them, or at least enough of one of them that they'll still vote for him, and not Ralph Nader.

Neither job will be easy, and both strategies run a good chance of failure.

In Bush's case, the administration and the Pentagon don't have much choice. After the collapse of Saddam Hussein's army, and the establishment of the U.S occupation authority, a process of radical de-Baathification was begun. Anybody who had been a member of the ruling Baath Party was tossed out of her or his job, including civil servants who had simply signed on the dotted line in order to be able to hold a job. It's pretty standard procedure in one-party states—every professor in China, for example, has to be a Communist Party member. L. Paul Bremer's approach of chucking everyone with a Baath Party card out of his or her job was clumsy and stupid, leaving the country without anybody who knew how to run anything, and creating a whole lot of angry desperate people—especially among the military. It was also cruel, since many decent people were tossed out of work. But at least it had the advantage of making it clear that there was a clean break between the new colonial power and the old regime.

Now, the opposite is happening. Instead of bringing back those decent folk who had been purged, Bremer and the Pentagon are bringing back the top military brass—the very people who really benefited under Hussein's brutal dictatorship—who, indeed, made it happen and did Hussein's dirty work, and who rightly were purged from the military.

Bush needs these guys, because the Iraqi colonial army he has been trying to create to take over the dangerous job of being cannon fodder at the front of the U.S. occupation army has shown itself unwilling to line up and be shot by soldiers of the rapidly expanding insurgency. The hope in the Pentagon and the White House is that these bloodstained officers from Hussein's army will be able to intimidate the new Iraqi army into doing America's bidding.

Maybe they will, and maybe they won't. If they can't pull it off, the occupation is in big trouble, because the killing of U.S. troops is going to continue to rise through November. If they do succeed, however, in getting Iraqi soldiers to do most of the dying in the struggle against insurgents, all the U.S. will have done is demonstrated to Iraqis that it has no intention of establishing democracy and freedom in Iraq; just another vicious dictatorship, this time under America's thumb. That will only feed the insurrection.

Bush's challenge is to try to tiptoe along this knife-edge through November, tamping down the insurrection with as many of the occupation's casualties as possible being among the Iraqi troops, not American forces.

Kerry, for his part, appears to have wholeheartedly adopted the losing strategy of Al Gore. Trapped by his unwillingness to condemn the Iraq War as a hopeless disaster, he is finding less and less that he can point to that distinguishes his own Iraq policy from Bush's. That leaves him struggling to find an issue on the domestic side that will fire up the masses. So far, all he's been able to come up with is a limp call to require companies to announce their plans to outsource jobs in advance, and a call to reduce the deficit by shifting more taxes onto the wealthy. And even that proposal is so Bush-like in its focus on tax cuts that Kerry has been forced to say he will probably not really do many of the progressive things he earlier said he wanted to do, because he won't have the money to do it—a classic Clinton line.

It's hard to get very excited about a plan to warn people that they're losing their jobs in a couple of months. And let's face it, nobody but a few academics working on tenure or promotion projects gives a rat's ass about the deficit. Tax reform might make a potent campaign theme, but Kerry is so lukewarm on this topic that nobody's really paying much attention. If he wanted to get people excited, he'd call for a massive cut in the

Social Security payroll tax, application of the payroll tax to all income, with no cap, and an increase in the tax on upper incomes to a 50-percent rate. Add to that restoration of the estate tax for inheritances of over $1 million and a tax on stock transactions, and you'd have a bunch of excited Democratic voters—and no budget deficit.

The trouble is, Kerry can't do this. He's so in hock to the Lieberman wing of the Democratic Party—what Howard Dean used to refer to quite accurately as the Republican wing of the Democratic Party—that he can't take such a progressive position.

That means he too has to walk on a knife edge, offering up campaign proposals that are cold oatmeal to an electorate that's hungry for red meat, and hoping that by running as a smarter, friendlier, less racist Republican he can eke out a victory in the fall.

It might work. Al Gore came close, after all. But what Kerry and his strategists seem to be forgetting is that for all his negatives and all his problems, last time Bush was the governor or Texas. This time he's the president and the commander in chief. That gives him a lot of votes right off the bat that he didn't have the first time around against Gore.

Of the two candidates, my guess is Kerry is the one who's going to get skewered on his blade first. His only hope is to recognize the dead end a centrist Clinton/Gore-inspired campaign is leading him towards, and to come out, and soon, for a radical program of ending the war now, shifting the war budget to domestic human needs, and reforming the tax code to make corporations and the rich pay more.

Don't hold your breath. The Bush campaign already has Kerry backtracking on his 1971 claim that he and his fellow soldiers in Vietnam committed atrocities. Astonishingly, he's even claiming Vietnam was a noble, or at least misunderstood, effort. As Alex Cockburn and Jeff St. Clair reported in *CounterPunch* magazine:

> He's got his medals back up on the office wall and here's what he wrote in "A Call to Service", his campaign bio: "I could never agree with those in the antiwar movement who dismissed our troops as war criminals or our country as the villain in the drama. As a veteran of both the Vietnam war and the Vietnam protest movement, I say to both conservative and liberal misinterpretations of that war it's time to get over it and recognize it as an exception, not as a ruling example, of the US military engagements of the twentieth century."[12]

Before long he'll be claiming the Iraq War was noble, too.

—*CounterPunch.org, April 20, 2004*

Even as the POW torture stories dominated the news, as the American death toll in Iraq passed the 800 mark, and as the administration's "sovereignty handover" charade lurched from crisis to crisis, Kerry continued to ignore the issue, missing perhaps his best chance to offer an alternative to war and mayhem as American foreign policy.

Where is John Kerry?
A Campaign Coasting Toward Disaster

Three decades ago, it was John Kerry, the decorated Vietnam Vet, who dramatically asked a timid Congress who should be the last young soldier to die for a war that was already lost?

It was an excellent question, then.

It is an excellent question now, too, and Kerry should be asking it again. But this is healthcare issues week on the Kerry campaign schedule.

If Kerry loses this election to George Bush, we'll be able to trace the loss back to this week, when he missed a unique chance to turn an uncertain and troubled public around on the war.

Instead of taking a leadership position and declaring the war a lost cause, as he did in younger days, Kerry has simply called for the firing of our Secretary of War (let's do away with that Secretary of Defense nonsense) Donald Rumsfeld—a move that even many Republicans probably would endorse. Note that in calling for Rumsfeld's head, Kerry is in effect exonerating the president of guilt in the torture scandal, by implying that Rumsfeld is guilty of poorly serving his boss.

He should be calling for the president's resignation or impeachment (as Nader has done), for authorizing the establishment of a torture center in Saddam Hussein's old house of horrors in the first place—probably one of the dumber things that the Bush administration and its foolish viceroy L. Paul Bremer III did in the course of their one-year rule of terror in Iraq.

Kerry has been stumbling over the Iraq War issue now for nearly a year and a half. Unable to explain his cowardly and stupid vote in favor of an invasion of Iraq back in the fall of 2002, the presumptive Democratic nominee has instead called for yet more troops to be sent there. Unable to call for an end of the war for fear of being called soft on defense, he has been reduced to claiming he could do a better job of fighting it.

The torture scandal, which has scuttled any chance the U.S. had of winning that war (if there ever was one), or even of emerging from it with a relatively pro-U.S. government in place in Baghdad, gives Kerry one brief window of opportunity to correct his mistakes. He could now plausibly say that while the war might once have been won, and democracy brought to Iraq, the ideologues and fanatics in the Bush White House had sabotaged that chance. He could say that by acting like a conquering empire, by taking shortcuts, by deliberately encouraging soldiers and intelligence agents to ignore and violate international rule of law on the handling of prisoners, and by needlessly alienating average Iraqis, Bush and his national security team had blown it.

He could now say that the war has been lost through hubris and incompetence, and that it's time to call it quits, cut our losses, and bring the troops home.

If Kerry were to do this, he would be a hero again. Even people who might disagree with him would have to respect his courage and conviction. And people who already planned on voting for him would be energized to go out and get others to vote for him too.

Then he could go back to talking about health care or the environment, and people might even pay attention, might think he actually had something bold and new to offer.

As it is, the Kerry campaign is coasting to disaster. The torture scandal has become the main event. The war is at a turning point, and Kerry is AWOL.

He isn't even able to get on page one.

And rightly so. What news value is there to yet another cobbled together plan to "reform" the American medical system? Everyone knows that these plans are just campaign blather, forgotten the moment the ballots have been counted.

If he wants to get back on page one, Kerry should take a page from the Spanish left and say that his first act on taking office next January would be to order the troops home, and that his second act would be to take the money budgeted for the war and, after setting aside half of it for Iraq aid and reparations, spend the rest on all the badly needed social programs he earlier had said he wouldn't have enough money to fund.

Sadly, it's not going to happen though. The script calls for Kerry to be talking about education next week, or was it transportation?

—*CounterPunch.org, May 13, 2004*

Chapter 7

Other Indignities, Assaults and Affronts

While war, elections and the ongoing assault on our civil liberties have provided some of the big shockers in recent years, they are hardly the only outrages we start each day contemplating. I find there is plenty more going on every day that can give me that morning jolt. Take the death penalty for example. Where state-sponsored execution is concerned, much of the media focus has been on Texas, certainly America's leading killing field. But the truth is when it comes to putting people away for good, my own state of Pennsylvania is right up there with the worst of them. And our governor, Ed Rendell, a man who put a fair proportion of the state's doomed men on death row as Philadelphia's district attorney, seems as comfortable playing god as the faux good ol' boy from Texas who currently occupies the White House. Shortly after taking office in Harrisburg, Rendell was presented with a study that ought to make him think twice about ordering another execution. Certainly it would give any decent human being in his position pause.

Will Rendell Act?
Race and the Death Penalty in Pennsylvania

The death penalty moratorium movement, fresh from a big win in Illinois, has now focused on a bigger target: Pennsylvania, the state with the fourth largest death row in the country with 244 people awaiting execution, 70 percent of them non-white.

On March 4, 2003, a committee of prominent legal experts appointed by the state's Supreme Court (no slouch when it comes to upholding death sentences), issued a 500-page report detailing the evidence of rampant bias in the state's criminal justice system. Not only does the report demonstrate that minorities—especially blacks—are disturbingly more likely to get the death penalty than whites—they are more likely to be convicted of crimes at all levels. The report, called

The Pennsylvania Supreme Court Committee on Racial and Gender Bias in the Justice System also documents how Pennsylvania prosecutors regularly remove as many blacks as possible from capital juries during the death-qualifying process of jury selection, making conviction of black defendants easier.

Faced with the incontrovertible evidence it found of this racist contamination of the judicial process, the supreme court racial and gender bias committee has called on all three branches of the state's government—the governor, the legislature, and the supreme court itself—to establish a moratorium on executions until the problem can be addressed through court reforms, new rules for prosecutors, and changes in state law.

Lissette McCormack, director of the committee and lead author of the study, says that each of the three branches of government is capable of independently instituting a moratorium on the death process. "The governor has the authority to order a reprieve for all prisoners on death row," she says. "It cannot be permanent, but it could last until reforms are made in the system." She adds that the legislature could pass a law imposing a moratorium, while the Supreme Court would be able to block executions on a case-by-case basis.

The committee's dramatic call for action puts enormous pressure on the state's new Democratic governor, Ed Rendell, to do something. A former prosecutor himself, Rendell, who served two terms as district attorney of Philadelphia from 1978 to 1986, helped put over 40 people, most of them black, on Pennsylvania's death row. (Among those condemned to death during Rendell's term of office is Mumia Abu-Jamal, one of the state's longest surviving death-row inmates. Abu-Jamal's case is slated to move next to the Third Circuit Court of Appeal, where his lawyers plan to present evidence demonstrating that the DA's office deliberately used peremptory challenges to improperly bar 11 of 15 otherwise qualified black jurors from serving on his jury.)

During his run for governor last fall, Rendell promised he would impose a death penalty moratorium if he saw evidence that the law was unfair (polls have shown that 70 percent of residents in the state would support a moratorium), but prior to issuance of the committee report, had said he had seen no such evidence. Rendell, who took office in January, has already signed one new death warrant.

Now that the committee has spoken, it will be harder for the governor, who won his seat largely thanks to the black vote in his home area of Philadelphia, to make the ludicrous claim that the state's capital punishment system is fair and without problems.

In fact, the Philadelphia DA's office has long been, and continues to be the main cause of much of the inherent racism in the state's justice system. Fully 85 percent of the prisoners dispatched to Pennsylvania's burgeoning death row by Philadelphia prosecutors have been black, though the city is only 44 percent African-American.

Death penalty proponents have long discounted such statistics, claiming that blacks commit far more homicides, but McCormack fires back that this is an intellectually dishonest argument. "They'll never explain how they're defining those homicides," she says. "Are they talking about homicide convictions? If so that's a tautology. If they're talking about people charged with homicide, then that doesn't tell you anything either, because the process of charging people is also racially biased." White killers, she observes, are often charged with manslaughter where blacks committing the same offense get charged with first-degree murder.

Jeff Garis, executive director of Pennsylvania Abolitionists United Against the Death Penalty, has called for a stepped-up campaign to press for a moratorium on executions in the state. Citing the committee's call for a moratorium on death, he says, "Now is the time to seize the momentum and demand, demand, demand that officials at all levels of state government abide by the recommendations in this report" he says, adding, "Opportunities like this can become turning points—if we capitalize on them."

—*CounterPunch.org, March 8, 2003*

So far, Rendell, like most of the governors of the other 35 states that have a death penalty, has ignored this damning study, and continues to sign death warrants, even as the courts have released several people from the state's death row, finding them to have been wrongly convicted. Meanwhile, the state's longest-term death-row inmate, Mumia Abu-Jamal, whose shamefully mishandled case was prosecuted by Rendell's office in 1982 (and about which I wrote about in my book *Killing Time*),[13] recently received a gratuitous kick in the teeth by yet another leftist looking to buy himself some street cred among conservative readers.

There He Goes Again!
Michael Moore Proclaims Mumia Guilty

Michael Moore, the Cannes celebrity ("Fahrenheit 9/11") and Academy Award-winning filmmaker ("Bowling for Columbine") and general muckraker, has done it again.

A few weeks back, while Gen. (ret.) Wesley Clark was still holed up at his Arkansas headquarters ostentatiously mulling whether to enter the Democratic presidential nomination race, Moore made a public plea for him to run, calling him a peace candidate. Moore hadn't done his homework though: Gen. Clarke, it turns out, had been a supporter of the Iraq war until very recently, and also has an unsavory history as a military commander that includes actions that should be considered war crimes, such as the deliberate terror bombing of civilian targets in Serbia during NATO's Kosovo campaign. The general also risked getting the U.S. into a shooting war with Russia when he ordered NATO troops to push Russian troops from an airport in Kosovo (a rash and stupid move that was only foiled by the insubordination of a British officer who refused to comply with the order).

Now Moore has ignored the facts again, this time saying long-time Pennsylvania death-row prisoner Mumia Abu-Jamal "probably killed" Philadelphia police officer Daniel Faulkner back on Dec. 9, 1981.

Moore's comment appears on page 189 of his hot new book, *Dude, Where's My Country?*, and it is expressed with typical Moore flippancy, and with no evidence to support it.

Here's the quote in full:

> Mumia [the campaigning Pennsylvania journalist who was sentenced for the shooting of a police officer and has been on death row since 1982] probably killed that guy. There, I said it. That does not mean he should be denied a fair trial or that he should be put to death. But because we don't want to see him or anyone executed, the efforts to defend him may have overlooked the fact that he did indeed kill that cop. This takes nothing away from the eloquence of his writings or commentary, or the important place he now holds on the international political stage. But he probably did kill that guy.

It would be interesting to know how or why Moore—who back in 1997 wrote in the *Nation* magazine, " I want Mumia to live, I've signed the petitions, I've helped pay for the ads—hell, I'll personally go and kick the butt of the governor of Pennsylvania!" and who in 1995 signed an ad in the *New York Times* saying Abu-Jamal was "probably sentenced to death" because of his political views—came to this peculiarly incongruous conclusion.

As the author of the only independent book to investigate this controversial case, I can state with confidence and conviction that the evidence that was used to convict Abu-Jamal of first-degree murder was weak at best, and in some cases probably falsified (while other evidence that might have exonerated him was improperly and illegally hidden from the defense). I've concluded that the only two witnesses who claimed at the trial to have seen all or most of the actual shooting of Faulkner were probably (and unlike Moore I use this word advisedly) not even at the scene of the shooting as they claimed.

On what do I base this damning claim? Nobody who was a witness at the trial, including police officers testifying for the prosecution, said they saw prostitute Cynthia White on the sidewalk where she claimed she was standing when the shooting occurred or afterwards. And nobody except for that same White claimed to have seen taxicab driver Robert Chobert, or even his taxicab, which he claimed he had parked directly behind Faulkner's squad car (a taxicab is a hard thing to miss!). And even White only said she saw the taxi there after the shooting was over (a crime scene drawing she provided to police, which included cars not involved in the incident at all, and which I included as an illustration in my book, did not include a taxi). Adding to suspicions about White, she was the only alleged witness to the shooting that police did not bring to the paddy wagon to identify the wounded Abu-Jamal. Curiously, though she was the prosecution's star witness, she was rushed off directly to Homicide without being asked to ID him as the shooter. Subsequently, the prosecutor argued strenuously (and successfully), based upon a false assertion to the pre-trial judge, that White was not going to be an identification witness, against her having to ID Abu-Jamal in a line-up. Yet at the trial, White was asked by the prosecutor to point him out.

As for the claim that Abu-Jamal had shouted out a confession at the hospital, I make clear in my book that this testimony by a police officer and a hospital security guard reeks of being a perjured story manufactured weeks after the shooting. Neither the cop nor the guard who testified about the confession had mentioned it to police investigators for months after the shooting (a wholly incomprehensible lapse, especially for a police officer), and indeed in two interviews with police investigators, one done the day of the shooting, the police officer who had been assigned to stay with Abu-Jamal from the time he was arrested at the scene to the time he was operated on for a bullet lodged near his spine, stated flatly that during that entire period, "The negro male made no comment.".

The truth is that this trial stank from the beginning, with the trial judge, Albert Sabo (who sent 31 people, 29 of them non-white, to death row), actually being overheard (by a fellow judge and his court stenographer) to tell his court crier, while exiting the courtroom at the end of the first day of Abu-Jamal's trial, "Yeah, and I'm going to help them fry that nigger."

Sadly Moore, who I guess is trying to be funny, or perhaps to make a case he's been working at for several years now that the left is "out of touch" with mainstream America, has joined a short-list of other purported leftists like Todd Gitlin and Marc Cooper, who seek to bolster their "independent" credentials by trashing Mumia and his supporters.

It matters little that these people, like Moore, generally hasten to add that they don't support the death penalty. Even the fact that Moore, unlike Cooper, at least concedes that Abu-Jamal "shouldn't be denied a fair trial," a backhanded way of implying that he didn't get one the first time, hardly compensates for the damage he does with his ill-founded assertion of Abu-Jamal's "probable" guilt.

If he didn't get a fair trial—and he surely didn't, as I document clearly in *Killing Time*—then on what possible grounds does Moore come to his conclusion that he "probably did kill that guy"? If the evidence presented at the trial was weak, cooked and hidden, how can he or anyone come to any kind of "probable" conclusion based upon it?

I actually sent Moore a review copy of my book back last fall, when I was seeking prominent readers to provide me with blurbs for the back cover. He never responded to my request.

Judging from his comments in his own new book, it seems clear that he never cracked mine.

His apparent lack of curiosity is unfortunate. It is also inexcusable in a journalist.

People like Michael Moore owe their readers more than to spout this kind of uninformed and ignorant drivel while posing as journalists. Everyone is entitled to an opinion, but unless it's just barroom argumentation, those opinions ought to be based upon the facts.

Abu-Jamal deserves a new, fair trial, not this kind of ignorant passing of judgment by people who should know better.

—*CounterPunch.org, Oct. 17, 2003*

One of the things both Michael Moore and Ed Rendell surely know is that murder trials are inherently unfair in most jurisdictions because prosecutors routinely purge blacks from juries. Rendell particularly knows this because his own department, over the course of two terms, had a scandalous record of such manipulation of the system, with his prosecutors removing otherwise qualified black jurors from the jury box 74 percent of the time through the use of so-called peremptory challenges (challenges that don't require any reason or explanation to the court). That's bad enough, but I recently discovered that the purging of blacks and other likely skeptics from juries is done even more insidiously across the country, out of sight of defense attorneys, making a joke out of the "justice for all" tag-line in the Pledge of Allegiance.

Not My Day in Court:
How the System Rigs the Jury Pool

I planned to go to jury duty on Friday, but they told me not to bother.

It turns out that in Montgomery County, PA, as in many jurisdictions across the state and country, if you're honest and answer, on your jury summons questionnaire, that you have been convicted of a crime—any crime, however long in the past—the computer blackballs you.

Now my particular crime was no big deal—arrested during the Mobilization Against the War march and sit-down demonstration on the mall of the Pentagon back in 1967 at the tender age of 18, I was charged with, and pleaded "no contest" to trespassing and resisting arrest, was fined $25, and handed a suspended sentence of five days in federal prison.

I suppose a lot of people would say being able to avoid jury duty by reporting on some minor 36-year-old conviction is a pretty good deal. But think about the implications.

There are an awful lot of people in Montgomery County—and in other counties with similar practices—who are being barred from juries because they are honestly reporting minor convictions. DUI is a crime. So is shoplifting. So is creating a nuisance or disturbing the peace. And remember, there is no time limit. I did a random check of counties in a number of states; three quarters of those I called are barring from jury duty people who have ever been convicted of a crime, any crime. Sometimes, they're even more explicit: in Nebraska's Jefferson County, for example, prospective imprisonment, if they've ever been convicted of a charge "involving a motor vehicle other than speeding tickets," and if they've ever been convicted of a crime "other than traffic." In Mississippi, the state bars from jury duty not just felons, but "bootleggers, habitual drunkards and common gamblers" (it must be hard to gather a jury there, if people are honest. Imagine if they tried this in Las Vegas!).

In Philadelphia, the rules are a little looser. You don't get bumped out of the jury pool for a minor crime, but you still get bumped automatically if you have "ever been convicted of a crime punishable by imprisonment of more than one year." Again, there is no time limit, and even if you got off with a fine and no prison time for your special crime, or say you got probation—the fact that the crime itself was "punishable" by a sentence of a year makes you ineligible to serve.

The federal courts are a little less strict. They reject as jurors anyone who has been sentenced to prison for a year or more, but are willing to waive this rejection if the potential juror has had her or his civil rights restored after serving that time (there's a box to check if this is the case).

What do these restrictions—especially ones like Montgomery County's—do to jury pools?

Well, given that 22 percent of black males under 35 have been in prison, it reduces young African American males' potential involvement in juries by that amount right off the top. Given that poor people who get arrested are much likelier to get convicted of serious crimes because they can't afford a lawyer who can get the charges reduced, or even beat the rap, it means that poor people are disproportionately going to be bounced. And because our nation's courts have for the most part been computerized, these determinations, which might once have been made by some court clerk (who could at least consider at the reasons for a conviction, the punishment, and the date of the offense), are now being made automatically by some computer program. (In my own case, when I complained about being bumped, I was told by an official in the county court's jury selection office that given the minor nature of my particular offense, and its antiquity, I could "probably" serve, but that in order to do so, I should "lie" and check "no" in response to the question about prior convictions the next time I got a jury summons.)

It's a fundamental premise of our legal system that a defendant has the right to be tried by a jury of her or his peers. But in our lock-'em-up-and-throw-away-the-key society, an awful lot of those peers are people who have had some minor experience with the law like mine.

How can we say someone is getting a fair trial if those people like me, who have had a glimpse of how the system operates, are barred from serving at trials? Who ends up judging defendants instead? People who have never faced a judge, never looked at the world through bars, never had their fingers inked and rolled—and people who have used their money, connections or social standing to beat the system.

Now there may be reasons why a particular person shouldn't serve on a jury, but we have a system for dealing with that—the voir dire, where two competing attorneys question jurors and try to convince a judge as to whether a jury candidate is fit to serve or should be excused. Attorneys even have the right to bar a few jurors for no reason, through what are called peremptory challenges.

What should clearly not be happening is having a computer arbitrarily knock off a whole class of responsible citizens before they even get to the voir dire.

It is truly ironic that while people can be defense attorneys and prosecutors, and even judges, even if they have a minor criminal conviction on their record, average folks like me, with the same kind of record, are barred from that one important office which we all are expected as citizens to share in filling—juror.

Hey, I want to serve as a juror. The crime is, they won't let me.

—*CounterPunch.org, Nov. 29, 2003*

Messing with justice is a nasty business, especially when the death penalty is involved. But it's hardly the only place our leaders are playing games with our minds. One place where deception, deliberate misinformation and abuse are particularly rife is the Social Security system. Here's an area where scare tactics, divide-and-conquer strategies, and outright fraud are the rule. But there may be a day of reckoning at hand.

Bush's Scare Tactics May Backfire: The Coming Senior Revolution

The Bush Administration has been developing the concept of the Big Lie to an art form: Iraq is developing nuclear weapons, Iraq is linked to Al Qaeda, unprecedented deficits will create jobs, invasion is liberation, anti-missile missiles actually work, and so on. But the latest whopper is really something.

Over the next few months, American taxpayers will be receiving their annual statements of account from the Social Security Administration. Those are the letters you get each year summarizing your wage-earning history and providing you with an estimate of the monthly check you can expect to receive when you retire and begin collecting Social Security.

This year, though, your account will come with a new statement—a disclaimer by the Social Security Administration that the funds you expect to receive cannot be relied upon. Why? Because the Social Security Trust Fund will be dried up by around 2040.

As the new statement reads:

> For more than 60 years, America has kept the promise of security for its workers and their families. But now the Social Security system faces serious future financial problems and action is needed soon to make sure that the system is sound when today's young workers are ready for retirement.

It goes on to say:

> Unless action is taken soon to strengthen Social Security, in just 15 years we will begin paying more in benefits than we collect in taxes. Without changes, by 2042, the Social Security Trust fund will be exhausted. By then, the number of American 65 or older is expected to have doubled. There won't be enough younger people to pay all the benefits owed to those who are retiring. We will need to resolve these issues soon to make sure Social Security continues to provide a foundation of protection for future generations as it has done in the past.

A spokesperson at the Social Security Administration denies that the new statement is alarmist. "The purpose is to educate people about the future of the program," he says. He claims that the changes from a prior statement, in use through last year, are minor and "all factual." In fact, the prior year's statement makes no reference to there "not being enough" younger people to pay for retirees' benefits. Rather, it states simply that "payroll taxes collected will be enough to pay only 73 percent of the benefits," and that "We'll need to resolve long-term financial issues to make sure Social Security will provide a foundation of protection for future generations as it has done in the past."

The new, more alarmist warning, coming right after tax time, is sure to worry and rile American workers, who see nearly eight percent of each paycheck snatched away to pay their Social Security tax each pay period.

It's bad enough you have to lose nearly a tenth of your wages off the top paying for Social Security and Medicare, but then to hear you're not even going to collect someday?

The note as currently written is, however, a bald-faced lie. Social Security is not a pension, though the right wing and the Bush Administration would like you to think so. It will be there in 2042, and it will be paying whatever benefits Congress decides it should pay.

It's true that if present trends continue, the trust fund will be exhausted in about 2040, but scary as that sounds, it really doesn't mean anything, and the Social Security Administration knows this. The trust fund is an accounting fiction. It is actually just a part of the U.S. government, and the U.S. government can't go bust.

Even today, although there is so much money in the trust fund that the government routinely borrows from it to finance the federal deficit (remember that dreadful "lockbox" the insufferable Al Gore used to keep referring to?), current Social Security beneficiaries get much of their monthly check courtesy of payments into the fund by current workers.

All that happens come the arrival of all those dreaded Baby Boomers at retirement age is that current workers, who will be far fewer relative to retirees than at present, will have to pay more in Social Security taxes than workers pay today—or someone else will have to take up the slack. Since most workers have parents on Social Security, even if future workers had to pay 10 or 12 percent of wages as a Social Security tax, instead of 7.5 percent, this is not the ugly generational battle that conservatives love to warn against. Most people, if asked, would rather see their parents supported decently on government payments than have to support them out of their own pockets (how many workers do you know who resent their parents' benefit checks?).

But here's where the plot thickens. Higher taxes for workers are not the only available cure for Social Security's "problems."

At the same time as there will be nearly twice as many elderly retirees pulling Social Security benefits as the bulge of Baby Boomers begins to hit retirement (the first Boomer retires in 2012, just seven years hence), the senior political lobby—already extremely powerful—will be twice as large. And it gets better (or more frightening, if you are a conservative politician or a corporate titan): Whereas today's seniors came of political age in the quiescent 1950s, tomorrow's retirees will be people who came of age during the rebellious 1960s and 1970s.

In a few years, we will see a senior lobby that knows how to organize politically, that knows how to do street politics, and that has demonstrated its ability to fight hard when its own interests are at stake (remember those struggles for the vote and against the draft and the Indochina War?). And once they near retirement, this group of Americans will be seeing Social Security and Medicare as their number one political issue. If Social Security is already the "third rail" of electoral politics, not to be touched, in a few years, it will be the Molotov cocktail, blowing up the political status quo.

Corporate America knows this. Those people in the boardrooms and the right-wing think tanks aren't worried about 2040. They don't think that long-term. (If they did, they wouldn't be so cavalier about the environment and global warming.) They're worried about 2010, because this new senior revolution is just around the corner. That's why there is an increasingly panicky effort underway to destroy Social Security before the Baby Boomer population realizes where its real political interests lie. If Social Security is effectively killed off before it becomes a core Boomer issue, it will be much harder to re-establish it. Hence all the lies about Social Security going bust, and this most recent scam in the mail courtesy of Bush's Social Security Administrator Jo Anne Barnhart, former Republican staff director of the Senate Committee on Government Affairs.

Consider a moment. Doesn't all this feigned concern in conservative and corporate circles about the fate of Social Security seem a trifle out of character? When's the last time you heard a company president or a Republican elected official express concern about the fate of poor people on welfare? Yet when you really come down to it, that's what Social Security is—a welfare program for the nation's elderly. The rich don't need it—it's chump change for them. It's the poor and working class who are dependent on those checks for their very living.

The Right doesn't really have much time on this one. It appears, to judge by the marketing folks at the American Association of Retired Persons (AARP), which offers memberships to everyone turning 50, that somewhere in their mid-50s, people start to think seriously about retirement. Today's earliest Baby Boomers are just about to hit that milestone now.

When today's Boomers really start to contemplate their retirement, the picture will not be pleasant. Property values—where many have placed their faith and their savings—are stagnating, not rising, and post-Enron, those 401K pensions that the middle class was all excited about are now smaller than they were five years ago. Meanwhile companies are whittling away pension programs as fast as they can, doing away with "defined benefit" plans that paid benefits based upon set formulas in favor of plans that pay depending upon what employees put in, and how well the investment portfolio performed—even as those investments that have been made with workers' contributions have been languishing or shrinking in value (if they weren't being pilfered, as happened at Enron). What's left? Social Security and Medicare. Given the sorry state of their private safety net, it's a safe bet that it won't be long before a movement springs up among the new elderly not just to "save" Social Security, but to radically change it into a true retirement program.

Tomorrow's senior lobby won't feel constrained by current law, which makes workers foot half the bill—a key assumption behind the false threats of the Bush Administration of looming trust fund bankruptcy. We can expect to see future Congresses pressured into passing reforms that will remove the income cap on the Social Securities tax, so millionaire investors will be paying taxes on the full amount of their incomes, not just the first $85,000 (this one reform alone, if made today, would push the trust fund's demise off into the future well past the Baby Boom retirement "crisis", but it didn't even get discussed by the latest Social Security "reform" commission, which was instructed to exclude any tax increase from its deliberations). We can expect to see private pensions made fully portable, so that employers can't pocket years of contributions every time they let go workers before they are "vested." And we can expect new laws that will shift the burden of Social Security taxes onto employers, so that young workers won't be overwhelmed trying to pay the benefits for their retired parents (there's nothing magic or sacred after all, about a 50/50 split in payroll tax payments. It could as easily be 25/75 or 10/90).

We can probably also expect to see a movement to expand Medicare from a niggardly program that only barely covers the medical care of the elderly, to a full-fledged national healthcare program that covers everyone.

Why?

Because it will be in the political interest of the much more powerful and radical senior lobby to give everyone a vested interest in a real healthcare plan.

No wonder the Bush Administration and the Right are turning to outright scare tactics in mass government mailings.

There's a senior revolution brewing.

—*CounterPunch.org, May 8, 2003*

Social Insecurity: Fear Mongering for Privatization

Here's an interesting question: Why does the corporate media keep parroting rightwing pols and "experts" when they prattle on about a crisis in Social Security?

Take *Business Week*, which in its current issue runs an interview with new Bush Office of Management and Budget Director Josh Bolten. In an August 11 issue Q&A, *Business Week* Washington writers Rich Miller and Howard Gleckman quote Sen. Kent Conrad (D-ND) as saying that now is the last chance to reduce the national debt before the retirement of the baby boomers. Bolten replies that the Social Security and Medicare systems are "structured in a way that our resources ultimately will not be able to pay for them," and that "we need to take a very hard look at their fundamental structure."

Bolten goes on to say that while "the environment hasn't been ideal to pursue a major change in Social Security," President Bush "will want to pursue it at the earliest opportunity" and that "reform" ideas are all "built around personal accounts."

Like the rest of the mainstream media, Miller and Gleckman don't question Bolten about the nature of the alleged crisis in Social Security, nor do they challenge his assumption that the only valid approach is privatization.

In fact, if reporters would just talk to the technocrats, as opposed to the politically-appointed wreckers in charge in the Administration, Congress and at the Social Security Administration, they'd learn that the alleged "crisis" facing the system is no crisis at all.

First off all—the magnitude of the problem: the funding deficit facing the Social Security Trust Fund, which would see the system paying out more than it takes in, beginning in 2018 (thanks to the baby boom rise in retirees), and which would exhaust the Trust Fund in 2042, assuming no changes in payroll taxes or payout levels, could be completely eliminated by simply increasing the payroll tax paid by employers and employees by a combined 1.92 percent. That is, for a person earning $30,000 a year, the social security tax on employer and employee would have to be raised by $288 each.

How often have you seen that little number bandied about in the media when they talk about switching the system over to voluntary private accounts on which workers could lose their shirts?

But that's not all. According to Social Security's green eyeshade analysts, if the cap on income taxed by Social Security—currently set at about $80,000, were lifted, so that all income was taxed, almost all the Trust Fund's looming deficit would be eliminated, even allowing for paying out higher benefits to those rich folks paying the extra taxes (the same rich folks who just got the lion's share of Bush's mammoth tax cuts).

According to the analysts, it would at that point only require an increase in the payroll tax of 0.15 percent (divided equally between employer and employee) to completely close the gap. That would mean an extra Social Security deduction of $22.50 a year or about 44 cents a week on that $30,000 income.

Some crisis!

But beyond this, there is the political matter of who could or should pay to solve the problem.

For some reason, the idea of having employer and employee share the contribution to workers' Social Security on a 50/50 basis has been treated as sacrosanct. It's been this way since the program's inception, but the truth is, there's nothing magic about this formula.

Instead of making workers pay more into the fund to prepare for the arrival of baby boomer retirees, why not shift the burden onto employers? For example, instead of increasing the tax on workers and employers by 0.96 percent to eliminate the future deficit, why not just hit employers with the whole 1.92 percent increase?

And while we're at it, why not shift another 1.5 percent of the employee tax over to employers?

Conservatives, and many conservative economists, argue against such a shift in the calculus of Social Security taxation, claiming that shifting the tax onto employers would not really reduce taxation on workers. They claim that employers would simply take the higher taxes out in the form of lower wages or higher prices for goods and services.

This is false, however. If one assumes that the U.S. operates as a free labor market, wage rates are determined by the laws of supply and demand, and workers, especially in times of relatively full employment, work for wages which they consider adequate for the work being performed. Employers can't set wages arbitrarily at any level they choose, any more than they can determine how much they will pay for raw materials (if they could, companies like McDonald's would be paying the minimum wage, not $8 an hour). Similarly, in a global economy, employers can't set prices for their products based simply on their cost of labor and materials. Prices are determined by demand. In other words, by and large, higher Social Security taxes on business would have to come out of profits.

The proof of this is the furor that is created among business leaders if anyone even suggests shifting the Social Security tax burden onto them. If they really could just pass the tax increase on to workers in the form of lower wages, they wouldn't really care about the split.

The other advantage of shifting the tax more onto employers, of course, is that the tax cut for workers would be highly progressive (the Social Security tax itself is highly regressive, hitting the poor the hardest, so reducing it would be highly progressive). In other words, cutting the employee share by 1.5 percent would put an enormous amount of cash into the hands of people who would immediately spend it into the economy, giving the economy a huge boost. (That $30.000 wage earner would gain $450 a year with a 1.5 percent cut in the payroll tax—$50 more than the Bush child care credit rebate which left out 8 million of the lowest income families.)

Why don't we hear about these facts?

Why is the talk in government and media always about "crisis" and "bankruptcy" when it comes to Social Security?

Well, for one thing, the media is composed of big business entities, and they don't want to pay those increased taxes.

More importantly, the conservatives ruling in Washington aren't really interested in saving Social Security. They want to destroy it through privatization. Want some evidence? The blue ribbon bi-partisan commission appointed by President Bush to develop solutions to the Social Security "crisis" was told that any kind of payroll tax increase was off the table. With its hands thus tied, of course the commission turned to privatization.

Meanwhile, liberal politicians are so cowed that they don't dare offer up any alternatives, though the answers are staring them in the face.

It's time for progressive politicians to call the conservative Establishment (Republican and DLC Democrat) on this.

Social Security needs real reform, and the way to do it is to raise taxes on the rich and on business.

It's also time for the media to report honestly on Social Security reform.

—*CounterPunch.org, Aug. 4, 2003*

It's bad enough that our leaders in Washington are trying to scare us into giving up on Social Security. Worse yet, they all have taken care of themselves quite nicely. The president, for example, just for "working" (or in Bush's case *working out*) four lousy years in the White House gets to collect half salary (that's $200,000 a year, folks) plus a housing allowance, not to mention an unbelievably huge tax deduction for his "papers". Members of Congress have voted themselves a cushy retirement scheme too that doesn't require too many years of "service" to the public. But the most grotesque of all has to be Alan Greenspan, he of the Central Bank, whose pontifications move markets and who recently announced from his lofty unelected perch that it would be a good idea to cut the benefits Social Security is supposed to pay to us baby boomers when we retire. This from a guy who's going to be cooling his heels in Palm Springs or Beverly Hills on the retirement scheme he's got all set up. Talk about shamelessness.

Hypocrisy at the Fed: Greenspan's Pension

Federal Reserve Board Chairman Alan Greenspan has caused a political furor by calling this past week for a cutback in the benefits that the Baby Boom generation can expect to receive from Social Security when they retire—something that will start to happen in 2011.

Greenspan made this proposal during his latest appearance before Congress, claiming the hit on boomers would be necessary because of the staggering deficits facing the U.S. in the wake of President Bush's unprecedented tax cuts.

Now aside from the fact that Greenspan failed to suggest to Congress the obvious alternative solution for eliminating those staggering deficits—rescinding the tax cuts that are causing them (in fact he said he favors making them permanent, instead of letting them expire as would currently happen without any Congressional action to keep them)—it seems fair to ask what Greenspan himself is doing about his own retirement.

In fact, Greenspan, who was born in 1926, has been very careful to prepare a very comfortable retirement for himself. According to some accounts, one key reason he left Wall Street and went into government service was for the pension. As the story goes, Townsend-Greenspan & Co, a pension management firm that Greenspan founded, actually did such a poor job of predicting the direction of the market that the enterprise was about to go belly up and had to be liquidated. As one former Greenspan competitor, Pierre Renfret, recalls, 'When Greenspan closed down his economic consulting business to go on the Board of the Federal Reserve he did so because he had no clients left and the business was going under. We even went so far as to try and hire some of his former employees only to find out he had none for the 6 months prior to his closing. When he closed down he did not have a single client left on a retainer basis."

According to Renfret, it was the failure of Greenspan's company that led him to turn to government employment, initially going to work for the Ford Administration, and later taking a job with the Federal Reserve Bank.

Since the early '90s, when he hit retirement age, Greenspan has been cashing a monthly Social Security check that is at the maximum benefit rate—currently just over $1800. That might seem chump change for a guy who's pulling down a salary of $172,000 a year, but it will rise when his wife, NBC journalist Andrea Mitchell, starts collecting her Social Security and retirement pension checks, too.

Then of course, there will be that fat federal pension check that will start arriving when Greenspan finally decides to step down from his sinecure at the central bank. According to people familiar with the workings of the federal pension program, Greenspan can probably expect to collect close to $100,000 a year in his dotage, making his total personal retirement take just from pension and Social Security about $121,600 a year. Of course, it's unlikely that a man with Greenspan's income and background (he's trained as an economist, worked on Wall Street and is the son of a stockbroker), wouldn't also have availed himself of the Keogh and IRA tax breaks available to him, which means he must have a sizeable private retirement fund too.

It's more than ironic—cynical and callous are probably better terms—that a man with these kinds of assets, and who has benefited so handsomely from the New Deal's most famous legacy, would be out front calling for diminished benefits for the next generation scheduled to begin retiring just after him.

It's particularly galling that this call for benefits cuts is coming from a guy who contributed so mightily to the mismanagement of the U.S. economy in the late 1990s—mismanagement that led to the collapse of the stock market two years ago, and the needless and wanton destruction of millions of people's retirement funds. Writing in a Morgan Stanley research report, analyst Stephen Roach says Greenspan, despite admitting in closed meetings of the Federal Reserve

Board that there was a dangerous stock market bubble developing, publicly endorsed the ludicrous theory that America has entered a 'new economy" in which earnings didn't matter, and failed to advocate any significant measures, such as an increase in margin requirements or a major increase in short term interest rates, that would have deflated that bubble, preventing the subsequent crash.

It ill befits those who are well fed to tell the starving classes to eat less. Neither should those who will retire like kings advocate taking away the meager income of those who will have little or nothing to live on when they are too old to work.

—*CounterPunch.org, March 4, 2004*

If the system for providing retirement security to elderly Americans is under assault, the medical system for those without private insurance is already in tatters. Indeed the crisis in health care in this richest of nations on the globe is perhaps the most damning indictment of America's capitalist system. And things continue to get worse, not better, as even those with private insurance find themselves being required to pay more and more for less and less coverage as time goes by.

Marketplace Medicine: America's Healthcare Scandal

Politicians are fond of saying that America has the finest system of healthcare in the world, and no doubt it's true that if you have endless resources, or a gold-plated health plan—the kind that is becoming increasingly rare as more and more companies shift more and more of their workers into ever stingier HMO's or take away their healthcare benefits altogether—you can get medical care that is as good as it gets.

But for most of us, the picture is a lot grimmer.

Because healthcare in America is run on a for-profit basis, it is basically controlled by the paymaster, meaning the insurance industry. Medicare is an exception, but as the government continues to lure and push Medicare recipients off onto private HMO-type plans, even that is becoming increasingly a for-profit operation.

What does this mean? That the people who are making the decisions—both in terms of broad treatment policies and also in terms of individual patients' treatment—are primarily motivated by cutting costs and maximizing profits.

Worse than that, because we're talking about American business practices here, the people and companies that are making these critical medical care decisions aren't even thinking about cutting costs and maximizing profits in a long-term sense. Given that most corporations consider long-range planning to mean looking a year ahead, they're not likely to be thinking about what healthcare measures or individual medical treatments are likely to be cost-effective over a five or ten-year period, much less over the life of a patient, but rather, what will be the cheapest health policy or treatment over the next three weeks or three months.

For example, it would obviously be immensely more cost effective as a matter of national health policy over the long term—and certainly for individual patients—to have a national program of free vaccinations for the flu, which annually kills tens of thousands of elderly or infirm Americans. Saving those lives, and reducing the millions of person days the rest of us spend miserably nursing the flu each year, would obviously represent an enormous cost savings even for the insurance industry that has to pay for all that care, but the initial outlay for all those vaccinations would be an upfront cost that would not be recovered for months. The result: no national flu vaccination program. In fact, most private health insurance plans don't even pay for vaccinations for anything!

The same thing could be said for high blood pressure. If insurance companies all paid for routine screening and treatment of high blood pressure with the most effective medicines available (instead of fobbing off only the older, less effective treatments on poorer patients), heart disease could be reduced dramatically, which would actually be a huge cost savings for the insurance industry (and for Medicare and Medicaid). But again, because the initial cost of such a program would be large and would not pay for itself over the short term, no one is doing this.

The list of such idiocies is endless.

Meanwhile, we are treated to scandal after scandal, courtesy of our vaunted free-enterprise medical system.

Consider the tale of Tenet Healthcare, one of the nation's largest for-profit hospital chains. A few days ago, Tenet agreed to pay a $54-million fine to the federal government, in the words of the *New York Times*, "to resolve accusations" that the company's hospital in Redding California had in conjunction with several of its doctors conducted unneeded heart operations on hundreds of patients who did not need such costly, invasive and life-threatening procedures. As is common in such corporate settlements with the government, Tenet (no stranger to scandal) was allowed to settle without having to admit guilt—a thoughtful concession by the government, since it makes it much harder for those hundreds of victims of the surgeons' knives to sue for malpractice damages than if the hospital company had been forced to admit its craven behavior.

Here's a scandal that simply could not occur in a society with public medicine: Unnecessary heart surgery, performed on hundreds of people because the doctors and the hospital saw a way to make millions of dollars.

Tenet, in fact, is a new name adopted by a company once known as National Medical Enterprises. The name change was in large part an effort to distance the firm from its sordid past (about which I wrote in an earlier book, *Marketplace Medicine*),[14] which included an enormous scandal involving NME's psychiatric hospitals, which were hit with one of the largest fines in the history of the U.S. Department of Health and Human Services for reportedly keeping psychiatric patients overlong in the hospital, often against the patients' wishes, so as to collect more from Medicare and insurers. After a change in top management, the company emerged from that scandal, largely intact but with a new alias, though not, as the Redding Medical Center case demonstrates, with a new ethical standard.

Tenet is no exception, though. Columbia Healthcare, another large hospital chain, also has paid huge fines to the government for bilking Medicare—and in the end, much of that bilking inevitably involves unnecessary medical treatments. Smaller scandals, which occur routinely, don't even make the national news. And we're not even talking here about mega scandal—the denial of adequate treatment, or of any treatment at all, to tens of millions of American citizens who are without health insurance.

The sorry state of America's healthcare system—the costliest in the world by far—should have the public screaming for massive reform. So far, however, all we've got on the table are Bush administration calls for more privatization of Medicare, and a bunch of pallid calls for some kind of minimal private insurance coverage for all from some of the Democratic presidential candidates. Only progressive candidate Dennis Kucinich is calling for a publicly funded national insurance program, though even his healthcare scheme continues to rely on private physicians and hospitals to actually deliver services—and even that modest reform is being ignored by the media (along with Kucinich's entire campaign).

Maybe it's time for a health victims' march on Washington. The heart surgery victims of Tenet Healthcare could be the vanguard of the march, chests bared to expose the scars of their needless operations.

—CounterPunch.org, Aug. 23, 2003

The right wing's answer to the health care crisis in America, as with everything, is privatization and deregulation. And healthcare deregulation has had quite a run. Hospitals were deregulated, and across the nation hundreds of vital community hospitals were promptly gobbled up, and many of them then shut down, by for-profit hospital chains that then began shutting their doors to the poor. Insurance companies were deregulated, and promptly began barring sick people from coverage, leaving them to the whims of the various states' wholly underfunded Medicaid programs. Little wonder that as the rest of the world continues to make dramatic gains on disease and life expectancy, America is seeing those critical measures of the health of a nation—infant mortality, life expectancy, average height, etc.—actually deteriorate. We don't hear much about this scandal from either our media or our politicians, however, because it flies in the face of our national religion: the free market. If you want to see deregulation and the workings of the vaunted free market in all their glory, however, just check out the U.S. power industry.

Lights Out, Baby:
Where's Arnold When We Need Him?

The Republican Terminator has shouldered his way into the lead in California's electoral recall carnival with a promise to "clean house" in a state that suffered through blackouts, brownouts and extortionate electric rate hikes thanks to the corruption and collusive behavior of several Republican and Democratic administrations. Angry at the failure of their air conditioning and at their high electric and tax bills, Californians, pollsters tell us, are turning to Arnie for help. They've seen him in action in countless movies, and know he doesn't fool around!

Now that the Northeast's electric power grid has been shown to be an even worse disaster than California's—a direct result of the same passion for electric trading and marketization that led to the Coast's energy crisis—we need Arnold to come back East and clean house here too, before New Yorkers and Motowners start behaving like electricity-deprived Iraqis in the summer heat, popping off police officers and stripping the copper from transmission lines.

Arnold hasn't said how he plans to clean up California's energy crisis, but given his long-term friendship with Kenny Boy Lay, the godfather of electric power trading, we can be sure that it will involve even more deregulation of the power industry. Just as President Bush has one solution for every economic problem—tax cuts—Arnold the Barbarian…er, Republican…with Bechtel veteran Charles Schultz and stock market investor Warren Buffett as his key advisers, can be expected to have one solution—deregulation—for every power problem.

Just what we need in New York and the rest of the Northeast.

See, it used to be that power plants were designed to serve a particular region. You figured out what the peak usage for a certain region would be, and then built plants in that region that could handle that load, with a certain added margin of safety. The government would estimate the cost of that service, add on a certain level of profit, and there was your electric bill. It was a quaint system, but wholly out of keeping with the national zeitgeist.

So along came the free-marketeers. They argued that electricity should be like stocks or oil or cotton—fully fungible and tradable. Spot and futures markets were established for electric power in short order. Of course, that meant that at some point, somebody would have to take delivery, which meant that you couldn't have discreet regions anymore. You had to have massive interlinked grids, over which huge amounts of electrons could be shuttled by computer switching. If a grid in the Midwest was willing to pay more for electricity on a given day than the grid in Pennsylvania, Pennsylvania power companies could ship their electricity through several intervening grids to the buyer. In theory, this would mean lower prices in the Midwest, and higher prices in Pennsylvania.

Left out of all this of course, is the fact that transmission losses are enormous, with as much as 30 percent of transmitted electricity vanishing as heat in the big power trunk lines that had to be built across the heartland. But hey, that's just economic "friction". The ratepayers can eat that.

It was, by most accounts, the shuttling around of some of this current that fried parts of the system in the Northeast, and led to the chain reaction of shutdowns of 21 power plants on Thursday.

No doubt the usual crowd of East Coast liberals will blame everything on deregulation, and call for more government control over the power industry, but this would be a terrible idea. Everyone knows that the only things government can do properly, and without screwing up, are: 1) executing people, 2) making war, and 3) preventing sinful behavior.

We need Arnold to take time out from the California recall campaign to come back East, take on these wimpy liberals, and make that case for more freedom for the power industry. If we could just make it easier for them to build more nuclear plants, burn more coal, and eliminate all those energy-wasting stack scrubbers, and if we could allow them to erect more and bigger transmission lines all over the countryside, we wouldn't be having all these annoying power outages.

Hasta la vista, baby.

—CounterPunch.org, Aug. 16, 2003

Another story you don't read much about is energy policy. There have been endless stories written about the wonderful tax rebates and tax cuts we've received from this administration and the Republican Congress. How often is it pointed out that we've lost far more than that thanks to the rising cost of energy that government deregulation policies and the War in Iraq have brought us? In one pocket and out the other.

The Great Oil Gouge: Burning Up That Tax Rebate

Remember that $400 family credit that you got from the IRS (assuming you weren't one of those 8 million poor families that the Republicans and the president decided didn't deserve a tax rebate)?

Well, if your family has the typical two cars and two drivers, and you each drive the typical 15,000 miles a year and get the typical 20 miles per gallon, that windfall will be more than eaten up by New Years Eve by what might be called the Bush/Cheney oil price surcharge, which has seen gas prices soar in recent weeks to the high they reached last March on the eve of the war against Iraq. And that's not counting the even more additional money you'll be forking over for heating oil this winter, which for a typical home in the Northeast or Midwest, could be $450-500 (not to mention your higher electric bills, since a lot of U.S. electricity is generated by oil-fired plants, besides which coal and natural gas prices rise in tandem with oil prices).

Think back a bit to when oil prices were surging last March. The oil industry at the time blamed those record high prices on the unusually cold winter, which had depleted crude oil reserves, and on concern over threats to the Middle Eastern oil supply as a result of the coming war—concerns which caused oil traders to bid up the per-barrel price of crude oil.

Of course, the war never did produce any delays in Middle Eastern oil deliveries, and in fact, some Iraqi oil is now being added to the world market, which should be bringing prices down, not up. And there certainly hasn't been any unusual demand placed upon supplies.

So why the record increase, which the Lundberg Survey says over the past two weeks has been the largest price hike on record since the outfit began keeping records 50 years ago?

According to the oil industry, the problem this time was temporary refinery shutdowns caused by the East Coast blackout, and by a break in a pipeline in Arizona.

Does anyone really believe this malarkey? The blackout lasted a couple of days, and was not nationwide. Indeed, it was in an area—the Northeast—not particularly known as a center of oil drilling and refining. There was no blackout in California, or in Texas, or even in the Southeast—all areas with far more refinery activity. And as for that pipeline in Arizona, it is not that crucial to U.S. oil supplies except in Arizona and New Mexico.

What's really going on here is collusive price gouging by an industry with a history of such behavior, and one that in this current political environment has become almost synonymous with the national government.

In recent years, the number of oil firms in the country, and the world, has been dramatically reduced, with the mergers of Exxon and Mobil, of Amoco and Arco and British Petroleum, and of Texaco and Chevron. That means a lot fewer companies competing.

In addition, the oil industry long ago learned how to collude on pricing without having to technically violate the anti-trust laws by sitting together in a single room or chatting on a single phone hook-up. Because these companies share refineries, share tank farm storage facilities, and share pipelines, it's easy for each company to know all the details of its "competitors'" production plans, reserves, distribution and pricing. There are few if any secrets among them. That's about all you need to have collusion in an industry where the main product is a commodity, priced the same the world over. And collusion clearly suits this industry far better than competition.

Everyone has seen how collusion works at the retail level. In my own community, I have three gas stations all within a block of each other—an Exxon station, a Sunoco station and a Texaco station. Every time one garage raises its price by a penny, the other two follow suit with a speed that makes your head spin. Rarely are any of them out of synch by more than a penny.

The other thing you've probably noticed is that whenever some incident happens in the news that might logically be construed as crimping oil production or delivery—say a pipeline break or a blackout—prices at the retail pumps jump.

Immediately.

Yet the gas in the tanks underground was put there days ago, and was refined weeks, or even months ago.

Notice what happens when the pipeline gets fixed or the lights come back on though.

Did the pump price drop right back down?

No. That takes weeks, if it happens at all.

That is not the behavior of a competitive market.

And at the producer level, the situation is even more corrupt and non-competitive.

We Americans, who live and die by the automobile and by the oil that fuels it, are quick to condemn the slightest increase in our taxes (and to praise any politician who reduces our tax bill by even a tiny amount). Yet so indoctrinated are we with "free market" ideology, that we accept without a word of protest any increase in our fuel prices as a natural disaster over which we have no power or say.

Not that this Administration, whose key members almost all hail from the oil patch, would ever order an anti-trust investigation of the oil industry, even if we did start rebelling.

—*CounterPunch.org, Aug. 26, 2003*

In the end, though, maybe the people who evangelize about deregulation, and all the politicians who foist it on us, will end up paying for it themselves. If they really believe what they tell us, they may end up doing themselves in. Back when California orange growers were facing an outbreak of Mediterranean fruit flies, the pesticide-promoting state agriculture department commissioner drank a glass of pesticide-laced water to prove it was "safe". Now we have our anti-FDA-regulation president pooh-poohing concerns about mad cow prions by scarfing down untested beef. Who knows where this will end, but we can at least hope.

Beef, the Meat of Republicans:
Deregulating Themselves to Extinction?

Things may be looking grim for progressives these days, given the Republican grip on the media, the American public's seemingly willful obsession with crime and celebrity news, the few really competitive seats in the already Republican-dominated Senate and House, and the increasingly conservative and politically activist U.S. Supreme Court.

Looking at the short term, then, there might seem little hope for a political turnaround.

Longer term, though, there is dialectic at work that favors progressive political change.

The latest mad cow outbreak gives us a clear picture of how this could work: Beef, after all, is above all a Republican food. How many progressives do you know who like to chow down on a 16-oz steak? Many of the progressives I know are vegetarians—even vegans—and those who do eat animals tend to favor poultry. Yet beef-loving Republicans (like President Bush, who this past weekend announced "I ate beef today, and will continue to eat beef), don't want to impose any regulatory costs on the agribusiness firms that raise, slaughter, butcher and deliver beef to their tables. That means that millions of mad cow prions could be finding their way onto the $1000 plates of the GOP fund-raising circuit, where they can gradually enter the Republican leaderships' bloodstreams. It's only a matter of time before even the gray matter of the Republican brain trust begins to resemble whatever it is that resides in the Bush II cranial cavity.

And Mad Cow is only one example.

With Washington firmly in the pocket of corporate interests, the nation's entire regulatory apparatus is now only doing the bidding of the industries its various units are ostensibly regulating. That means that there will be cover-up after cover-up of industry problems and crises, and that corporate evildoers will be given a free hand to commit their moneymaking atrocities.

But the interesting thing is that many of those corporate crimes will end up striking the very folk who are enabling them.

Take airlines. The FAA and the National Transportation Safety Board have always been as much about promoting air travel as they have been about monitoring airline safety, but under the Bush Administration, they have pretty much jettisoned the latter function altogether. Despite clear evidence that pilot compartments need to be secured, most U.S. airliners still don't have hardened doors to the flight deck, making it as easy for a hijacker to get to the flight controls as it is to go to the lavatory. Airliners are routinely permitted to fly, with passengers, past their engine overhaul deadlines, and planes that have only two engines are now allowed to fly over vast stretches of ocean, even though failure of one of those motors would doom the flight. The list goes on and on.

But think about it. Who flies these days? Most working class people can't afford such luxuries. My guess would be that the percentage of Republicans on airplanes is probably at least double the national average. Add to that the evidence that survival rates in a crash are much higher in the steerage section located at the rear of the plane than in the first class section at the front where the ride is smoother, and you can see how this calculus works to the advantage of the progressive movement.

The same might be said when it comes to housing.

Republicans, increasingly, are moving into gigantic McMansions. A family of four Republicans in a 26-room McMansion would not be unusual. But because of lax building codes designed to placate the construction industry, these ostentatious chipboard palaces are actually toxic wastelands. Sealed up as tight as drums with plastic wrap, double-glazed windows and the like, they are filled with deadly carcinogenic fumes from insulation, glue-filled particle-board siding, formaldehyde-soaked wall-to-wall carpeting and vinyl-based plaster. Walking into these over-sized structures is like entering a chemical plant, and the results of living in such settings are predictable.

The lower classes, progressives among them, are left with older housing stock, which, even if it was built with similar chemical-laced material, is so venerable that most of the volatile chemical stew has long since leached away. Besides, the windows of most progressives' homes I've been in are so leaky that the air inside remains relatively fresh even in winter.

It's easy to see who's going to win out in the longevity stakes here.

Medical care too, provides an example of how this demographic story is playing out.

We hear all the time how working people are losing insurance coverage, while the rich in America have access to gold-plated medical care, and this is all very true. But at the same time, with access to medical care comes overuse of medical care. Granted, the Republican rich are able to get rid of arthritic hip and knee joints so they can continue to stroll an 18-hole course while their poorer countrymen have to hobble around the house or shoot a few hoops in the driveway with inflamed joints. But those same metal-jointed conservatives (we used to call them rock-ribbed, but this is a dated term now), are also getting a lot of risky surgery. And before long, we'll be seeing the wealthy getting replacement organs from pigs and other animals. It's only a matter of time before the viruses that plague the animal kingdom will be plaguing the recipients of these frankensteinian ventures.

The increasingly impoverished middle class, unable to access modern high-tech medicine, will be stuck with their own organs, and will have to resort to long walks or jogging to keep their tickers healthy.

The same kind of story can be repeated over and over looking at each regulated industry.

My guess is that over time, we'll see the American ruling class, like the lead-poisoned Roman elite before it, reduced to doddering idiots, at which point the progressives and working classes, healthier by default, will take over.

—*CounterPunch.org, Jan. 2, 2004*

While we're on the topic of doddering idiots and moldering Republican brains, there is the matter of Ronald Reagan, America's 40th president, who mentally took his leave of this world sometime in the middle of his second term of office in the mid-1980s courtesy of Alzheimer's Disease, but who hung around corporally until the 2004 election season. His interminable interment, which dominated the airwaves for a week in June, provided limitless opportunity for fawning TV talent and pandering politicians to glorify the so-called "Great Communicator"—the man who brought us voodoo economics, unprecedented government corruption, secret wars and CIA-sponsored terrorism abroad, a war against the poor, the lovely slogan and philosophy "Greed is Good," and, to top it off, the biggest military budgets since World War II.

And so we had the sorry spectacle of the wildly unpopular and unappetizing George W. Bush, fresh from trying to claim he was the new Franklin Roosevelt confronting a new Hitler, trying to claim the mantle of the strangely popular Ronald Reagan. Worse yet, we had the even sorrier spectacle of Sen. John Kerry, the prospective Democratic nominee for president, solemnly (and the dour Kerry does solemn really well) attending a Reagan memorial service, and offering words of praise for this wretched proponent intolerance and racism, of class war from above, and of government by secrecy and deceit—all in the vain hope of winning over some of the small-minded bigots who once had proudly called themselves Reagan Democrats. (Kerry and his advisers probably forgot that most of those party switchers from over two decades ago had probably long since passed on or, after losing their jobs or homes or Social Security and pension benefits to the vagaries of Reaganomics, switched back.)

Memorializing a President Who Could Really Lie: Put Reagan on the $3 Bill

The gushy praise of the late Ronald Reagan as a "great communicator"—which is polluting the airwaves from Fox TV to NPR—is enough to make anyone not suffering from political Alzheimer's retch. Still, all the public fanfare makes it clear we have to do something to acknowledge the guy.

My suggestion: let's put his face on a special limited-edition three dollar bill.

So much of the Reagan patter that so endeared him to the racist and reactionary public that was his target audience was fraud and mirrors. Just consider his vicious anecdote about an alleged "welfare queen" driving a Cadillac—a blatant fabrication. What he really ought to get credit for is being a very congenial and convincing liar, which was just what his pro-corporate handlers wanted and needed. The trademark winning smile and the charming bob of the head were great devices for deceiving his viewers and listeners.

Truth is that the two terms of the Reagan administration, far from being an era of good communication between the government and the governed, were an era of government based upon secrecy, fraud and deceit.

It was the Reagan administration that pardoned FBI agents who had been convicted of Cointelpro abuses committed under President Nixon.

It was also the Reagan administration that effectively gutted the Freedom of Information Act, one of the more profound open government reforms to result from the Nixon scandals. That undermining of FOIA—an essential first step that allowed Reagan's government of lies to operate—was never fully repaired during the Clinton years, and has been carried further under the current Bush administration.

The Reagan administration also began shutting down crucial information about government—for example eliminating much important information gathering about medical costs and outcomes that used to be collected and disseminated by the Department of Health (then the Department of Health and Welfare). The idea behind these measures was to make it harder to monitor the impact of Reagan-era budget cutting of human services.

Reagan lied too about U.S. foreign policy, which began to rely, perhaps more heavily than ever, and certainly more heavily than in the Carter years, on secret wars and secret destabilization actions—the Contra war against the government of Nicaragua being the most blatant of these, but hardly the only example. Military backing of the death squads in El Salvador and Guatemala were two other particularly ugly cases.

Reagan's entire government budget policy was a humongous lie, as budget director David Stockman belatedly admitted—a lie which was secretly designed to simply bankrupt the country to force an end to the welfare state.

It's hard to imagine a bigger fraud being perpetrated upon the public than this deliberate wrecking of a nation's finances to achieve a public policy result that was not supported by the majority of the public.

And now the man who oversaw this program of government-by-deceit—a man whose presidency, it should be added, spawned the current equally mendacious presidency—is being praised not only as a great president (sic) but as a great "communicator" (truly sic).

I suppose in a perverse way, one would have to agree though. Reagan did do a good job of putting things over on the public. He and his handlers and physicians even managed to hide the rot that was destroying his brain during the last years of his presidency, during which he was reportedly little more than a speaking puppet for the men behind the curtain who were making policy.

The only problem with commemorating President Reagan with issuance of a $3 bill is that the money would actually be worth something.

Maybe a more appropriate place to imprint that wrinkled visage would be on a $50 U.S. Savings Bond. Those bonds have always been a classic consumer fraud, paying interest rates that are pegged at below the rate of inflation and leaving the "investors" poorer at maturity than they started out. The irony is even better because the bonds deteriorate in value faster the bigger the deficit, as the underlying currency declines in value and as the interest rate on other investments is driven higher.

—*CounterPunch.org, June 9, 2004*

Given the massive corruption and illegality of the Reagan administration, and the low wattage of the president himself, it's hard to believe they can be talking seriously in Washington about putting him on a piece of currency, and we may have to eventually get used to walking around with Ron's face jingling around in our pockets for years to come. At least, if they settle on putting him on the dime he'll appropriately be on a coin that matches the man's intellect. Fortunately, it's probably safe to say that we won't have to worry about another dim president eventually gracing the penny or the nickel. George Bush the Lesser is making such a hash of it even Republicans may want to try to bury the collective memory of this 43rd presidency.

Just look at what happened to Bush & Co.'s plans for a glorious hand-off of "sovereignty" to Iraqi officials. For a couple of months, the White House had been trumpeting plans for a June 30 handover which they said would be a glorious new dawn for Iraqi democracy and freedom. But when the day came…well, actually it never came. Fears of a disastrous attack on the ceremonies by an ever more powerful and audacious Iraqi insurgency led to cancellation of those plans in favor of something much more furtive. And no doubt worse is in store, and reminiscent of something we've seen before.

Saigon Revisited?
Bush's Evacuation Moment

It may have lacked the drama of the helicopter evacuation of the last Americans from the US embassy roof in Saigon, but the American "handover of sovereignty" in Iraq on June 28 was at least as humiliating as that last American retreat almost 30 years earlier.

Instead of a brass band, marching Iraqi troops, and a salute by American fusiliers, we had a secret ceremony featuring U.S. occupation proconsul L. Paul Bremer and what was described in the press as a "handful" of Iraqi officials, conducted deep within the high walls of the U.S. compound in Baghdad's heavily guarded Green Zone.

Even the timing of the ceremony was secretly moved up by two days.

Why all the secrecy? The U.S. and the provisional Iraqi government were so afraid of attacks by the mushrooming insurgency that they decided to surprise Iraqi rebels by conducting the handover early.

And so we had Bremer handing off authority to his handpicked Iraqi replacements and then rushing off under heavy guard to the Baghdad airport, flak Don Senor and staff in tow, to fly back to the U.S. in a C130 military cargo plane only two hours later. No celebratory dinner. No evening fireworks or public flag raising. Significantly, the new real power in Iraq, John Negroponte, flew into Baghdad only hours later (again to no ceremonial welcome) to take up his ambassador post, from which he will direct the affairs of state through the network of U.S. "advisers," who will be working in all the offices of the new Iraqi government.

How must the families of the nearly 1000 American soldiers who have been killed in Iraq, and the 140,000 troops still ducking RPGs and AK-47 rounds over there, feel to see the US government so anxious about security in Iraq 15 months after the invasion that leading officials have to sneak in and out of the country unannounced, and hold symbolically important ceremonies in secret?

The real truth about who is now running the country was revealed after the little secret ceremony, when invited journalists in attendance attempted to interview Iraq's presumed new leaders. While those leaders were apparently anxious to talk, the reporters were hustled away by American security officers. If they want interviews in the future, they'll have to make arrangements through the Pentagon, which is handling the job of public relations for the new Iraqi government.

Where the real power lies was also revealed in the fact that the same 140,000 U.S. troops who have been occupying Iraq for the past year or more are still in place, doing exactly what they've been doing: chasing insurgents, kicking in doors, bombing neighborhoods, killing civilians, and dying.

It will be a while yet before the helicopters evacuate the last Americans off the roof of the huge new Iraqi embassy being constructed for Negroponte and his legions (it's the largest US embassy in the world, because it needs to accommodate the behind-the-scenes government of Iraq, and of course a huge CIA staff, so they'll need more than one chopper).

The Bush administration desperately hopes that second humiliation will come sometime after the November election.

The mainstream media certainly continue to try their best to help that happen. Most TV news coverage focused on the minimalist handover ceremony itself, or on President Bush's little note ("Let freedom reign") scrawled in the margin of a message announcing the successful handover that was passed to him during a head-of-state confab in Turkey. The shameful circumstances of the Green Zone proceeding were soft-pedaled. The *N.Y. Times*, in a Baghdad-datelined article by Dexter Filkins, actually credited the secret ceremony with having been "designed to foil attacks by guerrilla insurgents," as though it had been a clever bit of gamesmanship, not an act of desperation. Filkins went on to observe that Bremer had "arrived last May (sic-he meant May of 2003) to a country in flames," but failed to make the obvious parallel observation that the leader of the American occupation was also leaving a country still literally in flames.

But whatever efforts the American media might make on Bush's behalf, the image of Bremer holding a clandestine handover ceremony to a puppet government and then scuttling off back to his New York City consultancy, his plane switching on missile avoidance systems to avoid being shot at during takeoff (the fate of an earlier flight a day before), has to have been embarrassing enough.

The new U.S. embassy would be well advised to keep a fleet of evacuation helicopters gassed up and ready.

—*CounterPunch.org, July 1, 2004*

Epilogue

Making Eating Breakfast Safe Again

No doubt about it. We are living in shocking times.

We have a president who can't read, leading a nation that can't defend itself in a war that can't end against enemies that can't be located, facing an election battle against an opponent who can't stand up, with an electorate that can't think for itself, and instead prefers to be spoon fed propaganda by a media that can't tell the truth.

The astonishing thing is that as bad as all this sounds, there are some remarkable things going on.

For one, the president and his chicken-hawk cabinet and circle of advisers are losing their little war—a big fat reality that even the most craven media can't ignore.

Secondly, despite all the billions of dollars that are being spent by the big corporate media on news programs that dull the mind, a vast amount of truth is getting out to millions of people via new forms of communication—most notably the Internet and email.

Third, new forms of organizing are being developed, entirely separate from the ossified political duopoly of Republicans and Democrats—as evidenced, for example, by the wave of anti-Patriot Act resolutions that continues to sweep the country, or by the incredible demonstrations in recent months against the Iraq War and in defense of women's rights.

Back in the '60s and on into the '70s and even the early 1980s, as we saw our efforts to create a new world crumbling, we on the left were wont to speculate that maybe what was needed was for things to get so bad that people would finally recognize how they were being screwed, so that they'd rise up and turn it all around. That kind of whistling-past-the-graveyard thinking (often assisted by tokes of the weed), helped us survive Richard Nixon, and later Ronald Reagan and George I. (The two terms of Bill Clinton kind of confused the picture, as people couldn't really tell whether he was a step forward, a step backward or just a respite from the onward march of the right—and in fact he was probably all three.) Now, in the reign of George II though, it's starting to look like this desperate dialectical theory may have been correct after all.

The Bush Administration, desperate to aggrandize its power after taking office through the theft of an election it actually had lost, may just have over-reached. In its haste to stack the courts, enrich the wealthy, deregulate corporations, gut the Constitution and crush the opposition, it appears to have unleashed demons beyond its control. Iraqi insurgents, armed only with hand weapons, are defeating America's colossal military. The economy is tottering under Bush's massive deficits, and increasing numbers of Americans are recognizing Bush for what he is: a grandiose ignoramus surrounded by a band of crooks and dangerous ideologues.

Writing in May 2004, it's hard to predict whether this overreaching will lead to a wave of revulsion that will throw the rascals out in November or not. Certainly John Kerry and the Democratic Party will deserve little of the credit if this were to happen. But in a sense, it won't matter that much what happens in November. The important thing is that the people are waking up.

My advice: Hang onto your capacity for shock and awe. You'll need it. And don't start sipping your coffee until after you've opened the morning paper and perused the headlines. Finally, keep reading, and financially supporting, the alternative media.

Great Websites

For Alternative News And Information

Here's a list of my favorite sites for getting news and information that you won't find in the mainstream U.S. corporate press or by watching TV "news" programs. It's hardly a complete survey of what's out there, but it's a good start—and a great antidote to the official propaganda. Many of these sites have links that will take you to more good sources of alternative news, so explore.

www.counterpunch.org Daily news and commentary from a left perspective

www.salon.com Daily news and commentary, paid subscription or put up with watching an advertisement for a day pass

www.inthesetimes.org Updated irregularly

www.riprense.com Check out Rip Rense's excellent, eclectic "Daily Links"

www.thememoryhole.org Brought us the images of all those flag-draped coffins

www.truthout.org Daily columns and news stories

www.news.independent.co.uk News from a British perspective

www.guardian.co.uk Ditto

www.zmag.org/weluser.htm News and commentary from the left

www.commondreams.org Excellent source of left and liberal news

www.tbwt.org Online site of Black World Today, a compendium of columns and reports from the African-American media

www.thenation.com Left/liberal news and articles, updated weekly

www.democraticunderground.com Just what it says

www.alternet.org A daily collection of the best progressive news and commentary

www.workingforchange.com A publication of Working Assets

www.mediamatters.org Excellent place to see what the mainstream media is doing wrong

www.fair.org First-rate media criticism, updated monthly

www.tompaine.com Excellent opinion columns

www.capitalhillblue.com Great place to go to keep a jaundiced eye on Congress

www.democracynow.org Website of the ground-breaking Pacifica news program of that name

www.informationclearinghouse.info/index.html As this site says: News you won't find on CNN

www.amconmag.com Site of *American Conservative* magazine—definitely worth a visit now and again

Notes

1   Counterpunch.org, May 27, 2004

2   *Philadelphia Inquirer*, March 27, 2003

3   Lindorff, Dave, "Oiling Up the Draft Machine," *Salon.com*, November 3, 2003

4   Lindorff, Dave, "Dishonorable Discharge," *In These Times*, November 26, 2003

5   Dennis McCafferty, "This Thanksgiving, more than ever, we should Count our Blessings," *USA Today*, Nov. 11, 2001

6   *The Nation*, March 15, 2004

7   CounterPunch.org, July 21, 2003

8   Salon.com, July 25, 2003

9   Kornbluh, Peter, *The Pinochet File: A Declassified Dossier on Atrocity and Accountability*, National Security Archive, 2003

10 "The Times and Iraq," *The New York Times*, May 26, 2004

11 Weapons of Mass Destruction? Or Mass Distraction?" by Daniel Okrent, *The New York Times*, May 30, 2004, p. WK2

12 Cockburn, Alexander and St. Clair, Jeff, "Campaign Diary: Kerry—He's Already Peaking," CounterPunch.org, Feb. 20, 2004

13 Lindorff, Dave, *Killing Time: An Investigation into the Death Penalty Case of Mumia Abu-Jamal*, Common Courage Press, 2003

14 Lindorff, Dave, *Marketplace Medicine: The Rise of the For-Profit Hospital Chains*, Bantam Books, 1992

About the Author

Award-winning investigative reporter Dave Lindorff has been working as a journalist for 30 years. He ran the *Daily News* bureau covering Los Angeles County government, spent several years as a correspondent in Hong Kong and China for *Businessweek*, and has written for such publications as *Rolling Stone*, *The Nation*, *In These Times*, *Mother Jones*, *Village Voice*, *Salon*, *The London Observer* and the Australian *National Times*. He is the author of two other books, *Marketplace Medicine: The Rise of the For-Profit Hospital Chains* (Bantam, 1992), an investigative report on the for-profit hospital industry, and *Killing Time: An Investigation into the Death Row Case of Mumia Abu-Jamal* (Common Courage Press, 2003), the only independent examination of this important capital case. A two-time Fulbright Scholar (Shanghai, China and Kaohsiung, Taiwan), he is a 1975 graduate of the Columbia University Graduate School of Journalism, and received a B.A. in Chinese in 1972 from Wesleyan University. For the past seven years, he has lived with his family just outside Philadelphia.